*Also by asha bandele*

Absence in the Palms of My Hands and Other Poems

# *The Prisoner's Wife*

## A MEMOIR

# a s h a   b a n d e l e

*Scribner*

SCRIBNER
1230 Avenue of the Americas
New York, NY 10020

SCRIBNER and design are trademarks of Macmillan Library Reference USA, Inc.,
used under license by Simon & Schuster, the publisher of this work.

Designed by Colin Joh

Set in Galliard

Manufactured in the United States of America

3 5 7 9 10 8 6 4 2

Library of Congress Cataloging-in-Publication Data
bandele, asha
The prisoner's wife: a memoir/asha bandele
p.    cm.
1. bandele, asha—Marriage. 2. Women poets, American—20th century—
Biography. 3. Prisoners' spouses—United States—Biography.
4. Married people—United States—Biography. 5. Afro-American
women poets—Biography.    I. Title.
PS3552.A47527Z47    1999
811'.54—dc21    99–12117
[B]
CIP

ISBN 0-684-85073-7

For Rashid
over and over and over

*. . . if i know anything at all,*
*it's that a wall is just a wall*
*and nothing more at all.*
*it can be broken down.*
—assata shakur

# *Acknowledgments*

There's no way that a book like this cannot be considered a collaborative effort. Trying to tell a very personal story while you're still in the midst of the drama requires a particular and consistent kind of support. It's the kind that comes at four in the afternoon and four in the morning. It's the kind that comes even when you think you don't need it. It pays your little attitude no attention and just walks right in, grabs you and holds you, until you laugh or cry or talk. Or write. You begin to write and when that happens, that release, you feel as close to freedom as this life will ever allow. There were so many people who, in a myriad of ways, gave me that gift. And they gave it to me again and again. I swear I don't know how to begin to thank them, but I do know I must at least call their names, say publicly that the best that this book has to offer is surely a reflection of their love and humanity.

First of all to my parents, who have resigned themselves to simply loving their difficult and strange daughter. Thank you. To my sister, who listens and listens, and who always works to understand, and to T'Kalla, Asale Ajani, Christa Bell, Robin Templeton, and Laila Jenkins, who took my relationship seriously from the very beginning, and who read and critiqued the manuscript along the way. Thank you. To the membership of the New Afrikan Independence Movement—with a particular affection for the Brooklyn Chapter of Malcolm X Grassroots Movement—for vision, for strength, for an end goal, asante sana.

To Khadijah Diouf, Monifa Akinwole, Vera Beatty, Tanaquil Jones, Kim Wade, Talibah Nomakhosi, Christian Fabian, Letta Neely, Reggie Richardon, Michele Brown, Dagmar Schnau,

Ahmed Obafemi, Jalil Muntaquin, Sekou Odinga, Mutulu Shakur, Lumumba Bandele, Safiya Bandele, and especially to Dr. Errol Henderson for never letting me backslide into mediocrity, asante sana.

To Bob Shacochis, who suggested once that perhaps living well was not the best revenge, and that writing well was. If this book in some way rises to the occasion, it is in no small part due to the attention you paid to it. Thank you. To Meri Danquah who believed in my work "just based on your spirit," she said, and then introduced me to the most incredible and brilliant agent in the whole world: Victoria Sanders. And Victoria, who always makes me feel like I'm the most important, the most talented. Should we even speculate on what kind of basketcase would I have been without you?

Writers always seem to have countless war stories about slash-and-burn editors with whom they can never find peace. While I don't want to invalidate their experiences, I do want to throw mine into the discussion as well. I want to say that I wish they'd worked with my editor, Gillian Blake, who saw fifty pages of disconnected writing, and said, here: this is the needle and this is the thread. All you have to do is take it one stitch at a time. Thank you.

And to the incredible and complex people of Brooklyn, New York, from East Flatbush to Bed-Stuy, from Fort Greene to Crown Heights: for everything we are and everything we are not, for all the swagger and strength, the inspiration and beauty and truth, for providing me with a home into which I can one day welcome my husband.

And at last, to the women I ride the vans with, the ones with whom I've traded stories and laughter while we've waited and waited on this side of the wall. May the time pass quickly. May the hurt be mitigated by the love.

# The Prisoner's Wife

# *this is a love story*

*t*his is a love story like every love story I had always known, like no love story I could ever have imagined. It's everything beautiful—bright colors, candle-scented rooms, orange silk, and lavender amethyst. It's everything grotesque, disfigured. It's long twisting wounds, open and unhealed, nerves pricked raw, exposed.

This is a love story, awake and alive. It's a breathing document, a living witness. It's human possibility, hope, and connection. It's a gathering of Spirit, the claiming of dreams. It's an Alvin Ailey dance, a *rainbow roun' mah shoulder.* It's a freedom song, a 12-string guitar, a Delta blues song. This story is a reprieve.

This is a love story, threadbare and used up, yet sometimes fat, weighty, stretched out of shape. It's polyester, this story, man-made, trying to be pretty, not quite making it. This is a story desperate to hold itself together. This is a story with patches in the knees.

This is a love story, my love story and thousands of other women's love story. It's a story that's known, documented, photographed, videotaped, audiotaped, filed, photocopied, watched over, studied, caricatured, questioned, researched, and noted.

This is a love story. It's the one we keep close, sheltering it from judgment. It's lovers denied at family dinners and at office parties. It's secret glances at Polaroid pictures. It's whispered names. This is a story hidden within midnight bus rides and 5:00 A.M. van rides, behind metal detectors, electronic doors, and steel slamming against steel.

This is a love story, the one not generally discussed in polite or even public conversation. But if there's one thing that I do know about myself, it's that I know I hate secrets, that secrets mean shame, and that I am not now, nor will I ever be, ashamed that I am a woman who has loved someone, and that someone has loved me.

And even though so many people have asked me if I have lost my mind, if I am lonely, or desperate. Even though so many people have wondered if I was having a crisis, or determined that I was just going through a phase, I will continue loving the man I am loving. I will love him even though he's got an ugly past, skeletons, and sorrow. Even though he doesn't have a great job or position or power, and even though he's a prisoner at a maximum-security correctional facility, which my husband, Rashid, is, I will continue loving him.

And this is our story.

≈

The first time I ever went into a prison, it was for a class I was taking on the relationship between Black people and incarceration in the United States. Months later, long after final exams had been taken and grades received, my former professor called me and asked if I would come with him and a few other people to a place called Eastern Correctional Facility in upstate New York. It was just about eighty miles from Brooklyn, where I lived. He wanted me, he said, to participate in a Black History Month program.

*Don't you write poems?* he asked.

*You could read your poetry,* he said.

I agreed and we all went to do the program, and this was how we met, Rashid and I, convict and student, gangster and poet, resident host and visiting performer.

Rashid is fine as hell, which I tried not to but couldn't help noticing the very first time I saw him. He looks like this beautifully symmetrical collaboration between Africa and India. He isn't huge, not an overwhelming presence, contrary to the usual celluloid interpretation of Black prisoners. Rashid is 5'7", with a brave smile and bright eyes. He is, I remember thinking this then, just the right size, and I could look directly at him, nearly eye to eye. His voice, which was never loud, told a story of a transplanted Afro-Caribbean.

*Where are you from?* I wanted to know.

*The Boogie Down,* he responded, meaning the South Bronx.

*And before?*

*Oh, oh,* he said, understanding my question. *Guyana. South America. It's the most beautiful place in the world. That's a hell of a thing in one life, huh? To have seen the most beautiful place in the world and the most horrible place. And I'm not even thirty yet!*

After that, a number of other men came over to me to tell me how much they enjoyed my performance, and would I be willing to read their work, when was I coming back up, could they write to me to discuss poetry, did I know I reminded them of this sister they used to know back in the day? In the midst of these questions, Rashid left me. I watched him as he walked across the huge auditorium where the program was being held. He weaved easily through the nearly one hundred men gathered there, through the orange chairs, across the stage, the back of it, and found another guest to talk to, a poet like me. A very talented poet, I should say, and a very attractive one. I waited for him to come back over to me. I tried to will him to come back over to me, but finally I was left there annoyed because Rashid did not return until it was time to say good-bye.

After we were in love, Rashid would tell me that it was me, my fault, that I was hard to approach. He told me that while I was an animated and exciting performer, offstage I was quiet, withdrawn, cool and distant.

*Besides,* he admits now, through a series of childlike giggles, *every dude knows when you really want to talk to a sister, you don't step to her directly. You step to her friend, and that's what I did. I talked to that other sister, the poet who performed before you, because that way I knew I'd get your attention. I mean, what I'd look like trying to talk to you when all of them other dudes were running they game on you? You know what I'm saying?*

Rashid is *so* pleased with himself as he tells me this story *five* years after our first encounter. After all, in the moment of his confession, we are in a visiting room, and I lie, as fitted as possible, in the crook of his arms. And in that moment, despite every hurting and hell I have had to endure to love this man, there is no other place that I would rather be.

When we began, I was twenty-five, a student and organizer, a wife on the verge of divorce from my first husband, a poet full

of secrets and sadness, an emerging woman hampered by insecurities and anger, a human being fighting off loneliness while
craving solitude, needing an open love, long honest discussions, a quiet touching at my core.

When we began, he was twenty-nine, inmate number
83*****, a convicted killer doing twenty years with life on the
back, a model prisoner, a program coordinator, the father of a
nine-year-old boy he had never been able to raise, a lawyer
without a law degree, a devoted Muslim, a man on the verge of
divorce from his first wife, a human being fighting off loneliness while craving solitude, needing an open love, long honest
discussions, a quiet touching at his core.

We were exactly the same and we were completely different.

We were never meant to be together.

We were always meant to save each other.

# home

**W**hen I look back at us now, the group of students who traipsed up into the prisons all those years ago to participate in the various programs, I always remember how we felt like Rashid was home from the very beginning. There was something about him, his warmth, his lack of an agenda that made it appear that there was no division, no difference between him and us, his world and ours.

Speaking at a prison can be a very overwhelming experience. Prisoners, already isolated, often make an intensely appreciative audience, and if you say things which in any way reflect their thinking, you can really get bombarded by requests at the close of a presentation. Folks are seeking pen pals, people to review their poetry and writings, any kind of connection to "the street." And as much as we may have wanted to, it was simply impossible for one or two or four people to serve that kind of mass need. But at such young ages, with virtually no primer before going into the facility, we didn't have any idea how to respond to what usually amounted to a hundred different requests for a hundred different things from a hundred different people.

This was why Rashid stood out, not just with me, but with all of us. He never asked us for anything. He just talked and talked with us. We talked about the struggle for equal education, world politics, social justice. We talked as though we were painters, using words like fluid strokes across the broad canvas which was our collective imagination. And the more we visited, the more we talked. And sometimes we agreed on things, and sometimes we disagreed on things, but it never got heated, ugly, or nasty. We were talking like we wanted to learn something. We were talking like we wanted to heal.

We were talking as though we believed our talking could change things, restore balance, make somebody free. It was unifying talk. And Rashid knew it, we all knew it. Rashid knew, as we knew, that he had become our friend, a member of our little clique, and this is what made it so difficult finally, when we would, at the end of a program, walk out of the prison without him. It seemed that if we meant anything we said in those long political discussions, there would just be no way we could have gone, leaving him behind then. Leaving him behind now.

When people have asked me how could I have fallen in love with a man who was convicted of murder, where I begin is as a student who was volunteering time and hoping that my poems and willingness to talk would somehow change someone for the better. Then I tell about the man who would become my husband, how his spirit engaged me, engaged every one of us, and how by the openness of his spirit, it was I who would change.

Back then, during those early days of friendship, I learned something about taking in different points of view, listening carefully, reserving judgment, and not having to win an argument for winning's sake. I learned by watching Rashid, who always spoke in turn, and who spoke deliberately, and who admitted being wrong if he'd been shown to be wrong.

*Prison,* he told me one day, *will teach a man to be polite.*

*The tension's so high here, you don't want to add to it by not say-*

*ing "excuse me" if it's right to say "excuse me." And that's good. I wasn't always like that. I used to be so arrogant.*

I've explained to people that I didn't, despite what it would seem, fall in love with a killer. I fell in love with a man who wanted to become his own more perfect creation, a man committed to the transformation of himself, of the world. And the world he imagined was like the world I imagined. It was a place that was just and fair and safe and livable. We could meet there, in that place. We could meet there as creators. We could meet there as equals.

*He valued my opinions!* I have said this to friends.

*Can you imagine such a man? He wants to consult with me about everything. Everything! He takes my advice,* I have said to whoever would listen.

When I talked about things Rashid had never heard of, he took notes. *But it's more than this,* I've said, trying to get in every point I could while they were still paying attention.

*He respects me enough to argue with me,* I told my girlfriend one afternoon.

*I never used to able to imagine that,* I said to her. To be engaged in a debate, and I didn't mean the way men usually argue with women in that, *Okay, dear, whatever you say* kind of way. No! I meant the way men argue with men, as though the other person was a worthy opponent. Rashid listened to me and he challenged me. That's who I fell in love with, I said over and over. A man who believed I was a woman who was worth it.

Sometimes when I've told people these things, they say they just can't see it. *Where's the ugly stuff?* I've been asked over and over. And I've told them yes, it was true, that there were some women for whom ugliness and hurt was the texture of their story, but it simply was not the picture that I had to draw.

*asha,* some have argued, *girl, you have blinders on. He might be great now, but who is he going to be when he comes home?*

*I don't know,* I respond. *Who will I be?*

*Rashid could come home and be horrible to you,* I've been warned.

*Yes,* I tell them. *Of course that's true. But Rashid could also come home and be wonderful to me. None of us know tomorrow, only this moment, now, this time, already recorded in history.*

And this moment when I am kissed, nurtured, rocked, and then set at ease by the love I have been given, this moment is the only real thing I know. That, and also this one other thing: that there are so many people who are lonely, without love and without passion in their lives, that I know that what I have, as difficult as it may be, is the most precious of all gifts.

And I couldn't just give it up without a fight, this rare, this desired thing, this thing which is life-sustaining. Could I? Could they, I ask? I want to know this. Could they reject the greatest love they've ever known just because it came from the worst place they've ever known?

≈

Still I am aware that all things happen in a context, and so, Rashid's many charms notwithstanding, it is also true that there was this confluence of events in my life, and together they probably assisted in making him so significant to me.

The world is so magnificent, the way it keeps rebirthing itself to you, if you're amenable. And if you're amenable, the way the world comes will be exciting, new each time, in different colors, different shapes.

For me, a brand-new world was born when I became a student at the City University of New York. I majored in political science and Black studies, not realizing that within each classroom I would find pieces of myself, scattered pieces of Black female me just waiting to be scooped up and reattached.

For the first time in my life, a life which had been dominated by white history, white cultures, white literature, white music, white sensibilities, a life where Black was a metaphor for less than, I was reading books with characters and experiences that I understood. I was finally offered a history that went beyond slavery to include that which was Black and successful, Black and intelligent, Black and encouraging.

Learning this left me with a range of emotions I think common to any conquered people. The greatest, the most profound one I had, was love, at last for myself, as a Black woman, a woman who indeed had a place in history, if not in high school textbooks. For the first time in my entire academic history, I was studying the literature of Black people: James Baldwin and Zora Neale Hurston, Buchi Emecheta and Chinua Achebe.

I learned that there was more to my ancestry than slavery and the Civil Rights movement, which during my grammar and high school years were the only contexts in which I'd heard Black people being discussed. I could, at that pivotal juncture in my academic career, study Malcolm X, not as an extra-credit project, but as an extraordinary international political figure who had moved from prison to the Bandung Conference to the Organization of AfroAmerican Unity. I am embarrassed to admit this but I know it has to be said. For the first time in my life, I was truly and completely proud to be Black. I had never felt that before. Not once. Not all the way.

But at the same time that I was virtually falling in love with my history and culture, I was also feeling a huge sense of grief over what had been done to my people, what had been lost, who had been murdered. There was, certainly, a rage, a nearly unmitigated rage, at the people who made the policies and laws and institutions which could only be called evil.

I tell you this so that you understand how easy it was in those days to determine who was friend and who was enemy. Later, as I matured, took in more and more information, nothing stayed simple and clear. But it was, then, literally and figuratively, a black-and-white situation. And it was through this lens that I first saw not only Rashid, but all prisoners.

Back then I saw all prisoners as victims. I told Rashid this.

*Yes, well, a lot of us also think like that in the beginning,* he said to me.

*And some people really are, straight-up, victims. At first we say we're all political prisoners because of the politics of the criminal justice system. And race is always an issue. But you know, as you get older, you want to take responsibility for all your life. Because if you live long enough, you do good things too. And I began to want to claim the good I had done. But if I was responsible for that, then I had to be responsible for the bad, too, right?*

≈

Yet it wasn't only this emerging worldview which influenced my choices. There were indeed some tangible and devastating things which happened all at once, in the year just before I fell in love with Rashid. There were these departures. Suddenly everything in my life was shifting aside, seeking a fast exit, and I was just there, crouched on a curb, alone, unable to see across distances, unable to get perspective.

The initial blow came when I was put out of school for protesting against the steady tuition increases and budget cuts which were closing more and more students out of an education. We had rallied, marched, lobbied, and then occupied the administration building of our school. And it was for this final act that a few of us were brought up on internal charges, found guilty, and removed.

For two reasons, this was a bigger loss than I had anticipated. First of all, I was president of my student government, and therefore largely defined by school activities. But second, my own parents had been administrators at the university. And to be sure, they disagreed with the tuition increases and budget cuts as well, but more than anything, they wanted me to graduate. They said this to me then, and as much as I wanted to comply, I would in fact make them wait some five years before I paraded in black to the proud hum of *Pomp and Circumstance*.

Fourteen years before, when I was fifteen years old, I had walked a similar parade to the same song down the aisle of my high school auditorium. There were many valleys, long drops down and down further between those two days, and in all that time, despite my often hostile outward behavior, what had always been of greatest important to me is what was of greatest importance to many children.

I wanted desperately to please my parents, to make them proud. My parents, I knew, had made incredible sacrifices for my sister and me, to have a nice home, to go to good schools, to be exposed to the arts. We were middle-class but never rich by any stretch of the imagination. Whatever we had, my sister and I, came as a result of the long, often arduous hours my parents put in at their respective jobs.

And they were jobs that were not necessarily dream jobs—not my parents in jobs that nurture your soul. My mother and father worked so that my sister and I could have that sort of option, to work in any field we wanted. It would be a long time before I was old enough to understand this, to see my sister and myself as the major works of my parents' lives, my sister and myself as their legacies. And only then would my studies become an urgent matter. In my generation, it seems, most of us struggle for position and status. But my parents, their struggle was for us, their children, and I believed I owed them.

I knew I had been a very difficult teenager, more sullen, a worse student than the other young people my parents knew. My various misdeeds, the hanging out, the skipping school, the drugs, the drinking, they had stolen away the chance for my parents to be proud as I pondered which Ivy League school I would attend; in fact I only initially made it into college because of people my mother had known. And then just as I had settled down some four years later, just as I transferred into the City University and began making all A's, this: the protests, the charges, and finally, the suspension.

In a sense, losing my student status in the last half of my senior year meant losing something of my parents. I felt a bit like they had given up on me. I was, after all, in my twenties now. What more could they do?

~

Against the disastrous backdrop of being put out of school, my precariously situated marriage toppled. I was twenty-three and two years married.

It was not that we didn't love each other, my first husband and I. It was that love was all we had. And we needed so much more. All couples do. We needed common passions and interests and goals. We needed to enjoy speaking with each other. We needed, then, some great omniscient who could have explained him to me, me to him.

What we had, instead, was silence. And in the face of that hard, that unfriendly quiet, my husband ran to work and stayed there for sometimes twelve, thirteen hours a day. I ran to school and did the same. By the time we'd come home, what else was there to do but sleep?

And we did, we slept. We slept fitfully, angrily, accusingly, but most of all, we slept singularly. We slept until there was nothing left to do except crawl out of bed, separately, and go on out into those two distinct worlds we had created for ourselves, his on one side of the universe, mine on the other.

And again my parents, with their happy, healthy, four-decade long marriage, my parents did not agree with or understand, how, after only two years, it could all fall apart. Everything had been so carefully constructed. I had, all of us had, listened to the experts, and tried to follow suit.

My first husband and I began life with an expensive, formal June wedding. I wore a white gown and veil. My father walked me down the aisle, and danced the first dance with me. We had joint bank accounts and credit cards. My husband said I didn't have to work, just go to school. I went to school. I cooked and cleaned. We had dinner parties. But in the end none of it worked because while we had the administrative part of it down, we were missing the creative. It didn't work because in the end, there were no words, no ongoing dialogues, no private jokes between us. And for many people, the absence of language is not enough reason to end a marriage. But for me it was the primary reason to do it. I know this now. I didn't know it then and this is why I could not run home to her, to my mother, who had, I'm sure, worked through and across silences to sustain her partnership with my father.

The bottom line was this: I wasn't running for my life from some kind of a monster, a batterer, a raging alcoholic. I was running from a man everybody loved, a man I loved. And this was why things got blamed on me. I had destabilized my own life, and then had the audacity to want sympathy, a shoulder, a helping hand.

I couldn't stay in a school. I couldn't stay in a marriage. I didn't have a job. So where could I stay? Who could I love? What could I do? What goal *could* I meet?

In the middle of the night, these questions would bang in my head. They would bang, like thick lead pipes against the sides of my dreams, bang and bang until I awoke. Awoke in fits of fear, sadness, isolation.

∾

I wanted love in my life again. I wanted to be important to someone again. I wanted to be accepted by someone again. My parents' disappointment, and my husband's disinterest, those things pushed and pricked like a thousand tiny pins menacing the soles of my feet. Whenever I walked, the pain of their rejection, what I translated as their rejection, would contort me; I suspected I looked like a sideshow act. That, or else an obvious failure. And I didn't know how not to be these things, how not to appear freakish, how not to be an outcast in the eyes of my family, and yes, in the eyes of men. That's the way breakups always seemed to leave me, especially at first, feeling undesirable, unlovable, ugly.

It was then no one single thing, but this terrific twister of loss and need that carried me into loving Rashid. For a year or more, he had been consistently inviting me up to the prisons to be part of their various cultural heritage shows, and I had gone each time, bringing other young people with me. One summer afternoon, I brought two young men I knew with me to do hip-hop poetry. One of the young men, a brother with a beautiful, sharp, carved face, stepped up to the mike. His tiny dreds stood firm on top of his head and it seemed like he was looking at everyone in the audience all at once, me, the prisoners, the police, everyone. Then he said, and I will never forget this,

> *Feel the rage of my warrior's wrath, as I pave a path of resistance.*
> *I want to put a head out. Now!*

As soon as those words hit the air, the stage was surrounded by more police than I have ever seen at one time, before or since, in a prison.

*All right! That's it!* one of the police said, and we were told we were going to have to leave the facility for "attempting to start a riot."

Before we were shoved out, I gave Rashid my home phone number. If we were being put out, I thought, what will they do to Rashid since he invited us up here?

*Call me,* I told him. I closed his hand around the tiny scrap of paper I had scribbled my number on.

*Call me if they give you any trouble because of this.*

Weeks, eight, maybe nine, pass between that incident and the first time I would answer my phone and hear what has now become an urgent and familiar recording:

*You have a collect call from . . . Rashid . . . an inmate at a correctional facility. If you wish to decline the call, hang up. To accept press three, now.*

And I did it. I pressed three and every part of my life, how I think, how I love, how I set priorities, what I pray for, what I treasure, what angers me, what I appreciate, how I organize my time, my money, every little thing in my life, and every big thing, changed. And it changed before I had a chance to seek consultation or ask a question. It changed before I had a chance to pause or reconsider. Or run.

# *this is the way you court a poet*

*t*he weeks that lead up to our first visit are now a blur of breathy phone calls and intense, biweekly letters. I told my girlfriends, the ones who asked me, that Rashid managed to romance me completely through those initial exchanges. I told them that it was those letters that hooked me. I told them that no woman has ever gotten a love letter until they've gotten a love letter from a man in prison.

Unlike my friends who have lovers whose range of feeling, they said, orbited within these two spheres: anger and lust, Rashid sweated out his emotion. *Every bit of it,* I told them. *He doesn't hold back on me the way so many men do.* All of Rashid's concerns and fears meet the paper, absent machismo, with a particular urgency: *Baby, I called last night, where were you?* Or: *asha, I didn't wanna love you like this 'cause I'm afraid you'll leave too, but I can't help it . . . you're so goddamn sweet.* But most often he just said: *Mama, if I could just hold you right now, if I could just touch you . . .*

Rashid was not a beautiful writer, no singing metaphors, no high art. But he was expressive, honest, and clear. He was vulnerable and so spiritually generous. Rashid gave me something I never had. Until we became involved, I had never been romanced. Surprise gifts, gooey cards, sappy words had never been mine.

When I fell in love with Rashid, already I had been married and had also lived with boyfriends, but still I was sure that romance was for other girls, delicate girls, the girls who I knew all throughout high school who heard their names called out over the radio: *That's "Ebony Eyes" going out to Yvonne from Michael with all of his love, always and forever . . .*

At twenty-five when Rashid sent me my first love letter, he dedicated a song by Luther Vandross to me in it. Maybe another woman my age would have thought this gesture was corny or juvenile. I cried. I thought it was oxygen.

When Rashid wrote, he wrote about my eyes. He said they were sexy, intimate, bedroom eyes. He said they were danger-ous eyes. At least dangerous for men, he said. No one had ever commented much on what my eyes looked like. Who sees your eyes when you're fourteen years old with *double D*-cup breasts? Or twenty-two, for that matter, who looks at your eyes?

The first time Rashid told me that he thought my eyes were one of my most beautiful features, I was insulted. I didn't know then that it was a compliment. I thought compliments could only be about legs, breasts, asses, and hips.

Let me tell you, that man courted me, all soft words and pure desire. No hidden agendas, no games, no emotional retardation, only reverence and passion from behind all of that stone and concrete, that steel and razor wire. It was out of a movie, an epic romance, the way Rashid loved, the way he wanted to be loved in return.

To this very day, his approach licks itself around my waist, tender, and without aggression. To this day, Rashid is unhur-ried, allowing me to direct the movement and pace, but always letting me know he is open, all the way, and ready for whatever I offer, whenever I offer it. No one, I am not exaggerating, no one had ever treated me like that, like a woman who ought to be handled with care.

I used to harass the mailman during those first few months. I used to stand there, staring over him as he dropped letters, bills, and magazines into other people's boxes, slowly making his way down to mine. I would sigh at him, dramatic and heavy. I would shift from one foot to the other, *real* heavy. When he did finally get to me, I would snatch that mail out of his hands and nearly knock him over as I pushed past him to race up the stairs to my apartment.

Once back home, I would throw, with disgust, all of my roommate's mail aside along with anything that came for me which was not clearly stamped *Eastern Correctional Facility*.

It was a ridiculous ritual.

I never even read Rashid's letters until hours later, when it was dark, long into the night. I wanted to be sure I wouldn't be interrupted by my roommate or the telephone. All these years later, I haven't changed this practice.

You have to understand, Rashid's letters are like dates. I have to get myself ready. I have to give them their proper space. Before I read his letters, I take a long, mango-scented bath. I burn white candles around the edge of the tub, and sandalwood incense, serenade my own self with Nina Simone songs (*Do I move you, are you willing*).

After, when I am dried and oiled and stretched out, when I have made a cup of vanilla tea, when I am dressed in something silk and loose, then I can invite Rashid in. *Come in,* I can say, and he does. And we sit for a while, speak softly and then rise, decide to go out, to breathe the night air together.

In those letters Rashid and I take long slow walks across the Brooklyn Bridge holding hands. Those letters, they are easy discussions over dinner. They're whispers on the slow, blue-light dance floor. They are 3:00 A.M. pillow talk. They are the embraces I crave, those letters. I dream by them, and they assure me that after an unsteady or else unforgiving night, morning comes. Morning always comes.

In the very beginning of our exchanges Rashid would also, in what I'm sure was an attempt to validate and provide context and history for our relationship, lift whole paragraphs out of *Soledad Brother.* And when he didn't lift words, he lifted arguments, until finally I complained. I told him that it didn't work for him to write as though he was George Jackson and I was Angela Davis. It was romantic, I told him, but we had a responsibility to be honest about ourselves. At this particular juncture in time, we didn't really have the skills to develop a theory that could liberate all Black people. One day. I could see it one day. But this day was just about us, which sounded so selfish, I cringed as I said it.

Still, if I was certain of anything, I was certain that we had to begin by learning how to love ourselves first, love ourselves fully first. If we could manage to do that, without codependence or control issues, we might really become useful to other Black people, I said. Useful to the world, I said.

# discovery

*R*ashid and I gave ourselves up to each other, publicly, in monitored phone calls, in scrutinized letters, and finally on videotape in prison visiting rooms. The months of our courtship fell without discipline and formed these odd mountains of time; before we knew it we were involved, an item, a tiny team climbing, our eyes shut tight, never looking down or back. And although it took many, many tries over many, many years, we did do it. We did reach the top of the mountain and we named that summit trust. We named it love, unconditional, and this was how we were able to thoroughly and completely turn back the years to each of our beginnings.

In the eight years we have now been together, through hushed and sometimes hesitating voices, we have excavated all of our years, the years of our lives that had been ripped in the center, the years without days, the years greater than the sum of their parts. We have examined these years, whatever has been left of them. We have laid them out and we have labeled them, but sometimes, when we have grown very tired, we have set them aside. We have left them alone for long, long periods. But we have never abandoned our journey (ourselves). We have always come back, always. We have faced our years and all that they have been, and all that they have not been, and we have tried, this I know for certain, we have tried as hard as two people have ever tried anything, to make some sort of peace with them.

Long into our relationship, I would see that our sharing,

our examining of ourselves, with all of its fervor, was, in a sense, a gift that the prison had given us. If strangers and even enemies could read our every letter, listen in on our every phone call, if they could witness our fights and our tears, if they could watch as the snot came down my face when I heaved, sobbed, and prayed for strength, what was there to hide from the person whom I loved?

But as incredible as our journey was and still is, it has also been intensely isolated, which is why friends question me constantly. They have often wondered out loud if I rushed headlong into some dangerous love affair, and I admit at first I had these intermittent doubts, not about Rashid, but about whether or not we could make a relationship something real, something we could touch, something that would sustain us.

Initially, I did tell Rashid we would have to go slow, just writing letters, just talking on the phone. A visit could come later, I said. But even those doubts, when I think about them now, I know they were really nothing more than background noise, and we easily blocked them out with all of our need, our nearly desperate willingness to love, and yes, even laughter, we blocked them with laughter as well.

Over two months, in thirty-two letters, twenty-four phone calls, and innumerable fantasies, we created ourselves, Rashid and I, as a couple, and in our eyes, a man and woman as normal as the men and women I'd see each day, together, holding hands, and taking for granted that very act, the holding of hands.

For us, and I mean the us who lived, not split in half by law and steel but the us from the letters and the fantasies, our romance was the truth. Everything else was a lie. This is what we believed then. And somehow, with so many of our dreams chipped or cracked or else ruined forever, this is what we believe now, today, in this moment of writing.

In a sense, an emotional sense if not a physical sense, our beginning really could have been anyone's beginning, imbued as it was with the familiar sort of nervous energy that undermined the struggle to be funny, charming, endearing, and brilliant in each statement.

Of course, back then my life had not become some imperiled landscape, a city existing upon a faultline; I didn't know then how it would be, living with the daily threat that everything I knew could break into unsalvageable pieces in a few violent angry seconds. I didn't know then how I would be stalked by the fear that in just one prison uprising, in even just one disagreement with a guard, what small joy Rashid and I might have created could be destroyed. I didn't know then what it would mean to consciously hand over the control of happiness in my life. Not all of it. But so much of it. Too much of it, there, held tight in the unpredictable hands of prison life.

# from the defense's files

*f*reedom, having the perfect love beside me, these things never seemed distant or impossible. Rather they were a tease, only barely out of my reach. If only I was granted one inch more we would be touching, Rashid and I, fingertip to fingertip. It made me obsessive, trying to figure out how to make my vision three-dimensional. It nearly swallowed me, the grasping and then missing, and then grasping once again. But I didn't lose hope. I just kept reaching, compulsive, like an addict. And Rashid, he fed this too, he was no innocent here.

How can I explain the way faith constructs itself within the narrow architecture of correctional institutions? They're not natural, these facilities, there's not ever enough space for a human being to live. And because of this, you have no choice, really. In order to survive, you must expand not only what you believe, but also how you go about believing it. You must expand it until you're nearly like a small child, accepting the implausible, the fantastic.

Rashid never believed that he would do all twenty years, which is the minimum time the state requires that he serves on his sentence. No one in prison ever thinks they're *really* going to take away all of that time from you, all of that life. He convinced me of this, that he would be home any minute. He convinced me because he was himself convinced.

Even when I was alone I couldn't really see any possible way they would keep Rashid, the man I was fast falling in love with. This man who had been my friend for two years, and my love for two months, surely he would be the one they would turn things around for, the one they would release early. Surely the ten years he had done *before* I'd known him was punishment enough. Surely now it was time to send him back out of prison and into my arms.

This is why I looked for him the way I did, always glancing around corners, checking faces on the subway, rushing anxiously home thinking that maybe. Maybe this day would be that day, the one when I would come home and find him there, in front of my apartment building, waiting, smiling.

It was a childish fantasy, I knew, not based in logic or reality. But that fantasy, sometimes it was all that could get me through, the idea that maybe today would be the day. If not, then perhaps the day after that, or the one after that. It was in this way that I would learn to measure Rashid's absence, to measure it and deflect its blows.

From very early on, Rashid's absence from the everyday of my life came out wild, swinging, some sort of renegade boxer. There were no rules, no referees. I had to structure a defense, one that I could sustain for this extended bout; when we fell in love, there was more than a decade left on his sentence.

Certainly though there were, in those initial weeks of ardent desire, these small spurts of nagging concerns when I wondered, What if he really has to do all this time, this whole other decade? Those moments, when they would come, it would feel like I had a choice, as though I was standing on the threshold between sanity and insanity. I couldn't figure out how to move, if to move, where I should go.

I couldn't imagine that the God I knew would have sent me the love I always wanted, the love I always needed, only to position it behind an unscalable wall. I prayed, I asked, *Was this my punishment for never being patient when I was a child? Was I to learn the lesson now, the one my mother tried but could not teach me, that patience is a virtue?*

When my fantasies would fail me as they sometimes did, the pain was free to snatch me up at gunpoint, make me walk a balance beam, not walk on it so much as run on it, jump on it. And maybe I would stay on and maybe I would fall off. I never knew, but either way, it made me exist within the fear that I had nearly no room to move. I used to think about falling off, how it could perhaps be a relief. No more fighting to keep balance. I thought these things, then, during week one, week two, week five, and week six of our relationship. I think these things, though less often now, in year eight of it.

But my fantasies, always they return to me, and still I walk home from the store, the gym, the poetry reading, the editor's meeting, thinking what if he's there, waiting on my stoop? What will I do? Will I faint, will I cry, will I scream, will I just grab him, pull him inside my apartment, and vow never to move from that space, that time?

They are like my own psychotropic prescription. They lift me, and although it is only for a moment, it's still enough to allow me to keep it and that I have, pushing on into the next letter, the next phone call, the next level of love, commitment.

*I am not crazy. I am not crazy. It is right for me to love him. It is. It is.*

I would chant these words when I awoke, chant them before I slept, chant them in the streets, chant them on the subways, over and over and over and over. I chanted until my chanting took on a physical form; it became something I could see, a picture, a painting. I saw our love in pastels bordered with brash dark oils. I could see this as if it hung on my wall, and for a time there was nothing else to be noticed, nothing else to be contemplated. I'm sure now that this is how they were able to advance on me, the years I've now spent going in and out of the prison. To advance, and then line up before me, poised, like some merciless firing squad.

# on the road:
## an update for the nineties

*t*he first time I visited Rashid not as a volunteer, but as a girlfriend, his girlfriend, it was the day after Christmas, the earliest part of the day, and I was sitting in a van, one of the many that a partner, a sister, a father or mother can take to get to one of the seventy prisons which are scattered across New York State.

Outside my window I watched morning pull reluctantly over the burnt edges of the South Bronx neighborhood, the place that served as the final stop the prison-bound van would make in the city before heading upstate. There was a coffee shop where we could go to the bathroom or buy breakfast. Most of the women piled out, and moments later, piled back in.

The van which transports up to fourteen people to the prison is always overwhelmed by the smell of bacon-and-egg sandwiches, coffee and hot chocolate, inexpensive perfume, hair pomade, nail polish, and skin laced with that last, desperately smoked cigarette. The air locks like a hangman's noose, a noose we have slipped our own necks into. The ride begins.

Two years into my relationship with Rashid, when he was transferred eight hours away from New York City, somewhere in north hell, to a facility that is walking distance from the Canadian border, and riding the van was not an option, I came to appreciate, even mourn its absence. The transfer, which was incorrectly ordered, was eventually overturned, but only after months and months of administrative and legal battles. And in the year before Rashid came back downstate, I learned how very nasty this life can get.

I learned from the very minute that I arrived at Columbus Circle in mid-Mahattan at 11 P.M. on one Friday night to meet the bus which would take me and several hundred other women to the faraway prison, the one up near Canada. And there, at Columbus Circle, waiting to head out, I was just half a mile from where I grew up. This is what I was struck by, standing in central Manhattan, under a midnight April rain: the proximity of the bus stop to my parents' house was far more predominant in my mind than that steady, cold showering, and the whimpering babies, and the impatient buzz of all those women, women like me, corralled, watching our faces fall down.

I fumbled in my bag for an umbrella and thought about how much my parents wanted to protect us, my sister and me, from anything and anyone and anyplace that would take away our choices, that would constrict our freedom. Private schools, summer camps, piano lessons, dance lessons, swimming, horseback riding, art classes, gymnastics, there was nothing my parents thought to refuse us if it would help us to become emotionally strong, independent women. What would they have said and what would they have felt if they'd seen me right then, about to board a bus where the first thing you're told is not the destination, but,

*No cigarette or crack smoking on the bus, and no drinking no kind of liquor or beer.*

When I was a teenager with no curfew, every weekend I roamed the streets of my neighborhood with my best friend Nicole, drinking beer and cheap wine, smoking cigarettes and spliffs, discussing nuclear destruction, sex, love, isolation, drugs, and music. Sometimes we would sit, the two of us, by the fountain at Lincoln Center. Other times we would wander over to Central Park, to the entrance at Fifty-ninth Street and Columbus Circle, past all of these women who were standing there amid boxes, bags, and babies, waiting to board buses that were headed to places we didn't know.

We knew nothing of prisons then, Nicole and I, as we passed the women nearly every Friday night. And as we passed, perhaps we whispered, but we never really wondered about them, the women, who they were, what they thought, what they were doing there. And we never feared, at least I never feared, that the sharp-edged world our parents tried to warn us about and protect us from could come slicing down into the heart of our dreams. Wherever Nicole is now, perhaps she is safe, perhaps she has avoided ever getting cut. I hope this is true, that she has never bled, in the way I have now bled, from the center of my life, from the very pulse of it.

But as a sad teenager who didn't see life past my twenty-first birthday, there was no way I could have ever predicted this moment when my life, the whole of it, was about to be pushed onto a bus and then squeezed into a seat which was not made to hold two grown people comfortably. Strangers we were, the woman and I stuffed in next to each other, swelled with stress, hoping to sleep for at least thirty minutes, an hour. We tried to sleep somehow without touching each other, without taking up space that didn't belong to us.

When Rashid was finally transferred back downstate, back within a two-hour drive from New York City, I called Freddie, my old van driver, and told him I'd returned. *Thank God*, I'd said. *Come get me, come pick me up*, I said, *on Thursday for a visit*.

He is a grumpy man, Freddie the van driver, but he is a good man, hardworking, like my father, exactly so. And being back on the van felt like coming home. I hated that it felt like that, but the familiar faces I saw in the seats, the door-to-door service, and Freddie holding open and closing the door for me, made me relax.

The first time I saw Freddie after the faraway upstate horror show, I wanted to hug him, but of course I didn't. In this world, it would be improper. It would be suggestive. With my man locked away, there are already suspicions that I, that women in my position, are lonely, even desperate. I simply said good morning to Freddie, as did he to me, although he mumbled his greeting. He grunted it almost.

*Freddie,* one of the women called out, *you got to open that window. And turn the music up too.*

I looked around at the women in the van, their young, old, and middle-aged faces were all locked up, just like mine. Their emotions were tucked into the corners and folds and wrinkles of their flesh. Their hairdos were protected by cotton-poly scarves, and their makeup was perfect. Their nails were long, curled, and colored. Their clothes, like my clothes, were, for the most part, their Sunday best. I absorbed those women, my sisters (myself), as though we were a masterpiece painting.

We were like an Easter Parade on crack.

# the edge:
## topography of a first date
## in a prison

*W*hen I went to see Rashid, we arrived for the six-hour visit at almost nine in the morning. Now, after these eight years of going up and back, the ride can feel endless, those four drawn-out hours from door to door. But my first time I was so excited and nervous, I thought we got there, to the prison, almost before I even found a seat in the van.

We pulled into the parking lot of the prison, the one I was so familiar with, the one that looked like a castle, the one I had been volunteering in for almost two years, the one which held Rashid. I followed the more experienced visitors up a long ramp, through two sets of unbelievably thick, heavy metal doors. It was not an entrance I had ever used before. But that was not the only thing which was different about this visit.

How I got treated by police had also changed; I was no longer a volunteer. I was a prisoner's lover now, his woman, his partner. Being a volunteer afforded me a tiny measure of courtesy, but being a lover, a girlfriend, afforded me mostly hostility and suspicion. Mothers, sisters, friends, fathers, cousins, and wives, all of us were treated with hostility and suspicion.

I entered a room with gray lockers and black plastic chairs, two bathrooms, a metal detector, and two police positioned behind a desk with no chairs. As instructed, I filled out a form, and when the police called my name, not my name, but Rashid's number, I walked over to the desk. I had put all of my things into a locker, except a change purse, a lipstick, a comb, and a pen. As a volunteer, I could always bring in my bag. As a visitor, the same bag became contraband. I handed over my change purse, form, and ID to an officer who did not look at me.

*Remove your shoes, coat, and jewelry. Place them on the desk.*

I did as I was told, and then began to walk through the metal detector.

*Not yet!* I was admonished. *Go back to the other side of the machine and wait until I'm ready.*

*Pen and lipstick ain't allowed. I'll hold onto them until you come out or you can put them back in your locker.* He said this, and then told me, *Now, go through the metal detector.*

I stepped through and it beeped.

*Do it again and don't touch the sides.*

I did as I was told, and went through once more without making a sound.

The officer motioned me through two electronically locked doors. The first one opened, and I stepped through. It closed, and then the second one opened, and I entered another large room with rows and rows of orange and black chairs, vending machines, and tables. I handed my entry form to an officer who was sitting at a desk in the front of the room. I took a seat at a table which was in the furthest corner of the room. I waited, nervous, feeling discomforted by the search process.

There would come a time a few years later when that search would seem like child's play, friendly almost. That time came after I married Rashid, and it would remind me of a story, a piece of history that had been trapped in my throat since I learned of it. It had been trapped there and it had been rotting.

It was the story of the Venus Hottentot. The first time I read about her, I did not know, I could not have known how she would follow me. But then the first time I read about the Venus Hottentot, the eighteenth-century Black South African woman who had been tricked into migrating to England, who had been stripped and forced into a British circus cage, who had been gawked at, talked about, trampled by a thousand hard, white eyes, I had never been inside a prison. What did I know then about cages, humiliation, forced exposure?

Getting processed into visiting rooms across New York State means police have the right to scan even my tampons and hold them up to the light. It is almost always men who do these searches. Almost every single time.

After we are married and granted conjugal visits, before I enter the trailer site where Rashid and I will spend our time, it will be my panties, diaphragm, and K-Y Jelly that male officers hold out in public often as a company of inmates is walking past five, maybe eight feet, from us. They have fingered my black silk panties, the ones I bought for only Rashid to see. They've shaken down my bra, my nightgown, even though it is sheer.

The first two or three times that happened to me, I felt immodest. I felt shame and embarrassment. Now I feel camaraderie with women who work the peep shows or who lap dance for a living. Except, of course, that I don't get paid. But you know I think I should. For every glance that gets held too long, for each time one of those police runs his fingers across my underwear, those motherfuckers owe me, in the very least, cash money.

∾

And then there was a morning when the wire in my bra set off the metal detector. The sergeant looked at my chest and then told me that,

*Of course you don't have to go through this kind of search. But if you want to get this visit, you going to have open up your shirt and let the female officer scan you. In the bathroom of course. It's a normal security procedure and the directive's posted over there if you want to read it.*

What choice did I have? I followed the female officer, a Puerto Rican woman who looked as though she could have been my mother, into the women's restroom. She did not want to search me any more than I wanted to be searched. She knew like I knew that it was completely unnecessary. A hand scanner could have been used over the top of my denim blouse. But in prison, those who have any modicum of power need neither logic nor decency to guide them through their decisions. Had I chosen to argue the point, even if I won, visiting hours would have been over.

Because she could not be hostile to the man who was her ranking officer, this female police was hostile to me. So much for sisterhood being global. It wasn't even local. In any case, as nasty as she got, barking orders as though *I* had offended her, her attitude had little impact on me.

Before I had even walked into that bathroom, I was gone, the soul of me was gone. It was disappeared out of my body. I was functioning but not present, split off and detached. It was a trick I had learned to do while having sex. It was an ancient trick; I could not remember a time when I did not know how to leave in this way.

My hands undid the first few buttons of my blouse, as my mind drew pictures on the walls, orange and green strokes dipped in screams. I saw myself dancing between the colors on the wall, uninhibited and unburdened. My body was see-through blue, a Caribbean ocean wave. I was rising in slow motion, all strength and untouchable, roaring, sky-bound, winged.

*Lower,* the officer said, *open your shirt up all the way. You're still beeping. And the jeans, take them down past your thighs.*

I unbuttoned, pulled down, turned forward and back. I outstretched my arms, shook out my bra, all the while, all inside myself, I was chanting and singing, visualizing and meditating.

In the end I was left standing there with my shirt and bra open and my pants pulled down. And for all of that, contraband was never found, nor was it ever really expected to be found. The reality is that if they truly feared I had some weapon stashed on me which was making the metal detector go off, why would they send me into a locked room with one of their unarmed officers, who was a woman twice my age and half my size?

*All right,* she growled, *get dressed and next time don't wear no underwire bra.*

I haven't worn anything but underwire bras since I was fifteen, maybe fourteen years old. In the all the years that I have been going into the prisons and through the metal detectors, I have never worn anything but underwire bras.

But those machines can be adjusted to varying degrees of sensitivity, which always makes us, the visitors, wonder if the metal detector has as much to do with harassment and power than with security. *If this was about security,* I complained once to another woman who had also just gone through metal detector drama, *the machine would always register that I was wearing an underwire bra.*

*Yup,* she said. She nodded and poked out her lip, frustrated. *You right about that.*

*I mean the thing would always be hypersensitive, unless of course the police felt it was okay to sneak knives or guns in one day, but not the next. You know what I'm saying,* I continued, and she agreed.

Given this, it has, therefore, been no surprise to me that in the years since the incident, the years where all of my bras have had underwire in them, not once has the metal detector ever gone off again. Not once.

When I told Rashid what happened to me, I expected him to be outraged about it, but he wasn't. Disturbed, maybe. Sorry that I went through the search. But not livid, rushing to his word processor to pound out memorandums and complaints to officials in Albany.

At some point I realized why my ordeal must have seemed small in his eyes. After every visit he has with me or anyone else, my baby gets strip-searched, often by men who openly despise him. In a small cubicle, he is told to remove all of his clothes and shake them out. He is made to run his hands through his hair, to open his mouth wide, lift his tongue, lift his balls, turn around and squat, then stand again, display the bottom of his feet, and then turn back around and face the police. Once, while waiting to be processed, a female officer bragged to me and two other women about how she could strip-search a male inmate if she had to. *It's in the rules,* she said to us, grinning and confident.

When I learned about strip searches, what they entailed, I was shocked. My stomach knotted up. Whatever I had imagined did not live up to the description Rashid gave me, and I knew that despite the arguments that explained why such a process was necessary, I could never, ever do such a job. No matter what. I couldn't participate in that sort of humiliation. Not of anyone. Not at anytime. I wondered about the police who did it, day in and day out, especially the ones who could brag about it to wives and girlfriends. What did they go home and tell their children? *Daddy looks up men's assholes for a living.*

I realized that Rashid was not outraged by what happened to me because searches were something he was nearly desensitized to; humiliation is the daily fabric worn to fray in the life he leads and the life I was choosing to live along with him.

Both of us knew, we said this to each other, that we had a responsibility to fight some of the battles the prison system instigated, but if we fought every single one that was thrown our way, what time would be left to laugh or to dream, to hope or to just be at peace? And then who would be the real winners?

We take the experience and shove it deep down inside ourselves. We crush it like trash to be bagged, compacted, taken out, and eventually, incinerated.

Inspections, interrogations, suspicions, and searches, there's a kind of freedom in being forced to place yourself in the hands of people who hate you, have them hold you up to the light, scan you, scrutinize you. This is what I have come to believe, finally, that there is a purity in sharing when there's nothing left to hide, no spaces for modesty or retreat.

I know that Rashid understands me as no lover has. I know

I am unburdened with him, never worrying that he will find out the woman I really am, the woman I hid or tried to deny with every other man I have ever been involved with.

We play no games, tell no lies, have no camouflage, are as naked and displayed as the Venus Hottentot, Rashid and I. All we have, all we are, and all we hope to be is out on the table, dissected and documented. We can either wither apart and give in to the madness, or else struggle, keep honoring that, despite everything, we can still love and make the love feel good.

And we wear our love in the way long intersecting roots wear the earth. And we wrap it around ourselves the way I've seen children wrap blankets around themselves. Beautiful, thick cotton blankets from Mexico with familiar colors and insistent patterns. That is what our love looks like. And we pull ourselves tight and together, beneath blankets, beneath earth, and we are warmed through and through. In cold, stark visiting rooms, we whisper that this cannot last forever, and we are warmed.

During that first visit, however, I was not very wise about how to survive within the walls of a prison. The first time, I sat at a table as far away from the guard's desk as possible; I thought that this would give us privacy, but later I learned that I had positioned myself directly in front of a two-way mirror. But that morning, sitting there dressed all in white, I did not consider such invasions, only the artifice and oddities of that large room with its plastic plants and its plastic chairs, the children scurrying everywhere, the women breathing back their tears, and all those men, those mostly Black men, those mostly strong, handsome men moving uncomfortably through the space in ugly, green, state-issued pants.

Suddenly there was a loud, jarring buzz, and then a door near to me opened and Rashid walked through. I recognized him immediately, although just the night before, when I had tried for several minutes, I found I could not call his face to me. I could not see it there, behind my eyes.

It was his voice, his handwriting, that I had come to know intimately. How to assign them, now, to that mouth, to that right hand? He greeted me, Rashid did, with a smile as big as the time he has served in these stone walls. I smiled back, but I did not stand, and I did not move. I did not know what I should do. In the two years that we had been friends, we had never hugged tightly, nor kissed, nor held each other's hands. In the two years that we had known each other, I could not remember a time when we had ever once touched for any more than a few brief seconds. Yet here we were, somehow together, in this bizarre place, having declared our love, but having never embraced.

*I should kiss him, full, my mouth in his mouth.*

That was what I thought as he approached me.

*I should hold him, pull him to me so that he can feel all the passion in my twenty-five-year-old body.*

*I should run my hands through his hair, ease my fingers down his back.*

*I should whisper sexy things into his ear.*

I thought those things, but I did not act on them. I did not move and I did not speak, until Rashid said,

*Hey, girl, can I get a hug?*

And I rose, I took him in my arms, not in the way that I

wanted to, but in the way that I felt was appropriate. I embraced him only lightly. I did not push my body hard into his. He kissed me on my cheek.

We were restrained, both of us, but for a long time after the hug was over, we continued standing. We stood and we held hands, and if either one of us had had the courage to have spoken right then in those slow minutes, we would have said, *I love you*. I am sure of this.

We would have said it with all the conviction we had said it in letters and even on the phone. But this was different, unlike the calls and letters, we were at once without barrier or boundary. My eyes were firm upon his eyes and there was no turning back. That visit seemed to be the difference between talking about how much you wanted to skydive, talking about it for months and months, and then finally the day coming, and you are there, being told to get over by the open door of the plane. Courage can take a walk in that moment, it can curl up in a corner, curl up into a place where you can no longer see it.

This was how we were: perched at the edge of a airplane, thousands of miles above an expansive and unknowable landscape, wondering, when the time came, would our parachutes work, would all those lessons, the ones we'd learned that had brought us to this day, be in any way useful, if we took a deep breath, and if we said a prayer, and if we closed our eyes and if we just did it, if we went ahead, if we jumped?

# conversations, 1: the fall

*i*f you're going to survive in prison, when you come in you got to be cool for a minute. Just watch until you can read the script, see what's up.

On our first visit I was full of questions about Rashid, about prison, about survival. We were sitting at the table. We were sitting very close. Our legs touched and a chill coasted down my back and as I was riding this chill, Rashid said he wanted me to know all about his case. In front of us were his transcripts.

*You need to know if you're going to be with me.*

I did not know then about prison protocol, how people rarely discuss their crimes even with their wives. Sometimes I talk to women now, women who ride the vans with me. They tell me how little they know about their husband's case, how they ask and ask, and how he won't divulge details beyond the nature of the crime.

What Rashid was doing on our first visit was setting up a foundation of honesty and trust. I see this now, but then I was not ready, and I did not understand. I was not prepared for Rashid, the man I was beginning to love, the man I was beginning to enjoy loving, to evaporate, and in his place, have a killer appear.

*Can we talk about other things first?*

I nearly pleaded this, and Rashid agreed, and instead began explaining prison life to me.

*Things here will get pretty clear to you—eventually—but if you rush, you'll make mistakes and offend somebody, and then it's a big fight and who needs that, you know what I mean?*

*When I first got locked down, I moved real easy. One of the things I noticed right away was how brothers acted in the mess hall. Okay, for example, you might be sitting at a table with somebody you don't know, so the whole time, you're not talking, it's total silence, but still you would never just get up or turn your back to him. When you get ready to do that, you knock on the table twice. Like this.*

Rashid knocked, two fast, hard raps, on our visiting room table.

*Really?* I said.

*Yeah. You know where that comes from?* he asked. But before I could respond, he continued,

*Back in the day, police couldn't speak to inmates so they used to knock on walls with their batons to signal when to stop and when to go. One knock meant stop, two meant go. So prisoners just got that into their way of communicating. Not speaking, but banging. All of us do it.*

Right then, we were interrupted by a couple who was passing by our table. Rashid introduced them and told me afterwards that the young man was locked in a cell near his. He told me that they were becoming friends.

*What'd he do?* I asked.

*I don't know, baby.*

*But he's your friend.*

*Yeah, but we don't speak about that. Dudes don't speak about their crimes too tough in here. I mean it's just not done. The only reason for me to know would be like, say, if I was helping him with his case.*

*The only reason?* I challenged. *What if he was a rapist or a child molester?*

*Come on now, baby. People with that kind of case, you know about, and obviously I wouldn't mess with him.*

*What if he was a wife beater? What if he killed his wife? Is killing a woman better than raping her?*

And that question hung between us by a thin rope until finally it fell, a loud, violent, crashing fall. Pieces sprayed everywhere. I picked up some of the pieces and Rashid picked up some of them, but still there was this mess. Frustrated, we walked away from it. We said we would come back. We said we would clean it up later.

# conversations, 2:
## did you drive away fast,
## did you drive away slow?

*d*id terrible dreams come split the night and render it useless, unsalvageable? Did you wake up with a start, the way they do in movies? Did your sweat drip down the air? Did your breath go tight? Did you slope into the morning, like a tired, unwilling guest?

Did you make love to your woman? Did you kiss her more intensely? Did you stare at her nipples before you put them in your mouth? Did she become uncomfortable with you staring? Did she tell you *Please just do it, Poppi, I can't wait any longer?* Did you tell her she would have to? Did you say if you went slow, you always would remember?

And did you? Remember?

Did you dance, man? Did you put Luther on the stereo? Did you pull your woman out of bed, and wrap your arms around her waist, and was it your naked arms, and was it her naked waist? Did you sing along with Luther when he said *A chair may be a chair, but a house is not a home if no one's living there?*

Did you run your hands along your books and records, along the fabric of your couch, along the clothes hanging in your closet? Did you jingle your keys? Did you lock and unlock your door? Did you throw your window open, stick your head outside unrestricted?

Did you see your boys on the corner? Did you go and give them each a pound? Did you all smoke cigarettes together? Did you all smoke a spliff? Did you ride around the block and say you thought the South Bronx was really beautiful? Did your boys say *'Cuzz you crazy, better leave that weed alone?* Did you laugh when they said this? Was your laughter a lie?

Did you drive out to Jersey so that you could see your son? Did you kiss him, did he gurgle, did you whisper that you love him? Did you leave his mama money? Did you tell her go buy herself something nice? Did she notice you seemed different? Did you say, yes? Yes.

Did you drive away fast, did you drive away slow? Did you look into your rearview mirror and see no reflection looking back? Did you feel terrified in that moment, all gangster bravado crumbled? Did you take a look again, in the mirror that did not reflect you, and did you scream, that second time, did you scream, did you know?

*What did you do on the day they came and got you, the day you were arrested? Was there some sort of foreboding? Did you feel that it was coming?*

I ask these questions of Rashid when we first become a couple, and for a long time he considered them.

*You never see it coming, asha.* This is what he says. *There wouldn't be so many people dead, and there wouldn't be so many people here, if we could ever see it coming.*

# conversations, 3:
## the charge was murder

*t*he charge was murder in the second degree. The man who was killed had been somebody's husband. He had been somebody's father. Rashid was nineteen years old, and acting in concert with his big brother and an older man named Lou. The transcripts told me this.

*The man had been Lou's partner. Lou said he was robbing him, and that upset me because Lou was sort of like my father.* Rashid told me this.

*But I was a little afraid of him, Lou, I mean. The thing was once he told me what was planned, I guess I felt if I backed out Lou might get me too.*

Rashid paused, and then,

*Not that that's an excuse. It's just the way it was.*

And that was what I wanted to know most of all, how it was, everything, the day itself, what was it like? I demand to know from Rashid, was it hot like the hot they say that can drive a man crazy? Was it cold, a mean, icy, stinging, wet cold? Was the moon full? When we did discuss the case in its entirety, I found I needed something to explain it beyond what had been recorded by the courts. *Give me some reason, some huge, terrible, beyond-your-control reason.* I urged Rashid, I begged him, I implored, *Tell me, tell me,* but he offered me nothing. He said only that,

*I can barely remember the day. Not in details like you're asking, asha. All these years, I've tried not to think of it. Thinking of it is*

60

*worse than doing the bid, if you can believe that. It's worse. That's
why I had to get rid of that person, that man I used to be. As much
as possible, I had to block out all the bad stuff from those days. If I
didn't it would have driven me insane. I'm telling you, girl, I would
have been a lunatic.*

I understood that and I told Rashid so. I told him and then
let it go for the moment. We began to discuss other things,
small things, lovers' things. We held each other. We moved on.
At 3:30 the guard announced that visiting hours were over. We
embraced before I left, and as I turned to walk toward the
door, Rashid asked me to wait a second.

*After, I threw up and was in bed for days. I remember that. I
remember that.*

It never goes away, not forever, the murder. No matter what
we do, no coercion or coaxing, no bribe, no begging, no physical force, no slap or scream, no denial, no good deed, no belief
in God, or life or love, can make it go away. At best, it retreats
for a time, at best.

Once, in the middle of a discussion about children, how we
love them, both of us do, I just inserted the question. I asked
Rashid, how did he manage to confront it?

*You can't possibly just block it out all the time, can you?* I posed
this as a question, but it was an accusation, really. *How do you
deal with it?*

*Without having the choice to do anything else.*

Rashid's voice was flat, but not sarcastic. He was looking
the other way from me.

*And I pray. I pray for forgiveness.*

*From who? From her?* I asked, *From his wife?*

*From God,* he responded, and then,

*I don't know how to ask her. But I've tried to anyway. In my prayers I've asked. I've prayed for her forgiveness. And his too. The child's, I mean. The man's son. His son, and also my own son.* He pulled his lips together tight, Rashid did, and he nodded his head slowly, and then he stopped speaking.

That was when I changed the subject. Again. Like always. Eventually, I always just change it.

# conversations, 4:
# visions, visitations

*t*he way I've learned to look at the crime is in small pieces, never as a whole. As a whole it would be too big. Taken all at once, it could knock me over, it could knock the breath out of me. I knew this immediately, which is why I crept up on it the way I did, one section at a time, from the back to the front, from the Rashid of today to the Rashid of yesterday.

There are young people who come into the prisons as part of a program designed to get them off the path of juvenile delinquency and steer them away from crime forever. Rashid heads this program. He has for years now. Sometimes when he talks about it, he tells me that he understands how those young people hurt, not just how, but also where.

*That's why they love you,* I tell him. *Why so many of them say you saved their life.*

I say this to Rashid, thinking of the letters that have been written to the prison both about him and the youth program. Rashid nods his head, and then almost smiles and then looks down. And when he does this, these three subtle movements, I know he is embarrassed. He is less interested in accepting my compliments, or the compliments of the young people, than he is in simply being polite enough to acknowlege that I have spoken. My partner is, he has become, a very humble man.

And I close my eyes around that image, the one of my life-saving partner, my generous partner, my modest partner, my loving partner. I paste it up, make it a permanent part of my sight. And I go to it, the current image of Rashid, that picture, when I can no longer avoid the murder or the face of a killer.

≈

There were these times when it was very, very still and very, very late that she would come to me, the widow, the woman left behind. Quiet, that's how she always was, never imposing, and never mean. She would come to me in my room, the one which was filled with pictures of Rashid and me holding each other, Rashid and me in love. She would sit there on my bed, and she would look at me, but it wasn't hostile, her look. It was a curious sort of look, one that asked questions, one that wondered, perhaps, who I was, who Rashid was, for me to love him the way I did.

I would always meet her eyes at every visitation. It was the least she deserved, this is what I felt, the very least, indeed. When she came, I would look at her levelly and continuously, until whenever she'd choose to leave. It was not an easy thing to do, never. But every time I managed to do it, to hold her gaze steady, woman to woman across a history cut short and cut jagged, I would feel rooted more deeply in the love I'd been given.

If I could still love Rashid in that moment when I was looking in her face, could we possibly be wrong then, could we possibly be a lie? I would ask her these questions, I would whisper them to her each time she'd come, but she would never answer me, and she would never stay.

# the place we go to,
# the way we get there

*f*rom the very beginning of our relationship, we have danced, Rashid and I, there in the visiting room, between the plastic tables and the plastic chairs, and beside the daylight that fails, that falters behind those old venetian blinds shut tight and weighed down by years of dust, years and years of it. We dance slow, and we dance steady, and I sing in his ear, and if anyone, other visitors or prisoners or even the police, if any of them have looked upon us as though we are strange, we have never noticed it.

In that room, all of us, with all of our differences and all that separates us, we still know this one thing. We know that to survive in prison we have to transform not only ourselves, but our spaces, our imaginations, that table, this chair, everything must change, everything.

This is what I think about, not always, but sometimes, when we are dancing, and when the visiting room is becoming our private room, and the bars have fallen away, and the doors and the locks have crumbled, and nothing and no one exists except our two bodies, our brown eyes, our locked hands, our barely moving feet, and the music we make together. That's all, nothing else is there, not one other thing.

*What is the moment your life changes course forever?* One afternoon I was holding onto Rashid as we danced, and that question came to me. I wondered how you would know that moment to identify it, to grab it up out of the air? I thought it probably wouldn't be the obvious one, the moment that announces its arrival, the one that crashes and splatters, the one we would note in our journals, and tell our friends about, and tell strangers even. If it were indeed that moment, I thought, then we could control it as it started to race toward us. We could make the decision to either get out of the way or else embrace it.

Later I argued that point to a friend. I said to her how you're never conscious of the moment of irrevocable change, but she told me I was wrong. She said it was indeed the big moment, the one of the impact. I asked her to imagine that she was crossing a street and then suddenly a drunk driver sped by and hit her as she stepped off the curb. What was the moment of change, I asked her? Was it the moment when the car hit, or the moment when the driver got behind the wheel, or when he started drinking that night, or when she, my friend, went outside, out onto the curb?

Dancing with Rashid has made me believe that my life didn't change when I told people it changed. My life changed long before the first phone call, or letter, or visit, and I now wonder if perhaps it was when I saw that my ex-husband would never make himself a great emotional presence in my life, and I realized I would need that. I would need it more than I needed a physical presence even, more than sleeping next to a man every night, more than sitting across a dinner table from him every evening.

Perhaps that moment of realization was when my life changed, but perhaps not. Perhaps my moment of change happens every time Rashid takes me in his arms and holds me tightly in the room we have made our own room, and begins to move himself and move me to the quiet rhythm of the music that we are playing in our own heads, and somehow, somehow, we begin to exist only in the freedom of the imagination we are sharing, as though we are one mind and one body, one vision and one thought riding the back of the sun to a place in ourselves that no one else will ever be able to see or separate, or touch or take away, or isolate or imprison.

# *when i was a child*

*R*ashid and I always came back to this discussion on transformation, the possibility of it. It was an idea that spiraled inward; we began with the need for reform in the prison and in the world outside, but the more we talked, the more we found the need to focus on the world inside. We became mirrors for each other.

Of course Rashid needing and wanting to transform was obvious. His history demanded this of him. But I was not without my own issues and they also required examination, their own process of transformation. This was not immediately apparent, however, and at first I suppose I did just sort of bask in the admiration Rashid had for me.

After doing all those programs in the prisons, after hearing all my poems and politics, Rashid had constructed me as this strong, sharp, independent woman, a woman with a tongue made of fire who could argue back the dark. I was, in his eyes, a woman with a spirit made of steel, an unbreakable woman.

And certainly it did, this image, have its bits of truth, as much as any illusion holds some truth in the eye of the believer, which Rashid was, and perhaps I was as well. I believed the masquerade that I had, myself, created. And not only did I believe it, I counted on it, on her, the pretend asha. I had envisioned her not as my understudy but as my replacement; just like in the movies, she would step out of the shadow of the chorus and take over for me. (I had collapsed somewhere offstage.)

Almost from the minute she emerged, the audience went

wild for the replacement asha. She had so much more confidence than I, so much more stamina. She could take the midair leaps that my legs always refused. She was the more dramatic performer, the funny one, the one with so much more charm, the one people remembered with a smile.

I got used to her being me, Rashid and I both did, and this was why it was completely devastating when she left the show, and I was forced to return to myself without any warning, and without any direction, and without even any rehearsal.

This is how it happened:

Rashid and I decided that we would tell each other everything, that there would never be any secrets between us. We didn't know then what that would mean, how it would strip us, leave us before each other without weapons, shields, masks.

This is what we knew:

Telling everything was the only way to understand how we could ever have arrived at this place. We believed it was the only way we would figure out how we would go from it one day, and, as George Jackson said, *leave nothing behind.*

When we talked, we discovered we could travel out of the prison, sometimes out of America. The fullness of our communication became, and still is, the road out of the prison, the road back home.

*Will you take me to Guyana?*

I asked Rashid this on one Tuesday visit when it was raining outside and we were leaning into each other and we were whispering. Rashid said he would take me to Guyana. He said,

*Of course. As soon as I'm home, we're going to go.*

*No,* I corrected. *I mean now. Can you take me there now?*

And he did, he took me there. He drew me the most incredible, the most vibrant and detailed picture of growing up in Guyana. And I could feel it, and I could taste it, and I could see it, and I could smell it, the splash and salt of that heated green sea. And I could see him there, Rashid.

I could see the way it once was: him, a small boy playing, running, making mischief, and all the mothers scolding him, and all the old men playing dominoes on corners, the boys scampering up the coconut trees, the girls in their Catholic school uniforms, and everywhere green, and mountains, and the tiny family shops, and wide, wide marketplace, and even the poverty, but the being together, at least that, the unity and symmetry of that world.

The way the prison had it, Rashid started and stopped in one moment, in one place, as a criminal, a convict, but I knew there was more. I knew his picture stretched back thirty years. And I knew his picture was a complex construction of color and lighting. Every time I looked at it I could find something different, and this is why I knew I needed to leave it hanging there on my wall where I could go back and study it, again and again.

*I wish I never came to this country.*

Rashid never said this to me, to say it would have been a sort of renunciation of our love, but I knew he must have thought it, even if it would have meant there would have been no us. And we were, so quickly, after the first few exchanges, with our openness, and our need, already, an us.

Yes, he and I, a couple, although there were no double dates, no Saturday nights at the movies. The only proof we had, the only tangible proof, was our communication, and we clung to it; in our relationship, it became exalted. When we were on the phone, I would close my eyes, and I would press my cheek closer into the receiver. It was an instinctual reaction; I wanted to be nearer to him, and in a way, when I made this almost imperceptible gesture, I was. On the inside, I was.

During those early phone calls, I would curl up in my bed and light my candles and burn my incense and play Coltrane's "Greensleeves," and refuse to allow the prison to be the sole arbitor of the atmosphere in which we had to live, in which we were going to build this love. Even now, not always, but often enough, there are quiet horns blowing from my CD player and incense and candles burning, a tenuous peace.

Talking with Rashid on the phone or in person made me think about how all my life I had walked into love like I was walking into a war zone, into a land that had been mined. I tried to move in camouflage, with guns strapped to my waist and a first-aid kit in a bag on my back. I felt every step made me more vulnerable, and eventually I would freeze. Eventually, I would stop going forward. I could not remember ever being another way.

Before Rashid, I could never rest with love, I could never relax with it, never fall back into its arms. I didn't trust the thing. With Rashid everything was so different. I was able, from our very first conversation, to be open with him, completely, to be all of who I was, the best and worst of who I was, and it felt strange, but it did not feel frightening. I was not scared, not even when we first started. I loved him from the first day. I loved him without any protective gear.

Rashid and I had been friends before we had been lovers. We loved each other intimately before we touched each other intimately, and I am sure this is what broke my defenses down without my even flinching; it never occurred to me or to him that there was any other way for us to be with each other except open, vulnerable.

I'm sure, too, what made a difference was that I felt that Rashid's own history would keep him from judging mine. I would conclude this finally when I began to wonder, out loud, in the presence of my lover, how I had become the woman I was. Why had I been so afraid for so long, so untrusting, so uncomfortable in my relationships? A book I was reading at the time told me that in order to explore every part of myself, in order to seek answers and resolution, I would have to be in a place where I could feel nurtured, at home. I knew that place was with Rashid, not just with him, but inside him, all the way, alongside his veins and heart and lungs. I was there, he was too, we both were.

Still, no matter how open, no matter how willing our hearts were, I have to confess that it was not only us. The prison itself played a significant role in solidifying how we were with each other, how close we would become. The prison, with all of its efforts to keep us unsteady, uncomfortable, and unable to love, became my adversary. Its stance against love automatically made me take a stance for love; I became a warrior. When I went to war, then, initially I thought I was battling against the bars and steel, the chains and cells, the brutal separation. I was a fierce soldier.

After enough time had passed that I was allowed some perspective, I came to see the battles quite differently, however. When all of my tactics and strategies had played out, when I had cursed and kicked and called the police all kinds of names, in the end the only one left in ruins was me. When the shock of seeing myself destroyed wore off, I realized it was not so terrible.

The me who had been killed was the me who had gone through life with shifty eyes, the ones that always greeted love sideways, looking at it askance, always as a potential enemy. I tell Rashid this, about how I had once looked at love, and he said he understood. He said that it was how he felt once, before me, before us. This was how we came to see ourselves as rebels.

We vowed a lifetime of battles against anything and anyone who tried to block our love from coming. We vowed a lifetime of battles against anyone or anything who could grab hold of our arms and pull us onto dangerous roads. And as we made our vows in the presence of ourselves and our ancestors and our God and the guards, we felt our apprehensions and our inhibitions come loose, and there they were and there we were, spilled like the pieces of two complex puzzles.

We stared at and played with those jumbled pieces of ourselves, the pieces which were piled on top of each other, the pieces that would get stuck sometimes on the wrong side of the puzzle. It would be a long time before everything fit together properly, years before things made sense. But that initial process of discovery, it was the most exciting thing, as though we were on the verge of uncovering some kind of miracle cure.

≈

I wanted to know everything about Rashid, I told him this over and over. I wanted to know every twist, every turn. Nothing should be left out, I said to him, and he complied. Rashid told me stories about a double-faced childhood; a beautiful country that loved and nurtured him, but a country where men too often beat everything in their path, including women and children.

In Guyana that's just the way it was.

Oh, God.

And my mother left when I was a baby.

Why didn't she take you?

I don't know.

Come on. Don't tell me she just left you alone?

*No. She left me in a suitcase. By my grandmother. That's what they say.*

*And then?*

*And then eventually we were all together again. Me and my brother with my father and his new family.*

The stories Rashid told were like happiness in a crate turned upside-down and shaken out of position. What would begin as multicolored, as rainbow tales about a little boy and the ocean and the countryside and secret hiding places, would end up monochromatic, painfully dull, sometimes the swelled purple of bruises, sometimes the mean scarlet of skin ripped off of bare backs, bottoms, and legs.

I would push and Rashid would talk, and the colors in the stories slipped, each one of them fell on their backs and slid together. Purple into scarlet into finally only black. But at least it was a safe black, Rashid told me. It was a shadow black, a black like the black of the second before you pass out, and then nothing. No colors, no shadows, no thing at all.

*That's why I used to run away a lot. I wasn't trying to be bad, but things were hard, asha. I can't even tell you.*

*Don't tell me,* I wanted to but never did say. I never took my hand from in front of my mouth. I held it there, held every whimper and every scream there, there, locked behind my palm and my teeth. I held it, although now I think I should have let it free. But then I believed that if Rashid wasn't yelling, how could I? If he could disappear his emotions, then so could I, and that was what we did together. We walked through the stories of his youth as though they were normal, the everyday bread of life. Except once. Once I said finally,

*I hate your family.*

*No,* Rashid argued. *No, asha. Don't say that. Don't feel that way. It was a different time and place. It's just the way things were. It wasn't abuse. If it was, it wasn't on purpose. But I remember that once I did drink turpentine.*

*Turpentine?*

*Yeah. Better to be dead. Know what I mean?*

*You tried to kill yourself?*

*I don't know about all that. I just didn't want to get a beating.*

There's a difference between wanting to die and not wanting to live. I believe this and I said it to Rashid. I said it to him because suddenly as he talked about the turpentine, I remembered something from my own childhood. I remembered a time when I wanted to die, and then I remembered other times when I simply didn't want to live. Wanting to die is an active stance, an offensive play. It involves planning, consideration. Not wanting to live is a passive play. And a passive play as opposed to a defensive play. Even a defensive play is more bold. Not wanting to live is simply a retreat.

The story of Rashid being nine and drinking turpentine, the way it hit me, triggered first a sympathetic ache, and then an empathetic ache, and then a watershed of memory. And memory in a way I wasn't used to having memory. Memory with minute details, faces, sounds.

Whenever we would talk and Rashid would describe his childhood, I would get an uncomfortable sensation throughout my body. My head would hurt. All of his memories going far, far back were virtual snapshots of people and places he hadn't seen in fifteen years.

*How do you remember all that?* I'd ask, trying not to sound defensive. For some reason, I didn't know why—knowing would come later—my own memories of childhood were disconnected and sketchy at best, but most often they were stolen.

My memories were mostly stories I had snatched out of my mother's mouth, my sister's. When my family would all be together at Christmas, I would have them repeat the same old tales again and again. Afterwards, alone, I would try to record them forever in some sacred, safe place in my brain, but it never worked. There were leaks, there were holes, there must have been! I couldn't contain the stories of my childhood for any meaningful amount of time, no matter how hard I would try.

When Rashid and I were in a conversation, and my turn would come to tell some story, some detail of my own life, I would speak in big, broad terms. I hoped Rashid would not notice, no one else ever seemed to notice before, not even me. Even I hadn't noticed the the difficulty I had in retaining experiences, especially experiences with men, until this relationship. Before Rashid, no one, not me, not my first husband or my best friend, not my sister, not anyone I knew, ever dwelled much on the past. We all lived in the current moment, or the moment coming just then, from right around the corner.

With Rashid, things were different. Time had, in a sense, frozen in 1983, the year he was arrested. The streets and subways, his home, his cars, his hangout partners, his women and escapades, everything stopped at that moment in January when he was hauled off to jail. To stay alive, to be an entity existing beyond the walls of the prison, he had to go back. Going back, telling me who he was before the strip searches, the cells, and the number instead of the name, allowed Rashid to hold onto his humanity. It was proof that once he had been, and in time, he would be again, a man, whole, in control of his environment and himself.

But when it was my turn to talk, I was scared Rashid would think I was somehow holding back on him in spite of our promise to tell everything, to travel with each other back down the years. If Rashid's life was a feature film, mine was a trailer. Mine had no dialogue, no clear storyline. I tried to fill in the gaps with long, thorough descriptions of my Manhattan neighborhood, my academic parents, the private schools, the ballet lessons and art classes, but I knew the picture was hazy.

I knew the picture was, in fact, less like a film and more like an unfinished collage, maybe not unfinished, but one in which pieces had been torn out, photographs had come unglued and blown away. This is why the turpentine story became so significant. It triggered in me not just one picture, but a whole photo album of pictures, color and black-and-white, slides, and blown-up prints, in focus, detailed. When Rashid told me that he drank the poison, I told him that,

*I tried once.* I said this fast, nervous.

*Tried what?* He thought that I meant that I drank turpentine too. I could tell by the tone his voice had taken.

*I tried to die.*

*You did?* Rashid said, his voice coated with surprise and disbelief. *What'd you do, asha?*

*I took pills. But before that, I can't remember when, only that it happened, I cut my wrists. It wasn't too deep though. I got scared when I saw the first little bit of blood. And plus it hurt. I was trying to end hurting.*

As we talked I remembered things I hadn't thought of in years. I saw them, and my eyes became a movie screen, and there it was, scene one, my college dorm room, and me at sixteen, swallowing twenty-five, maybe thirty pills. And there it was, scene two, the pills going down and I was not feeling sick, just lonely, isolated. I was aching for my faraway best friend and aching about my irreverent lover. I was just aching. And then there is a fast cut to my smug college roommate. This was scene three. My college roommate who had read my journal while I was in the hospital and told other people what it contained. She told them how crazy she thought I was. Someone eventually told me what my roommate had done, and for several years after that, I would record nothing of my life anywhere, not on paper, not inside myself, nowhere.

But on the night of the pills, when I still thought our friendship and trust was intact, my roommate came back into our room. I didn't know she was going to come back in the room. She was supposed to have been at a party, but had forgotten something. I surmised this later, but I did not know for sure. I never did know for sure why she came back in that night, at that time. Immediately after the pills and the hospital stay, I left school, and my roommate and I did not keep in touch. I assume I had been told of her betrayal and just did like the Peter Tosh song says to do: *Walk and don't look back.* Anyway, I told Rashid, I could not remember the exact sequence of things then, but I remembered that roommate, that girl, how she came back in the dorm, how she saw me, and how she screamed. She stood over me, and she just screamed.

I was lying in the floor almost passed out. Someone, not my roommate, called an ambulance. While we were waiting for it to arrive, other students, and the dorm monitor, came into my room and slapped me. They slapped me and they pulled me up and they made me walk in order to keep me awake, conscious. I went up and down the hallway, a woman on each side of me, holding me up. And I did, I stayed conscious, conscious enough to feel embarrassed because I had made myself a spectacle. I had been trying to go away, to extirpate myself, to somehow never be seen again, and instead I found that I had only succeeded in making myself more visible.

And being more visible was something I had not counted on. I never imagined that a possible conclusion to swallowing the pills was being rescued. And I certainly never imagined the particular kind of rescue that drags you up and down a public hallway while you are wearing only a nightgown. When I told Rashid the story, I told him that if I thought about it hard enough, which I rarely did, I could still feel that industrial hallway rug scraping beneath my bare feet. I could still feel the bruises pushing out onto my skin in the same place where the women held the upper part of my arms tight, tight, pulling, pulling. I told Rashid,

*They didn't have to pump my stomach at the hospital, you know. They only had to make me vomit; they make you vomit if it's soon enough after you've taken the pills.*

I told him about the doctor, a Jamaican woman, who tended to me. She was the first of two Black doctors who had ever treated me. This was probably why I have remembered her so well, why I can still see her face, not all the way, but her general features.

*She was the one,* I said, *she told me that, about the vomiting and pills.*

She'd told me that as she sat on my bed, in a room with a camera in it that stayed trained on me for twenty-four hours like a wagging finger or else a gun.

*Why'd you do it, asha?* Rashid asked me this. It would be the first of many times he asked me that question.

*I don't know,* I said. *I was sad,* I said.

*Nothing felt right,* I added. *It was as though the entire world was misplaced. It was as though I was misplaced. I had been skipped and so I graduated from high school at fifteen. I was really too young to head off to college. But you couldn't have convinced me of that then. So when I got there—the school was in D.C.—I knew right away I didn't fit in that setting. I didn't even last a whole semester. From the moment I arrived, I felt like I was living in the wrong time in the wrong place, making mostly the wrong friends, and always falling for the wrong man.*

*Nothing felt right,* I said again, because I began to feel sure. *I was always thinking that, how nothing felt right,* I remembered aloud. I remembered wanting to die because I was thinking that.

*After that,* I told Rashid, I tried again. I took some pills again, *but it was six years later and it wasn't like before. I never tried as hard as I had tried that first time.*

*The second time,* I began, and as I did, I also began to gain an understanding I did not previously have, *the second time I didn't want to die so much as I didn't want to live.*

It came back to me, how the life I was living was so pointedly lonely; lonely because my first husband and I had come apart. We were there, living together, but still apart. We were in a house with no conversations over the dinner table, no evening walks, no sharing of problems, no touching, no tenderness. And then, at twenty-two years old, I didn't really know another way to leave except by dying. But it didn't mean that that's what I wanted, to die, only that I didn't want to live in emptiness.

*That's the difference between wanting to die and not wanting to live. Does this make sense?* I asked Rashid.

*I think so.* He said this slowly after a long pause, and then continued, *Yes, it does,* he said. *Yes.*

One morning not long after Rashid and I had fallen in love, I woke up and at first everything seemed as it had been before I'd closed my eyes and faded into sleep. But the appearance was a mirage and I realized this, the trick, when I left my Brooklyn apartment, and began the five-minute walk down Fulton Street, down toward the train station.

As usual, there were crack vials littering the ground, like bread crumbs that lead you into, not out of, the threatening forest. I was counting the vials, counting them and losing count of them when all at once, for reasons I did not understand then and do not understand now, I heard a voice. It didn't fit the moment, that voice. It was incongruous, out of place, ancient and abstract. It was also familiar and it played like a note repeating on a scratched record. Again and again I heard a man saying to me, *I taught you how to neck. I taught you how to neck.*

I listened and I listened for more and more words, but nothing else came. But the voice in my head, the voice of the man, said nothing else, and I said nothing at all. I was not part of a dialogue. I was just there, silent, staring at him. I remembered that suddenly. And I remembered I was seven or eight, a small girl visiting my mother's office in the big building on the college campus where the man taught, where the man took me off into a classroom and showed me math tricks, and then asked me to sit in his lap, which I did. I did it because I liked him, everybody liked him. And this was probably why I did not scream or question or move when his hand began to travel up my leg, up my thigh, and then whatever memory should have come right after that, did not. Everything stops with the moving hand. Everything except when the man and I were walking across the campus, and he said to me that now I knew *how to neck*.

On the day these memories came to me I called my mother. I called her when I got to work and told her what I remembered. I described the man and she told me his name. She told me that she could not believe that he would have done such a thing, and when she told me this, that she could not believe it, I said simply, *Me, either.* But what I thought about was the pervasive sadness that haunted me for so long. I thought about the drugs and the drinking. And I thought that my life stood as irrefutable testimony that somewhere, something had turned down a wrong and dangerous path, and finally I was going to have to face it. Finally I was going to have to understand why.

Months and months after that day on Fulton Street in Brooklyn I read a book about sexual abuse and the book taught me that repressed memories often come back at a time when you are best able to confront them. The book said that memories often surface when you are emotionally strong enough to confront them, or when you have support systems around you, or when you feel safe, and maybe that's true.

Maybe Rashid being a presence in my life then, emotionally consistent, nonabusive, and loving as he was, allowed me to be able to face that which had contorted me for so many years. But I can only speculate on this, because when the memories came, they were so rude and so nasty that there was no time or space or energy to wonder why. They had just come, that's all. And they were uncontained, and uncontainable, those memories. They burst in at any time they wanted to, wherever I was. They would step right up and stand in front of me. They would block my vision and they would distort it. They made friends seem like enemies. I fought with everyone who was in my proximity, especially Rashid.

When they came, those memories, they were fast as the water converging into a truculent, unpredictable sea. Those memories, they were like waves that were strong enough to erode a beach and erase a landscape. Erase it forever.

There was never any question that something had happened to me, but what was it that had happened, and who was it that I should blame? This was the confusion that took over my life, and cornered my sun, and kept me moving in shadows, bumping into my past and breaking pieces of myself.

Of course I understood that the man from the college was wrong, because I was, after all, so very young then. But surely he, that man, could not have been enough to disintegrate my childhood and leave it as ashes and soot. Not one man alone.

*I cannot remember, I cannot remember.*

I would cry this to Rashid, that nothing was clear. I would tell him I could not find answers, only more questions. *I am frustrated, I am exhausted,* I said to Rashid. I said that the years I wanted to know about and finally understand were years that had been bent, slapped around, shoved, and kicked aside by silence and lies.

My memories, I told Rashid, were like FBI documents with days and months blacked out over here, years over there. I may have never repressed them, but neither have I processed them, or even thought about them much in the last five, ten, or twenty years. How to attach faces now, hands, and responsibility to the fast snatches of images that exploded in my head, exploded and then evaporated? How to do that and still sound credible?

The way abuse works is by erasing the horror of itself even as it is occurring. But not only the horror, also its victim, her opinions, what she sees and feels.

(*You know you want this, say you want this, say it now, bitch, comin' up in here lookin' like that, what the fuck you expected, say you need it*—I need it—*say you want it*—I want it—*say you love it*—I love it—*say who fuckin' pussy is this*—yours, it's yours—.)

For months these conversations kicked inside my head, stomped inside it, until finally they became the only sounds I could hear, and when that happened, when I could hear no other sounds, I began to see things. I began to see my life, not as it was right then, but my life as it had once been. My old life once more became a movie, but this time with only one scene playing over and over on my apartment walls, on subway windows, on the streets where I walked. I kept seeing my once-upon-a-time self. I was thirteen. Eventually I told Rashid.

*When I turned thirteen and got my working papers, I had a series of part-time jobs, and at those jobs, at nearly every one, there were all these men, and they were older than me, usually by ten, but often fifteen, twenty years.*

I said to Rashid that this was when things began to happen in horrible succession. I explained that unlike so many other survivors I was reading about, my home was a safe place. For me, it was the world outside that brimmed with violence and danger, and although I knew this, I would venture willingly into it, into all the cracks and crevices New York City had to offer. You could find me there, in those cracks and crevices.

*This is why I think maybe it wasn't abuse.* (This part was whispered.) *I remember that I liked it, not the sex, and not the touching, but being wanted, it validated me somehow. It made me feel special. It made me feel human. Being wanted. It made me feel human.*

When I said this, I felt ready to put the whole matter away, to accept the blame, and to move on, but Rashid argued with me. He was the first one to say it, to confirm that what I had experienced was abuse. *Because,* he said,

*You were a child, asha. That's what made it abusive. You were a child.*

Rashid was soft when he said this, but he was firm, convinced of his position. I was not, however, and I told him so.

*I can't remember that,* I said quickly, but after, when Rashid got up and went to the bathroom, I closed my eyes and tried to see what he told me he could see: me as a little girl. I did not succeed, though, not then, and when he returned I told him once more,

*I can't remember being a little girl. By the time I was twelve I felt all the way grown. I swear I did. I'm not exaggerating. If you saw me then, Rashid, you would understand. The way my body was, the things I thought about.*

Rashid stared into my words, he frowned into them, and this was when he asked me to describe how it was in the fullest possible detail so that we could look at that time together. Perhaps together, he explained, we could understand those days in a brand-new way. Rashid said this, but I was too afraid. I knew that in the moment I said to him all of what I remembered, I would forever be another woman in his eyes, and would he still love me?

*Can we do this later?* I asked, but Rashid did not agree. He reminded me that I was the one who said you cannot hide from your past, your life, yourself. And when he did this, when he reminded me of my own words, I began to tell him things, slowly. Over many months and many visits, I revealed the years between thirteen and eighteen. Initially I was vague, offering only minutia, but Rashid pushed and finally there was an afternoon when I told him specifics.

I told him that although the faces may have changed, and the places may have also, some things could always be counted on to remain the same: the pulling, and grabbing, and pinching, and slapping, and all those dirty words, and all those bad names, the leering, the propositions. But of all of those men, I told Rashid, there was one who stood out. There was one man who was so mean I thought about him regularly, unlike the others. The others I blocked out. I don't even remember most of their names, but that man, I thought about him again and

again. He would come to me in the night and kick me out of
my dreams. He would come to me in the day, when I had been
wrapped in the arms of another man. A man who was safe. He
would come to me and when he did, he could make good men
seem bad, frightening, and dirty. I told Rashid this. *I've had
flashbacks of the man and I've had nightmares of him. Sometimes it
didn't look like him. Sometimes his face was different, but I was
never fooled. I always knew who it was,* I told Rashid, and then I
said the man's name out loud. I said it and watched the surprise push out over his face.

*You said that man had been your boyfriend, asha, and you said
he was beautiful!*

*He was,* I explained, *not my boyfriend, but beautiful, my God,
he was so beautiful.*

I told Rashid how he looked: tall and brown, an indigenous
man from the mighty Sioux nation, an unrecognized prince
with a braid down his back, three black belts to his credit, a
wide, fast laugh, and $200-a-day cocaine habit.

*That was how I saw him when we first met.*

The man told me I was the prettiest girl he had ever seen.
The man told me that love was what mattered, not age, not the
fact that he was twenty-eight, and I was fourteen. *So what?* he
had said to me, I can still hear him saying it.

He worked in a movie theater as a security guard. The theater also employed my girlfriend, and sometimes I would fill in
for her, and sometimes I would go there and just hang out
with her. That was how I met him, I explained.

I told Rashid about the evening I went down to the movie
theater a few weeks after I'd met him. I told how the man said
he wanted to talk to me, and on the inside I smiled. On the
inside I felt special, and I followed him down the stairs into the

staff lounge, and once again he whispered in my ear that age did not matter. And once again, I had believed him. I had wanted to believe him. I believed him even when he backed me up against a locker, even when he began undoing the buttons on my blouse, and even when I said slow down and he did not slow down, not then, and not when when I said it again, *Slow down! Please!*

I said I was not ready, even though, I explained to Rashid, I thought I was ready. But being ready was not the point. The point was that I wanted the man to love me and to respect me, and all my life I had been taught that saying no was how you got those things: love and respect.

I told Rashid how it was such a conscious decision on my part, when I said *Slow down.* I remembered clearly thinking that if I told him to slow down what would happen was that first, he would slow down, then he would think I was a nice girl, a good girl. After that he would rebutton my blouse, and smooth my hair. After that, maybe not that night, but perhaps the next, he would bring me flowers, and then he would fall in love with me, and then I would begin to exist in the world as a relevant person, a person who was necessary because I was a person who was loved. But not just loved, loved by *him.* This is what was important, because he was grown, he was twenty-eight, and he was beautiful. I was fourteen and wrong. That's how I felt back then. Twelve and wrong. Thirteen and wrong. Fourteen and wrong. Alive and wrong and wrong and wrong.

And I wanted to be set right, just once, just that time, in front of him. He was beautiful, I was wrong. This was what I was thinking all at once, in the same moment, and that was why I said it to him, *Slow down, I'm not ready.* I said it to him, and then I prepared myself to be loved, caressed, and respected.

But that did not happen. The man did not say he loved me. He said I was nothing but a fucking tease, an ugly bitch, a cunt. He slapped me in my face, and then he punched the locker I was leaning against, and the locker reeled backwards and then forwards again, and it knocked me in my head, and the pain rushed through me, it buckled me, it broke down the air in me, and for a second I could not see, but then I could. My sight returned.

The first thing I saw after the darkness was the man raising up his fist again, and I didn't know if he would hit me or the locker, but either way I knew I would lose, and that was when I ducked my head and began to run. I headed toward the stairs and my shoe twisted, it nearly came off my foot, but it did not, and I ran and fell up those stairs out onto Eighth Avenue and behind me the man was screaming, *You nasty fucking cunt, you think you so fucking cute, you ain't that fucking cute!!* And then a cab came, and I got in, and it sped away. But that was not the ugly part of the story I told Rashid.

The ugly part of the story didn't come until weeks and weeks later, when it was summertime and I ran into the man in Central Park. We were both alone. We had not seen each other since the night at the movie theater, but when he greeted me, he smiled and did not mention the violence between us. He told me I looked beautiful and that he would like to sit with me. Would I sit with him? he asked, Would I smoke a joint with him? he asked.

And now, today, I know myself well enough to understand that there is a part of me who always wants to make what is ugly somehow beautiful. This is part of why I write, I suspect, why I love art, all expressions of it. But I didn't know this then, on that late summer afternoon, that the reason I went with him was to make a new memory, a memory I could enjoy, a memory that could sustain me. On that late summer afternoon, what I knew was that I was feeling mesmerized by everything, the easy heat on my skin, his beauty, the fact that he still wanted me, and the possibility of what sweetness we could create together.

And it was me. I was the one who said it. I said it of my own volition, *Yes,* I said to him. *Sure, let's go,* I said, and we walked over to someplace in the park more remote, and we sat and we smoked, and in the distance we could hear a radio playing, and we moved against the music and his arm was around my shoulder, and now he is telling me I am beautiful, and somehow I am actually feeling it, beautiful, I mean, and for a time the whole world is no more than me and the music and the summer air, and our bodies close, warm and soft. And the whole world is the sun, which is leaving the sky with all of this grace and dignity, and the moon, which is huge and gold, and the man's arm around my shoulder, holding me.

But suddenly it is his weight I feel, his weight overcoming mine, suddenly this becomes the world. And then the music disappears and the moon disappears and even the season, the summertime disappears, and of course I do as well. I disappear. It will not be the last time. It was not the first.

What remained after I was gone was a body that was no longer my own, and he kissed it, the man did. He kissed it with an anger so complete that he actually was biting the top of the lip that was once mine. And my ex-body did not scream or squirm. It did not move until the man slapped the inside of one of the thighs as a signal that it was time to open up, and the body that once was, but is no longer mine, opened up, the legs did anyway, and the man got between them.

The man undid his pants and he tried to push into my ex-body, but he found that it was hard to do with all the clothes between us, and that was when he dropped his arm across the face on my ex-body. His hand was across its eyes, his elbow poked in its ear. He balanced himself. He said, *I'm gonna fuck the living shit out of you.*

And for however long he was in the body that was, but is no longer mine, that was indeed what he tried to do. That was what he nearly accomplished in doing; not fucking the shit out of, but fucking the life, nearly up out of that body in the breaking night of summertime, behind dried bushes, on dying grass. And when we parted that night, there was no good-bye, no I'll call you, no see you later. When we parted that night, I would never see him again.

And I would never learn to call this rape or abuse because I went with him willingly, I got high with him willingly, and I did not scream, not once. But there would be many things I did learn from him, from that time. *I see it now,* I told Rashid.

I learned how saying no can get you beat. I learned how my age didn't matter because nothing about me mattered. I learned how I could just abandon my body if things got ugly, that my body could handle it while I sat on ceilings, on pieces of the sky, and watched the whole disgusting thing.

Waiters, bartenders, drug dealers, musicians, chefs, actors, students, camp counselors, and managers, when the workday ended, and the ties came loose, there wasn't a fucking difference between them. Beyond all other lessons that I would learn, that was what being a teenager in New York City in the 1980s would teach me most of all.

❧

Trying to heal, I would discover, was not a steady process, not by any stretch of the imagination. Despite all the candles I burned, specific candles for each day of the week, despite the early morning meditations, journal writing, prayers, and healing exercises from one of the thirty or so books about childhood sexual abuse I bought, things just did not move in a predictable straight line from awful to bad to manageable to good.

I could wake up in the morning feeling hopeful, filling myself with all the light of the early sun, and by afternoon I could be wondering what was the fastest way to kill myself. There were so many possible triggers for absolute despair: a news item about an abused child, a man on the street who said something to me too aggressively, a friend touching me on the leg in a way that seemed familiar, ancient, and terrible. Part of the problem was my approach to getting well. I didn't know this then.

I have always been impatient, since I was a small girl, a toddler rushing from one toy to the next, from one corner of the room to the next. As I grew up, I became notorious for my ability to consistently overlook the most vital part of an instruction manual, or trying to carry too many things at once. Inevitably I would drop one or two items, and sometimes they would break, and sometimes they wouldn't break, but always I made a mess.

What I did when I first began trying to heal was skip right to the end of my books where there were all these testimonials of women who were survivors. I ignored all the parts in the beginning about definitions of abuse, and the steps I should take, and instead I absorbed the most wrenching stories of women who had been sliced down the middle by fathers, stepfathers, uncles, and brothers. They had spent their childhoods being hustled between emergency rooms and social workers.

None of the stories I read sounded like mine. That was what helped to confirm me in my own mind as a liar, a fraud. The eight or nine testimonials I read and reread became for a time the only definitions that I accepted of sexual abuse. They were testimonies of incest or of a single abuser: an uncle, a family friend, molesting a child over and over. My story didn't fit. My story had many characters in it, there were many men, and generally, once they did it the first time, they left me alone. Generally.

There was something else. I had good parents, loving parents, parents who gave my sister and me everything they could. The only time I ever had to go to the hospital was when I had put things down my own throat, and when I thought about that, how I had sent my own self to the hospital, I thought about how I must have been a fraud. And the idea of me being, on top of everything else, a liar as well was more than I could stand, and it sent me out into the world looking for blood.

I felt I had to find a telltale trail of blood, and if not that, then at least a nasty wound, a swollen discolored bruise, a scab, anything. Anything. But that never happened. I didn't find it, and I know on some level I'm writing this all down now because I'm sure there must be other women out in the world looking for blood like I was looking for blood, and they won't find it like I didn't find it, but they should know they are not frauds. I was not a fraud.

I was a young woman whose memories came rushing in at a

time when phrases like false memory syndrome were thrown around, when therapists were accused of implanting ideas in their clients' heads and this and only *this* was the reason for the apparent epidemic of sexual abuse in our society. It would be a long time before I felt strong enough to defend myself against these sentiments.

And it would be even longer before I learned how Sigmund Freud's original work documented sexual abuse in the lives of his female patients. I learned that when he did release his findings, there was a huge social backlash. I learned that if the society was to believe its women, what then would they have to conclude about their men, the ones who ran the government and the banks and the businesses? Freud retracted his findings. But I didn't know about all of this back those nights when I'd lock myself in my bedroom and rock and grind and let the sweat and snot run down my face and forget to breathe and try to convince myself there was a reason for me to live. Even if I couldn't remember it right then. There was a reason.

No, back then, I had not read anything by Freud. I had read books by Nabakov. I had read *Lolita,* and I saw myself there, squatting between the pages, a nasty girl, a freak.

Of course there was a simple logic to this: If I blamed myself for everything, as I had all my life, then I could seek revenge on myself. The men were gone but I was here, and I could attack myself as I always had. I knew how to self-destruct, with drugs and alcohol, overdoses, unequal and abusive relationships, food. I could make anything a weapon. I could wield anything against myself. There was a certain satisfaction in it. It took so long for me to change, longer than all of my friends who got high and did stupid dangerous teenage things; I did them well into my twenties. I might still be doing them if I hadn't met Rashid, if we hadn't been involved.

When I became involved with Rashid, I still drank even though alcohol was beginning to make me sick. One beer and I would want to pass out. I still smoked cigarettes and weed even though I *hated* being high and my throat was sore all the time. I still had uneven friendships.

It's not that I think Rashid is or was some sort of miracle worker. My husband is a man, flesh, blood, and flawed like every one of us. But Rashid was willing to read the books and Rashid was willing to stifle his temper when I threw misdirected fits of rage. And he was, more than anyone else, in the line of fire, but he did not move. And there were times that I knew he did need to get away from me. He won't admit it, but I know it's true. And this is where the prison actually served our relationship; it forced us to be apart, and during that time, that was probably a good thing. I hate to say it but the separation probably saved us. No one can live in the throes of that sort of intensity and anger for too long, and when things would become very terrible between us, the phone would cut off, or the visit would end, and we'd have to each go back into our own separate corners. I slunk into mine.

There was one other thing. Rashid and I could not have sex. At that time, we were not married, which meant we could not have conjugal visits. And as painful as it seemed then—we used to go on and on about the need to be together—the reality was that I didn't need to be having a physical relationship with anybody. The reality was that I was not emotionally equipped to handle it.

We had little to distract us from the issue at hand, and when

I would begin disintegrating into all of my own fears, nightmares, and insecurities, Rashid would say to me again and
again,

 *You were a child, asha.*
 *(I didn't feel like one so was I really one?)*
 *What if it was your daughter?*
 *(Don't say that to me. I don't like you to say that to me.)*
 *What if you were your own daughter?*
 *(Please stop.)*
 *Imagine that.*
 *(No.)*
 *Just once.*
 *(I can't!)*
 *Please!*

And after he pushed me for what seemed like the thou-
sandth time, I tried. I covered my face with my hands and tried
to conjure up a picture of me as my own daughter, a little girl,
a teenager. I tried it a second and then a third time and then a
fourth time, and then a fifth, and finally, finally an image
moved into uneasy focus. If I blinked, it would disappear. She
would disappear. I knew this and so I concentrated, and as I
did, something inside me began to shift.

Once I read a book that said *What if you came home one
night and found everything had been ransacked, some stuff was
missing, some stuff was broken? What if a window was smashed, a
door kicked in? You would know that you'd been robbed, even if there
was no thief right then, in the vicinity.* At last I came to understand that that's how it was with abuse. That even without the
trail of blood, there was evidence, and the evidence was me, my
house, with its drawers roughly pulled open and rifled through,

its floors littered everywhere with shards of glass and rusted nails. My house with valuables missing.

And when I could see this, I knew that it could never have been simply teenaged angst, that it wasn't just puberty that had stormed through my house and made me crazy. The damage was too devastating, too complete. And because it was, there would be no storybook life like the one my parents had dreamed for me and worked so hard to achieve. And no matter what, I could not change or forget or drug or drink or sex or analyze or even love my own history away, and the best I could ever, ever do was rebuild. And this made me profoundly sad for a time.

For a time all I thought about was what would a never-molested asha look like? That question stuttered my movements, my breath, and my sight. Would I have gotten a Bachelor's Degree in four years instead of fourteen? Would I have walked away from the drugs? Would I be able to drive? Would I like my body? Would I have been able to say no to the food, the drugs, the alcohol, the abusive men, and all the years of hysteria and depression? Would I never have had the persistent and crippling sense that I was dirty, a whore, a funky bitch, not good enough, an undesirable?

I asked those questions of a friend one afternoon. She was also a survivor, and we were having lunch in a Thai restaurant in Brooklyn. I was whispering and crying and she was holding my hand, and she leaned across the small table, across the food, her face was inches from my face, and she told me that I was not a liar, or crazy or wrong or broken. She told me I was also not perfect. But I could stand, she said. I could walk, she said. I could write and I could tell the truth. And I could understand.

She said I could understand that in the end I would not be defined by my experiences. I would be defined by what I chose to do with my experiences, if I was open and willing, and uncompromising and honest.

# one day my soul sat down and rested

*i* come from people who prefer silence, who believe that refusing to give a name to a thing will send it away. They have lived like this, and they have survived, my people, and they have built their families and done their work, and found their joys. My own parents raised up, both of them did, out of childhoods that had been punctured by poverty, death, and departures, and they had rarely spoken about what had been lost to them, and what had been taken, what it was they mourned, and what it was in the long and hidden hours of their own lives that they cried for.

I was always different in this particular regard. Saying what I feel is something that I have done since I first learned how to speak. I have never been able to contain my feelings, although there were many times I wished I could have. Without some process for verbal expression, I know I will go insane, or else I will die. This is something I know for certain.

Silence already tried to kill me, not once, but many times. That was what I thought about immediately when I considered the possibility of never saying a word to anyone about the abuse. And not saying a word was absolutely a very real option. When the memories came I was tempted toward silence. The last thing I wanted to do was to alienate myself further from anyone; the abuse had already marked me, I felt. It had already made me an interloper inside my own self, and I didn't want people to see that. I didn't want my friends to see me as someone different now, or Rashid to see me as someone damaged now, or my family to see me as someone dirty, or worse, as someone indiscreet.

But finally I did reject it, the silence, because I knew the way it operated. I knew that whatever pain did not come, distinct and terrible, from out of my mouth would find an escape route in some other place. That was its history with me, the silence's. For fifteen years it had crept out through my hands every time I reached for a spliff laced with angel dust, a vial of cocaine, a glass pipe filled to its blackened rim with freebase, a tab of acid and a hit of mescaline, a taste of heroin, and two Quaaludes washed down with beer, speed taken with shots of tequila chased with Dos Equis, glasses of vodka tonics, Budweiser, Riunite, Canei Rosé, and Champale, that were followed later by pizza with double extra cheese, Oreos, a pint of ice cream, and then two fingers down my throat. I could swallow anything, put anything inside myself, there was no limit, except passing out, which I did, many times, in bars, on streetcorners, in unfamiliar apartments, and in the arms of men whose names and faces are lost to me now.

For years, as a teenager and young woman, I had lived like that, on the outside of my own body, watching my soul wander through cities and men and unequal friendships and drugs and food, and jobs I hated, and by the time I got to Rashid, and found myself facing him with this big, terrible thing that I did not understand and could not control, I was tired, so incredibly tired, that I had to tell him so. I could not hide it.

I told Rashid that I understood that I was no longer somebody's small precious little girl, and that I could no longer be held in my mother's soft, comforting lap. I could no longer have someone come in and rescue me out of my bad dreams. I had to rescue myself, I knew that, but I asked Rashid if he would please be a member of my team, and he agreed, and this was most clearly when we defined ourselves as that, a team, and afterwards we would never go back to being completely separate people; afterwards there would be this burn we shared, you can see it on him, and you can see it on me. On each of us the burn appears different, but somehow you know it came from the very same fire.

But on that day when I asked Rashid for his help, when we were sitting in the visiting room where I could see a small piece of the sky and I was wishing I could fly into it, I looked at my lover and thought for sure he would reject me. I thought he would say no, he could not help me, or that he would say nothing at all, but what he said was, *Come here to me, asha.*

He said, *I will not leave you, asha,* and he said that whoever I had once been did not scare or sicken him, and in the end his love for me would be bigger than all of my scars added up together. And this last thing, he did not just say it to me, he promised it to me, and when he did that my soul sat down for the first time that I can ever remember, it sat down and it rested. It rested for hours that became days that became weeks that became months that became years and when it rose from that rest, it was smiling, she was smiling, my soul was. She smiled for hours and hours and hours, she would not stop smiling, and even today, you can see, she has still not stopped smiling.

# red

*t*he irony of it all would hit me later, that there in a prison, suspended beyond time, caught in the small space behind Plexiglas, I would begin to feel free. I never did go to therapy for the abuse. I read books and talked with friends, but for the better part of the first three years of our relationship, it was mostly Rashid who worked with me. I went to him regularly to confess and to cry. I went to him stumbling and I went to him shrieking.

And Rashid stood firm. He studied the same books I studied. He became an expert on a topic that he had never thought about before except in passing. I cannot think of one wrong turn he made during that time. Not one moment of insensitivity. Not one word misstated. Not one look askance. Not one accusation that *perhaps I really wanted to, didn't fight hard enough, basically just gave my pussy away, deserved whatever I got because I wore my skirts too short, my lipstick too bright, should have known when I went there and danced like that and spoke like this, and besides everybody knew what kind of girl I was anyway, so what? What?* Rashid never said to me the things other men have said to me. Still say to me.

And it was because of how kind and smart and loving he was that it seemed particularly unfair that when the feelings of freedom began to stir, they only began to stir inside of me. Not inside of us. Not inside of Rashid and me together. Just me. As I was beginning to feel in control of my body, my lover was spending his days waiting in line to be frisked, strip-searched, passed through metal detectors, trying to get on the phone, and hoping for a piece of mail from me that sometimes came. That sometimes didn't.

Nevertheless I could not contain myself and cautiously I began having a conversation with Rashid about what I was thinking. I told him that something strange but also wonderful was happening. I told him that for the first time in a long time, I wasn't plowing through my days thinking only of the abuse. That hours and almost whole days went by without me feeling that it had me snatched up by the back of my neck.

*I feel so strong these days,* I told Rashid. *I almost feel normal,* I told him. *I feel in control of myself. I never felt in control of myself like this before. Like I have some power over my own needs. Like I have some power over my own body. I listen when my girlfriends talk about the men they meet, and I don't quite have the same sense of sovereignty over myself that they do, but I'm not where I was before.*

And Rashid said that this was wonderful, that it was the news he wanted to hear, but he didn't understand all the ramifications of my new feelings. He did not understand because I had not yet articulated them to him. I had not said how the initial rush of love which had carried me over our daily difficulties had begun to sputter. And although my feelings for him had not diminished, I was starting to see my life as though it was a child's brand-new coloring book: I was all thick dark outlines. Nothing was filled in or differentiated by hue.

I was in no hurry to say these things to a man I felt had just helped to save my life. And I was in no hurry to revisit a topic we'd discussed when we first fell in love—monogamy. When we first became a couple I had said to Rashid that I just didn't see how a woman could be monogamous with a man when he was doing big time in prison. We had gone back and forth, back and forth, and begrudgingly Rashid had acquiesed to my point of view. But aside from a few dates, there had never been much reason for the issue to come up. Not until now. Now that I felt free.

Despite my hesitation at raising the matter, at no point was I blind to or unmindful of what was happening inside me. Out of loyalty and guilt, I tried to shove my feelings away. I spoke, hypothetically, with a few women I knew from the van rides upstate. I hoped that I would find out from them how they balanced their love for their husbands with their own desires and need for attention. But much to my shock, every one of the women I talked to had *friends*. Every one of them said it was necessary. They need their *friends*. To keep them sane, they said. To ease the loneliness, they said, and to add a little color and spice to the bland soup of prison life. I was just like those women.

Like them, I knew I needed more colors in my life but I could not imagine where to find them. I suspected that the magical box of sixty-four colored Crayola crayons had been deemed illegal and was now also incarcerated. Sienna and burnt orange, canary and magenta. I thought they had been buried somewhere in the deepest, most solitary part of the jail where I could not access them. A part with no visiting rooms and no visitors, no windows and no views.

From a place behind my eyes I did try to see a world inside the prison that pulsed with the fullness of living and possibility, but I could not find it. Yet I did not just give up hope. There in the visiting room, in Rashid's arms, I would attempt to do what had always worked before. Once I could simply escape us both into my imagination—we would just leave, set up residence there, but now even my mind was failing us. On one visit, two visits, three visits, and four, we were stopped by the prison which had barricaded every door to our possible other worlds. If we were lucky, we'd get a fast glimpse of a better place, but as soon as I was away from Rashid, I'd forget the little bit of promise we had seen together. I told Rashid everything I was feeling. He looked at me helplessly. I looked at the floor.

If only Rashid could have colored me in! Draw in the lines, my soul used to plead during each of my twice-weekly sojourns upstate. I used to plead through my glances, and I used to plead through my touches. I used to plead through the switch of my hips as I walked toward the door at the end of my visit: *Follow me, Rashid, come home with me now. If you loved me, I know that you would find a way.*

How to survive? This became the overriding question in my life. I would wake up plotting. Everything I bought, everything I did, everyone I befriended was a tool designed to keep me alive, living, able to see at least some of the world's beauty because I could not live without color. Not live and be productive. Not live and be at peace. These were the matters that began to jumble and distort and compromise every other possible discussion Rashid and I could have had.

I told him that I loved him, but I loved myself as well. I said I had no choice but to pull on every resource I'd ever had, every bit of mother's wisdom, every healing book, every scripture, and to mold them into sinew and begin to move through the world refusing to capitulate to what the prison would have made me: old before I was thirty, bitter, brittle and breaking.

I begged, and I borrowed, I cajoled, and I conjured. In the end I found I had somehow cobbled together my own box of crayons, worn but still useful. Feeling inspired, I decided to reject any limitation at all. I set out to collect watercolors, pastels, acrylics, oils, and chalks. I painted my world with poetry, music and dance, politics and new places. And Rashid just watched me from behind that wall and gun tower. *You're just doing your thing,* he'd say to me as I began to travel more and more. More and more I began to find reasons to be away from the prison. More and more I'd forget to make decisions *with* him. I'd just say, when he called, that I was off to this women's conference, that campus to do a poetry reading. I began to cancel dates I had with him. I wrote letters less frequently.

At a conference one summer I met a woman who was getting ready to start a nonprofit organization. She needed a partner, she told me, someone who could codirect the program with her. She asked me if I was interested, I said I was, and in one unbelievable month I told Rashid about the offer, said I was going to accept it, and that in thirty days I was moving to San Francisco where the organization was based.

*San Francisco?* Rashid exclaimed, but after the surprise wore off, he just said, *Okay, baby, if it's going to make you happy. Okay.* He asked only that we make a schedule of when I would come to see him. *Sure,* I agreed, not knowing that the job would keep me on the road at least two weeks out of every month. I was able to travel back to New York City fairly regularly on business, but my visits to the prison still became infrequent. Even when I moved back to New York, as I eventually did, I never would go back into them as often as before.

I imposed a distance, not so much between myself and Rashid, but between myself and repression. I told Rashid that because what he and I shared was bounded by the rules of the jail, I had resolved to open up the other parts of my life. *I have to,* I said to him. I said to Rashid that it had not been enough embracing new cities, new jobs. Sometimes I needed love, I told him, other love, I told him, other men. Not scores of them, or even several of them. But a few of them.

Whenever Rashid and I talked about having an open relationship, he would tell me he could not understand how I could love him and yet go out with even one other man. I, on the other hand, marveled at the fact that it hadn't been hundreds of other men. Though even hundreds of men would never be an adequate measure against the intensity of the isolation.

*I need them,* I told him. Human contact, to feel desired, to walk through a neighborhood holding someone's hand. *I need that.* Not every day, I told Rashid, but some days. *I don't seek anyone out,* I said, *but I cannot resist loving the ones who seem to just appear before me, open and pure.*

It wasn't a question of sex, although sex was sometimes a part of the picture with a few of the men I met. It was going out to movies and dinner and poetry readings and clubs that I longed for and that made me feel almost normal. I explained to Rashid that the times I shared with those men often pulled me through the days when the days angrily threatened to leave me like a hostage, blindfolded and bound to bars and locks, razor wires and guards. Those men held me when I needed it, and some even loved me when I needed it. Then too, one nearly broke me.

There had been one man with whom I'd been friends for a long time. And from that safe place, as friends, we'd shared secrets and problems and sadness and dreams. And although he never said it, I knew that man saw my life like it was some tragic film. I knew he saw me like the heroine in the film, the woman tied to the tracks. And I did nothing to deny that vision. I waited to be rescued, and one night after a long-distance disagreement with Rashid, the man came to me. He united my hands and he untied my feet.

And for that one moment, we were like our favorite celluloid heroes. Of course it was only for that moment, since it is only in the movies where everything is scripted: the conversations, emotions. We had forgotten that we were alive, real lives. Neither one of us was prepared for the work that it would take to write our own story. Our plot ideas conflicted.

The man didn't want me to love Rashid anymore, and I wanted the man to love me only in the limited spaces I provided, just there, nowhere else. What happened next was not surprising. We became an ending before we had become much of a beginning. Our relationship, the whole of it, the romance and the friendship, ended after a long week of fighting. Still, we had created this havoc that laid itself for a long, long time, like some huge, heavy tarpaulin, across my life and across his life, and also across Rashid's life.

I suppose there must always be the risk of feelings expanding wildly beyond your initial agreement with someone. This is what Rashid always says he fears most, that what begins as a lunch date ends up as me falling in love, ends as me leaving him. He fears emotions as no longer cool, crafted things, but emotions as weapons, as crude shanks, rusty and dangerous.

When he told this to me one afternoon, I said I understood. I said, *Rashid, you are so right.* But it was something I knew only after I had been stabbed by those renegade emotions, and now my scars are a witness. Rashid's scars are a witness, yet his wounds seem uglier, more raw, infected perhaps. Some of them have never stopped bleeding no matter how much pressure or first aid we have applied. When he kisses me now, sometimes I can feel the place where another man's touch slit open the sweet taste between us. I try but cannot avoid what has become our truth: Rashid's tongue is lined with the unmistakable salt of blood.

We kiss and both of us drip red.

≈

During this time there was one visit where Rashid held my face in his hands and we were so close I thought he was breathing for me. I could not sense where my air stopped and his began.

On that visit, he said I came to him in his dreams. He whispered that to me, his mouth directly upon my ear. Even still I could not hear him. *Say it again?* I asked.

*We are together, away from the prison, back in Guyana, up in the countryside.*

Rashid began explaining to me. He said when he dreamt of me, that was how most of the dreams began.

*But I have other dreams sometimes, and those other dreams are the ones that tell me.*

*Tell you what?* I asked.

*I have dreams that tell me about you. They tell me when you go out, when you've met some man.*

*I don't understand.*

*I'm saying to you that my dreams tell me everything you do. I wake up and even though I can't remember details, I know. I have this horrible feeling in my stomach. That's how I can always call you the day after you've gone out with someone and say to you I know what you did last night. Or say to you if someone called you. You kept asking me,* How do you always know, Rashid? *You thought I had you followed but I don't have the money to have you followed. I just have dreams. I've always had dreams. I didn't always pay attention to them. I should have. Maybe I wouldn't be here. Maybe a lot of things. But the point is that now I'm different. Now I pay attention. Now I don't miss a thing. Never.*

Rashid and I had many disagreements over how restrictive our relationship should be. I felt that I should not live by the same sexually repressive rules which had been forced upon him. I felt that the difference between me and many other women in my situation was that I was completely honest about my feelings and needs. Most of the women I knew did not discuss this topic with their partners. Finally, I felt most emphatically that if the situation were reversed, no one would have even expected Rashid to wait around for me, let alone be monogamous.

Those were the positions I presented to Rashid again and again. I presented them and felt justified. But I presented them and then turned away quickly because after all, there was nothing I could say to stop the pain from wildly crisscrossing his beautiful face, crisscrossing it and kicking it, slapping it and distorting it. There was nothing I could say when Rashid would whisper to me, as he always did during these discussions,

*How would you feel, asha? If I was somehow involving myself with other women, how would you feel?*

One afternoon the visiting room was unusally quiet, and I'm
sure that was part of what made Rashid and me also quiet. We
had decided to try things his way. We had agreed, for a least a
time, to forget the idea of an open relationship, and for the
first part of the visit we nearly did not fuss or argue or even
talk. We did not need to talk, to sort things out the way we had
before this agreement. Now the way we touched was itself
conversation. The way we touched said everything. But as the
day pushed forward, I began to miss the sound of my lover's
voice, which is why I did eventually ask him,

*Are you okay, honey?*

*Yes. I'm fine. Are you comfortable?* Rashid responded because
I was lying against him, as much as I could, with him in his
chair on one side of the table and me in mine on the other side
of it.

*I am,* I said, and really did mean it. I was very comfortable
and it seemed Rashid was as well, which was why I did not
understand when he stabbed into the quiet with a bayonet of
words.

*So did they deserve you?*

*What are you talking about?* I asked. I nearly exclaimed it,
although I knew exactly what he was talking about.

*When you spent time with some other man. Did he, did any of
them, deserve you? I mean it's true that you might have deserved
attention,* you *might have deserved a night out, but what about
them? Did they deserve you and your energy and your time? Had
they worked to be with you, to earn a place in your heart?*

I did not answer. I did not tell Rashid that it was not a
question I had ever really considered: What I deserved. What I
didn't deserve.

Rashid leapt at my silence. He said,

*You don't have an answer? Never mind, then. I'll just tell you what I think.*

*I think you deserve a man who isn't afraid of you, and who isn't afraid of everything that brought you pain, and who will face that pain with you, no matter how ugly it is. You deserve a man who knows how to make you laugh, asha.*

*You deserve a man who will tell you when you're wrong, and who will listen when you tell him he's wrong, and a man who is going to be just as open as you are, and just as free with his thoughts as you are, and just as willing to struggle with himself as you are. And a man who wants to make the world a better place as much as you want to make it a better place.*

*You deserve a man who loves your poems, and who wants to hear you read them again and again and again. You deserve a man who's not afraid of being passionate, and who loves to kiss all of you, not just your mouth, but all down your back, on the bottom of your feet. You deserve a man who wants to cook for you, and raise babies with you, and be old and tired with you. And I think that these things are the least of what you deserve.*

*What you deserve is a man who will always protect you. Protect you with his life if he has to.*

*asha,* Rashid said—said like it was the one true thing he would ever say—*asha, that's me.*

## *what there is to lose*

*P*art of what allowed Rashid and me to lurch toward closure on the issue of monogamy was that I finally made an admission. It was as much an admission to myself as it was to him. It was an admission which allowed me to release some of the confusion and fear which came dragging in behind me when I fell in love with a man in prison.

I confessed to Rashid that on most days I woke up to the scent of the same old and persistent insecurity. It informed many of the decisions I made, and the fights Rashid and I had. And it had been there since we first fell in love. It was the insecurity with the sour breath and the mean, crooked trickster's laugh. Devoid of sympathy or softness, it would drop its hard judgments across my face and there was no escape. *asha,* it would say to me, *you know the man only loves you out of limited choices.*

Throughout the course of our relationship, people have warned me about the manipulative, dishonest, even abusive ways of prisoners. I have heard a warehouse full of stories about convicts who siphon off all of their wives' money for sneakers, food packages, and cartons of cigarettes. The end of the story is always the same: the man gets released and after a short time, leaves his wife with a broken spirit and an empty bank account. And in each story another woman is somehow involved.

It's not that I don't appreciate the concern of the people who love me. It's that their willingness to cluster all prisoners into one simplistic stereotype never leaves any space for Rashid's humanity. The prisoner, the man I have come to know and love, doesn't demand things from me. He doesn't order or even ask me to bring him money or food and clothing packages. We negotiate all aspects of our relationship, usually based more on my needs than his. Rashid's behavior defies all the stereotypes I have heard, but these questions remain, nevertheless. Most of the time I am the one who is doing the asking.

I think the greatest gift that can be given to someone you love is to give them the gift to see themselves as you see them. All your flaws in full recession, or at least perspective. I told Rashid that in the end, whether or not he proved to be an honorable man, I knew that was the gift he tried to give to me nearly every day that I had been with him. I told Rashid it was my own shortcomings which stood between his offering and my receiving. If only he knew, I said, how I wished I could see the asha he told me he could see.

Rashid sees a confident, funny, brilliant woman. He sees a desirable woman. He sees a woman other men would give their right arm to be with. He sees absolute beauty, unfailing intelligence, and an indescribable radiance.

I see the new pimple on my face.

I see every book I have not had the discipline to write. I see the fifteen pounds I always want to lose. I see the extra mile I do not run, the dessert I do not avoid, and the sugar I am addicted to. I see all the times I feel awkward and cannot think of anything intelligent to say. I see my hair out of place.

I see the men I loved who didn't love me back. I see the desperate need I had to convince them all that I was worthy of one more date, one more call, one more touch, one more anything. I see every mistake I ever made, every time I was unfair, every time I lost my temper, and every time I didn't try hard enough. I haven't quite figured out how to see radiance through all of that dark, cloudy shit.

I told Rashid that this was why sometimes I wanted to go out with other men. Sometimes, I wanted to go out with men who chose me from a sea of women. I told Rashid that, despite everything, sometimes it was so hard to believe that he *really* loved me. Sure, he thinks he does, I would tell myself, but just wait until he sees all the fine women gliding across the streets of Brooklyn. All the women who are everything I am not. The ones who have voices which never crack or sound hurried or strained. The ones who have only been touched by men who loved them, or at least respected them. The ones who have always respected themselves. The ones who went to the prom, or had a high school sweetheart. Those women.

The women with the skin that looks like sweet mocha-cream. The ones with the tight unblemished bodies which never, ever weigh in at more than one hundred and twenty-five pounds. The ones who have never been addicted, afflicted, in need of therapy or a personal library of self-help books.

I assured Rashid that I was not a series of various neuroses, but I was hardly the picture of womanish confidence that he envisioned. I explained to my lover that I tried and tried to push back the doubts and affirm the beauty. I said to him that I knew I was blessed to have him in my life. But no matter what I knew, there were times when I had nothing to fill the space his absence created in my life. *That's when I vacillate about us,* I said.

≈

*You have to understand, my girlfriend said to me once, when a brother is locked down, naturally he's going to feel insecure. You really have to see this, asha. You're out here running around the country, halfway around the globe and back, meeting all kinds of people. He knows other men are going to approach you and even interest you. And he knows he can't really compete with that. So, of course he's going to trip when it seems like you're trying to look all sexy. Plus he's Muslim and he's the Imam. And that makes you automatically the Imam's wife. Which of course is its own kind of drama.*

I was complaining to my girlfriend about a fight Rashid and I had over a dress I'd worn. We had faced the abuse, the question of monogamy, and my choice to travel to the prison less frequently. But now, when for the first time in a long time we finally had the prospect of some peace, Rashid had begun picking on me about my clothes being too short, too tight, too American. *What happened to all those long, flowing African dresses you used to wear?* Rashid would ask over and over, as he pulled at my skirt in a futile attempt to drop the hemline.

*People and styles change,* I said, as Rashid made faces and hissed.

*That thing is too damn short and you know it. Why do you always let all these men you don't know see so much of you?*

The dress, in my eyes, was quite an average, unsexy business dress. It came to just above my knee. On other occasions I had conceded that I had been immodest, but I refused to give in on this one. I felt he was unjustified. But after I'd talked with my girlfriend and she raised the possibility of Rashid being insecure, I did not do what I would have normally done. I did not send him a mean letter and tell him to relax. I sent no mail for few days and instead just reflected on her point.

I thought about how Rashid always exuded such an air of self-assurance that I had never considered the notion that he could also be insecure. My own doubts were so encompassing, I never took the time to wonder about his doubts. But the truth is that most men in prison have at least one *Dear John* letter shoved in their lockers. I knew Rashid had one shoved into his.

For both parties, then, prison romance is at best a calculated risk. Those of us who are in this odd and unnatural place learn to soothe ourselves with the kind of negative reasoning that says, Well, on the outside, relationships don't necessarily work out. Even marriages in America end in divorce 50 percent of the time, so what have we got to lose?

Love and insecurity are an ill-fated couple. Yet there they are, together all the time, rolling around in the bed, accusing and then assuaging, and then accusing each other again and again.

My thing was running. Always had been. Probably always will be. Get out while you can still recognize yourself, that's my philosophy. Get out before you hate somebody you used to love. I've picked fights with Rashid not conscious of what I was doing until after the damage was done. And I could fight about anything, the tone of his voice, religion, a simple request, an answer that came too slowly. I could make anything seem bad enough to prove that we really ought not be together.

No one needs a psychology degree to figure this out. There was something inside me that hoped Rashid would decide that I was not worth it. I was too argumentative, too difficult. If

Rashid got mad or tired of my rantings, maybe he would tell me to leave. If he told me to leave, maybe he would decide I should never come back. If I never come back, maybe the pain will subside, the loneliness.

*Rashid, believe me,* I said when we were discussing insecurities, *I am not a woman who likes to play games. I go back and forth because I am scared,* I told him. *I understand,* Rashid said. He said it and he held me. *And I also have this problem,* I continued. *I could never be strong enough to leave of my own volition. I'm a woman in love. In love and in trouble, my mother would say.*

# *power*

**f**or two years before Rashid and
I became a couple, I had volunteered, taught, and read poetry
at cultural events and programs in the prisons. Once or twice
word would come back to me that one or another of the prisoners had a complaint about me. Sometimes it was because I
used a curse word in a poem, other times it was because one of
them thought my pants were too tight. But most often when I
did a program in the prison, I received extended standing ova-
tions and repeated requests to return. The majority of brothers
I met were very kind to me, warm and respectful.

As soon as Rashid and I went public about our romance, all
of that changed.

Suddenly who I was became a point of contention with
many prisoners: the way I dressed (too suggestive); the way I
spoke (too profane); the way I offered myself to the world
(too friendly). Worst of all, my name was deliberately evaporated. I became known suddenly and solely as "Rashid's
woman."

Prison is a macho place. Security. Us against them. Pumping iron. Mean faces. From the superintendent's office to the
incoming convict, it's all about might makes right. Physical or
mental, everything in prison is a power play; who can out-lift,
out-survive, and out-will whom. And within all this, there we
are, the loyal women. We stand by our men. We bring up baby,
along with cigarettes, junk food, and expensive sneakers. We
women, we do it all despite weather and welfare.

As I write, I read pieces of this story to friends of mine. Many of them comment, correctly so, on how brave Rashid is, having parts of his life discussed so publically and graphically.

*You have all the power here,* a few of them said. *You being the writer. You're like God,* some said.

Still others pushed the issue further. Others proclaimed I had all the power in every part of our relationship. The life or death of our love rested precariously in my hands. It was me, I was told. I brought freedom and outside light to Rashid's dark, dank, caged situation.

There are months, so many months that I can no longer count them, that the phone bill comes in, five hundred, six, sometimes eight hundred dollars. Within the pages of the bill are lines and lines detailing the costs of the collect calls I accept. Collect calls are the only way Rashid can reach me. And me? I take $20 cab rides, run, cancel appointments, end dates abruptly in order to make it home in time to accept a call he and I had previously arranged.

*I don't know why you two just don't cut this phone business down,* Rashid's father said to me the one time we were all together at the facility for a big prisoner-and-family picnic day. I was annoyed by the statement, but not surprised. Others have said the same type of thing to me. They have said it as though our relationship didn't suffer enough communication lapses and distances. But people have tried to make me feel guilty for needing to connect with my husband.

There were years I took lesser-paying jobs because they allowed me the flexibility to visit Rashid during the week, which was something we both preferred since the weekdays were less crowded. When I go shopping now, I often buy clothes only if I think they will meet the dress code imposed on visitors by the prison. And later, after Rashid and I got married and were granted conjugal visits, there were times when I missed important events because they conflicted with the dates that the prison had scheduled for us to be together. Sometimes there were events which could have possibly propelled my career, but I couldn't imagine what would make me cancel time with Rashid. Besides, if I tried to get a postponement, it could have been months before we were rescheduled.

All of those daily realities made me wonder what my life would look like if I really was that God some people had determined me to be. What would my life look like if I was even a mere shadow of that God? What if I *could* write into existence all I ever wanted, or even all I ever needed? My words as magic wands. My words, not as a metaphor for power, but as the thing itself. My words as a synonym for creation.

Those people are, I suppose, so certain in their analysis that I have all the power, because I can come and go as I please without being frisked or shackled—as if my legs moving, walking, up and out are not connected to my heart, beating, feeling, needing. And my heart is always right there, trapped in that prison, no matter where my legs may find the strength to carry me. Nobody mentions that.

Others who have felt compelled to throw their two cents into the debate have commented that Rashid's ability to virtually command me upstate, that my changing the ways of my life in order to allow for prison rules and restrictions, gives him all the power. Rashid, a man who is told when, where, and how he can see and touch me, is constructed as a man with all the power.

In the meantime, and on numerous occasions, the phone company has blocked Rashid's collect calls not because I have paid my bill late, but because they *think* I might pay it late. It's their policy, the long-distance carrier has explained to me. If they think the bill is getting too high, they'll just cut me off. They'll cut me off without notice. They cut me off without repercussion. They'll cut me off no matter how lonely I am, no matter how much I may need to hear Rashid's voice, and no matter how much he may need to hear mine. Never mind that I haven't ever paid a bill late, no matter how costly it was.

One day recently, a guard terminated a couple's visit because he felt their six-year-old-child made too much noise. We, each wife and husband, each girlfriend and boyfriend, watched with disbelief as the couple was being separated. We held our own partner more tightly, and cursed the police under our breath, and wished terrible things on him, and then we thanked God it wasn't us being dragged apart two hours early. Of course next time it could be us.

We knew an unjust or incorrect accusation from a guard, a lie from a guard, could determine a prisoner and his wife's ability to see, touch, or smile at each other. A computer-generated restriction from a phone company could stop our ability to even talk. And those things could happen no matter who has the power.

That is what I tell people when they offer me their theories. The phone company can beat my ass, it can reduce me to long sobs of frustration and loneliness, but I'll keep coming back, crawling, money in hand, bruised, maybe broken in places, but I'll always keep begging.

Regardless of what anyone else might believe, I know there are no simple answers, no one-line solutions to this question of prison love and its relationship to power. I say there are no simple answers to most things in life, though often I've tried hard to reduce them down, choose sides quickly, and then maintain my positions forever and ever. For Rashid and me, however, this is not an option. In prison, there is no place for the simplified, the redacted, the easy way out.

To hold on to ourselves and our sanity, what Rashid and I must do is master the art of being fluid. We can neither make things too complicated nor too simple. We must be great negotiators, willing to compromise without selling ourselves short. We are unnetted trapeze artists, Rashid and I, balancing when to fight with police with when to ignore them, when to spend money for another collect call with when to fold our emotions into a package we put away for another time. A better time. A different time. A later time. Or else a time after that.

# marytr

*t*here was a time after we were married when Rashid sent me a letter detailing some of the restrictions which were being imposed upon incarcerated Muslims. Access to the room they used as the mosque was suddenly restricted, which in turn affected the ability of the men to pray together and to fellowship. Then, suddenly, the Department of Corrections wanted to control the food choices for Muslims on their holy day celebrations (food that the men pay for themselves). Rights were being chipped away at slowly but consistently, leaving the men in an odd predicament. The rights that they had lost were too small to provoke any widespread uproar, yet if things continued along the path they were headed, soon they would have no rights at all.

Rashid closed his letter to me with a quote which is reported to have come from the Prophet Muhammed. It read,

*Whoever of you sees an evil action, let him change it with his hand; and if he is not able to do so, then with his tongue; and if he is not able to do so, then with his heart—and that is the weakest of faith.*

I wrote a fast and thoughtless response to Rashid which thankfully I never did wind up mailing. Out of concern for his safety, I'd told him to leave all these issues alone, but I tore up my letter because if my baby didn't take a position, then who would take a position? The media and politicians have constructed prisoners as people who have adopted religion as a con game, and perhaps some have. Some prisoners may use religion as a tool to get a few small privileges. But most of the prisoners I have encountered are deeply committed, sincere believers. I mean, wouldn't you be, surrounded by noise, anger, violence, depression, and steel, wouldn't you give your life over to a greater power?

Rashid may be the most sincere man I have ever known. And he has always been religious. As a child in Guyana, he was a deeply committed, Sunday-school-going, Bible-quoting Christian. The years between Christianity and Orthodox Islam saw him embrace the Five Percent Nation, Masonry, and the Nation of Islam. His beliefs now, the longest held of all of them, seem to me a very natural progression.

And so the question was, how could I do it? How could I say to him, *Baby, please, hold back . . . let someone else do it . . . can't you just pray and be silent . . .* Me, a woman who lives all of her life in public, on the page, asking her partner to restrict his expression. I knew I wasn't being fair, but I didn't know what I was supposed to do. Was I supposed to willingly sacrifice the man I love to prove my own sociopolitical commitment? Was I supposed to be ashamed that I'm a woman who just wants her man to come home, and not in a body bag?

When he helps another inmate file a grievance or get their legal work together, when he refuses to allow the prison to discard his humanity, Rashid takes his whole life in hands, all the love that is in him, all that is right and just, all that is imperfect and all that is scared, he takes the father in him, the son, the brother, and the partner in him, he takes all that makes him rise and think and pray and dance and scream and make love and struggle, he takes everything and risks it, with one sentence, one challenge, one legal document, one disagreement.

For those who want to know, this is the real story of prison life. Not color televisions or weight rooms. Those things exist only to distract inmates.

After everything I've seen, the only story of prisons that I am able to write is the story of the intimidation and the fear that I live in every day of our life. If we argue with a guard in the visiting room, if there's some kind of policy change, if another prisoner gets attacked and needs assistance, what will it mean? Will it mean Rashid will be set up with drugs? Will a guard try to set him up to be killed? These things are not products of my imagination. These are things that have happened to us. And they are documented. They are known. They are everyday business. They are simply not stuff the six o'clock news ever chooses to cover.

I began a new letter to Rashid first by telling him that I didn't believe that I was made of whatever it took to be married to a martyr. History instructs us that they kill people who rose up and challenge the status quo. But as I was writing, I started thinking about how I believe in transformation behind the wall. How I believe in it and support it. I started thinking about George Jackson. And I started thinking about Angela Davis. And, it was in the middle of those thoughts that the memorial service for Dr. Betty Shabazz came on.

I set the letter aside and watched Myrlie Evers-Williams and Coretta Scott King as they stood there together, shaking at the podium, desperate to explain what it was to have lost their husbands to the movement. Coretta Scott King said that as she watched Medgar Evers shot down in 1963, she wondered if this would one day be her fate. She said that when, in 1965, she saw Malcolm X killed in front of his pregnant wife and four children, she knew that her turn was coming around the corner. Mrs. King said that she, Myrlie, and Betty were sisters, albeit sisters pulled into existence by tragedy.

I knew I never wanted to be part of that kind of sisterhood. That was the next line of the letter I wrote to Rashid, though I did not write it without a measure of guilt. It was not that I supposed my partner to be a Malcolm X, but like so many people I knew who had committed crimes and who now wanted to turn their lives around, Rashid embraced only the highest of moral positions. So much of his early life was handed over, he said more than once, to these base emotions: greed, lust, and selfishness. Today Rashid lives for others. Today he lives for God.

Sitting in my room that day watching the memorial service, trying to write that letter, and feeling the full weight of prison-imposed fears, I thought about all of the years I'd spent as a student organizer. I thought of all the protests, and I thought of my work with Black Panthers who were now political prisoners. I thought about my unwaivering positions on issues of self-determination, women's rights, and economic justice. And then, shocked, I wondered, could it be possible that in the end all I really wanted was the man I loved to be at home with me where I could see him and touch him, build and create with him? And at home, where I at least had the chance at trying to protect him.

Whatever changes Rashid was going to make in this world, I decided I had to be there alongside him. Not me as a distant witness, and not me on the other end of a horrible phone call. If ever there comes a time that we've got to go out, then we've got to go out together.

And that's what I finally wrote to Rashid as a response to his letter. If there's business to be handled, I said, either figure out how we're going handle it together or else leave it alone. Period. That's it. End of discussion.

# time

**p**rison toys with time, teases its meaning, confuses those of us trapped and defined by the fourth dimension. During visits and phone calls, minutes and hours disappear within a single greedy swallow. Whatever else may need to be said—and there is always something else which needs to be said—must be postponed, put on the back burner, minimized, or forgotten.

Waiting for the court to rule, *just to rule,* on an appeal which could free Rashid, is horrifically long, dragged out like his homecoming. The years stretched out, yawned, took their own sweet time to pass. They went on vacation, those years, and left me staring at calendars hoping that eventually they would indeed return and get the job of bringing Rashid home to me finally done.

Every time I looked up, there was always more time ahead of us than there was time behind us. As I write this, there are six more years left on Rashid's sentence, and that's just the time between today and the parole board where Rashid could get hit with more time. He's got life on the end of his bid, so there's no guarantee of anything.

I get lost when I think about what could happen in my life in the next six years, what has already happened in the past six years. I am not the same woman I was a half decade ago, not even close.

Six years ago, I was married to another man; the idea of falling in love with a man in prison had never even crossed my mind. Six years ago I spent weekends in clubs and bars. I smoked cigarettes and I drank alcohol regularly. Six years ago, the idea of getting my own book of poetry published by someone was a fantasy. I was barely willing to read my poems publicly. Six years ago I hadn't finished college, and didn't know if I was ever going to finish college. Six years ago the only emotions I could access regularly were anger and pain.

Six years ago I wouldn't have liked the woman I am today. I would have thought I was boring.

The woman I am today prefers to stay home, is still attracted to, but doesn't want to get caught up in, "the mix." Today I am a vegetarian who eats organic foods. Today I have finished my Bachelor's degree and am nearly done with my Master's. I am a published poet now, and have read my work before audiences in New York State prisons and before audiences in London, England. I don't go to clubs and rarely to parties. Today I set achievable goals, concentrate on them, and complete them in realistic time frames. Today I time-manage and write daily. I do affirmations. I meditate. I run. When people ask, how did you finish school finally, stop smoking, get published? I tell them, *Slowly*. I tell them about discipline and focus and isolating yourself into your own dreams and hopes. I tell them about struggling to never live in reaction to my fears.

*In six years,* I asked Rashid once, *what will happen to me? I think about how I could have six new lives in that time. How am I supposed to stay here with you? How realistic is this relationship? How do other women do this time?*

I looked to him for answers that I knew and he knew he would never have. Our relationship is strictly trial-and-error. Or trial by error. And I cannot imagine how I will make it. And I cannot imagine how I won't.

≈

*You know what the difference between you and me is?*

Rashid began speaking, his voice low and our faces huddled close in the visiting room. We always do whatever we can to resist the imposing *clang clang* sounds of vending machines, and the booming of police shouting, *Visiting room to central!!! Open!! clickclick . . . hmmmm! bang!*

The electronic steel door, which is controlled by a man pushing a button behind a two-way mirror, slammed open and a guard passed through. The door slammed shut quickly with all the same noise and drama, but we managed to resist the cacophony. We even managed to resist the sensory-depriving, noncolors of the walls, numbered tables, and hard plastic chairs. We choose the rich, defiant tones and texture of our flesh, eyes, and humanity instead.

*The difference between you and me is that with every day that passes, you see a little bit of your life slip away. Every day is one day further away from your dreams not being met. One more day without your family intact, without the babies you want to have, without your partner being home with you, without having any real home at all.*

*But every day that goes by for me is one day closer to having what I've always wanted: a beautiful woman I can cherish and be with, a family, a good job, being in the street with people who I can work with to make things better and stop all of these kids from coming into these jails.*

He was right and I was silent, saddened, and scared by the truth. Once again, our needs have collided and then exploded upon impact. Nobody is ever right and nobody is ever wrong. We are left there, trapped between nowhere and nothing.

Powerless, we are, as though we have been strapped in and forced to ride the passenger seat of our own lives.

And time, she moves, a dancer to her own drum, elusive as the wind, unconcerned, uncommitted, unsympathetic, and unavoidable.

# between god and religion
## and rashid and me

*a*ll of our struggles are not big, prison-imposed struggles. Some of them are regular, everyday sort of troubles, troubles that other couples, couples who have never even seen a prison, have. And while neither of us like to fight, when we argue over these every-couple sort of things, we know it is a blessing. Rashid and I crave normalcy even when it comes on the edge of an argument.

Islam, Rashid's religion, would be one of those everyday sort of battles, and it followed us as a source of dissension within our relationship. I never could reconcile myself with what I understood as its patriarchal doctrine. From the very start of our affair, Rashid began the process of attempting to convert me. He denies this. He denied it then, and he denies it now, but I know better.

During the two years in which our relationship was strictly platonic, never once did Islam creep into our conversations. And back then, we would have these long, winding discussions about politics and social issues. We were, all of us, the prisoners and the students, open, personal, and fairly unrestrained. Oddly, however, Islam was never mentioned.

Once Rashid and I shifted into romance, everything changed, and changed without warning. I became a sudden and unwilling audience for long passages from the Qur'an and even longer rationales on parts of the scripture which I found particularly disturbing. In one section I read the manner and

133

circumstance under which a man may beat his wife. Rashid said he would never hit me. I told him I was not comforted by that fact.

*In the first place,* I would usually argue, *I already have a wonderful relationship with God.*

*And if you ask me,* I said, *I think religion generally gets in the way of a good relationship with God.*

I told Rashid that I found no space for myself, my woman self, in Islam. Everything I saw in the religion taught me how I was supposed to be a good daughter, or else a good wife, but there was so much womanness in me between those two definitions. In the Islam I see, I can't find space for the asha who has all of this history. This history that's shaped me. This history that's hurt me.

In Islam, there's no space to forget for a moment, about being responsible to a husband or child or parent, and just go get my nails done, or go for a run, or wander aimlessly one afternoon, or buy a dress I don't need, or dance, or kick it with my girls, or laugh raucously, or gossip a little, or do a million other imperfect or else immodest things that I do to get through some of my days. I can't find the space to exist in all of the full sensuality of my regular expression.

The religion, I told Rashid, would harness me back from my own spirit. That scares me, I told him.

I told him that, *In Islam, I never find the room to fall apart. Never room to take a day off. There's always some neat answer to problems, and I just don't see life like that. Things aren't that neat, and sometimes the only right response to a problem is to fall apart. And believe me, when the man you love is in prison, sometimes, you have to fall apart.*

*Maybe you see something I don't see. Maybe there is room in the religion that I just can't find. Maybe there are things that I don't understand. But until I do, I have to leave it alone.*

I continued by explaining that the religion was too severe for me, that I did not understand the love of God based on this long set of rules. I explained that I needed a God who loved me for doing my best, even when my best isn't very good. And, I explained, I did not want to be in a religion where men cannot shake my hand or hug me unless we're married.

*I believe in human contact,* I say. *I don't think touching has to all be considered sexual.*

*In this society, it is,* Rashid argues.

*But we can't let something negative define our behavior. We have to define our behavior. I'm going to keep hugging people and holding hands, and if I have to say a thousand times I only mean this platonically until they get it, fine.*

*But what happens if you hug the wrong man?* Rashid asked.

Over the years, this is how we go, back and forth, point and counterpoint. I do not understand him on this issue, and he does not understand me. After a few rounds, we always agree to disagree until something brings the issue back onto the table. Of course, something always does.

But as much as I want to, I cannot simply dismiss Islam out of hand, because Rashid says that his religion saved his life. And religion beyond simply a belief in God, which he has always had, but religion as a code for living, a structure, a strict set of rituals, a chart directing him through every minute of every day. Islam, with all its specificity, was and continues to be Rashid's primary catalyst for transformation.

Beyond precise moral instruction, Islam determines methods and times of daily prayer, how to kneel. It tells you how to dress, what to eat, how to manage your money, and how to resolve conflicts. It tells you how to romance someone, how to make love, and how to raise your babies. It demands complete obedience, and when you have done wrong, it does not shirk from meting out punishment.

Islam, then, is the parent Rashid never had. This is what I have finally come to understand. In his life, it is an entity that has been as instructive and consistent as my own mother and father have been in my life. When there is no one else to love him, there is Allah, his Messenger and his message.

When there is no one else to love me, there is my mother and father, their particular morality, advice, and admonishments. And it is these which have always embraced me and kept me in a way Rashid's people never did. Not when he was a boy, and not now, as he is a man.

Once I asked Rashid about birthday celebrations he had when he was child, and celebrations he's had since he's been in here. He says he cannot remember ever getting even a card from his mom or dad.

*Maybe when I was boy. I can't remember though. Nothing since I've been here. No card from them. Nothing.*

Rashid waits a moment and recalls, *My mother used to send packages after she left and went to the States. But I don't know if they came because it was my birthday. I think she just sent packages sometimes. It's fine though. Really,* Rashid adds, but I do not believe him.

≈

There was a woman we would see regularly in the visiting room. She and her husband were Muslims, you could tell by looking at them. He wore his *kufe,* and she was always in the full *hijab.* She became the bain of my existence, that woman, always there as a reminder about how short and fitted my dresses and suits were. Rashid has never and would never ask me to be covered from head to toe, though I know if I did so he would not complain. I could tell by the way he'd sometimes comment on her outfits. I could tell by the way he'd comment on mine. Finally I fought back.

I argued to Rashid how the couple had two small children and on most visits the woman would bring them along with her. On most visits, too, she had some kind of intense sexual interaction with her husband, sometimes full intercourse right there, while her children looked on.

Rashid and I had no idea how they were able to carry this off. Most couples hug too long and suddenly there was some guard standing over them just waiting for a hand to slip into a forbidden zone. But those two, they really could go at it with no apparent repercussions every time they were together. I'm not accusing anyone of anything, but it was strange for any couple to have such freedom.

That curiosity aside, what was really relevant to me was not *how* they were able to do it, since they weren't friends or associates of ours. What was relevant was that they were Muslim, and as Muslims, a religion certainly defined by modesty, they were the height of immodesty.

*Look at them, honey,* I whispered one day. *She may dress the part, but look how she acts!*

*It's true, I may wear dresses above the knee, but I never behave like she does! I would never let you behave the way she allows her husband to behave!* I feel quite righteous in this moment as I motion toward the couple carrying on in front of their children. I sit back in my seat. I grin.

Rashid grins too. He grins and then says, *I think we ought never to compare ourselves to the worst of all possible examples. I think we ought always to compare ourselves to the best the world has to offer.*

Rashid looks at me. He waits for an answer, a rebuttal perhaps, and for several miserable seconds I search my brain for one. Finally I say quickly,

*Nevertheless, my point remains. You should judge me by my actions, not my clothes.*

Rashid opens his mouth to respond, but I kiss him instead and tell him I am hungry. *Let's get some popcorn,* I say, standing up to walk over to the vending machines, satisfied to have had the last word.

He smiles at me, aware of what I am doing. The conversation is over, the disagreement unresolved, but at least we are laughing.

*All right,* Rashid says. *Come on,* he says, and takes my hand. And when he does this, I look at him. This is a man who liberates, not oppresses, me. He liberates my thoughts and ideas, all of who I am.

Yes, my spirit is liberated, even here behind a wall, a razorwire fence, and four electronically locked doors. Here with Rashid, I have never felt so open, so free, or for that matter, and by extension, never so close to God.

# sight

**W**e lived on a land with no borders, *in a city with no center, down a street with no name, in a house with no walls, where there were windows with no bars.*

*We were free in this place, Rashid, we were free. And can you remember? How the days moved with no time, how the years did not stunt us? How we shared language with no words, how our silence was the singing that made the sky begin to dance? Remember this, beloved? The way the sky danced bold and the way the sky danced wide? The way she seduced us and the way she seduced herself with her beckoning arms and her winding hips? The way she claimed her space and the way she leapt and then changed colors?*

This was a dream, but it was not a night dream. It was a day dream, and it came to me one afternoon in the middle of Manhattan where I was walking, wondering if Rashid had ever walked here, on this exact street. I was wondering if he had ever walked here and felt the sun laying down on the back of his neck, the way I was, right then, feeling it lay down on the back of mine, and if he did walk here and feel that, did the sound of the cars and the people stop for him the way they had stopped for me? I could not hear them. I could not even see them.

I could only see Rashid. I could only see Rashid and me. I could only see Rashid and me, and the land with no borders, and the sky above the land, the sky that danced.

One day when were together in the visiting room I asked Rashid if he ever saw this place, the one from my dreams.

*It was so vivid,* I said to him. *I think you had to have seen it.* I pulled Rashid near to me. I said I thought he had to have seen it even from this place, this cage with no air, beneath a sky with no stars.

Rashid leaned back in his chair and then he closed his eyes and then he nodded his head slowly.

*Yes,* he says to me, *yes, asha, I saw it. I can still see the place when I look out the window, when I look just past the doors. I can see it every day.*

# a wedding at the prison

*e*ver since you and Rashid became involved, he's wanted to marry you. In Islam, there's no such thing as boyfriend and girlfriend! *He has argued this point to you from the very beginning, but you never did find it very compelling. What you have found compelling was how good the man has loved you for almost five years. What you have found compelling was the history the two of you have created, and that if you got married, you could at last be alone with him. One morning, swept up in a whirlwind of desire, love, and hope for the future, you tell Rashid, Yes, yes, yes. You tell him you can handle being married to a man in prison.*

*Two months later you are standing outside your apartment building, waiting for the prison van. You are alone and it is five minutes to five on a Tuesday morning. It is springtime, but it is cold. You remember how it was the first time you married. You remember that first the sedan picked you up from your parents' house, and later, an Excalibur drove you and your groom off to a five-star hotel where you stayed until it was time to fly off to your honeymoon in the Greek Islands. You wonder how things could have changed so radically. You feel very confused in that moment as you look down the road to see if the prison van is coming yet.*

*Freddie, the van driver, had said for you to be outside at ten minutes before five. He is late and now you are panicking. What if he forgets you, you wonder, even though he has never once forgotten you? Is the lateness an omen? This thought comes to you but you do not hold on to it. You snap it up, and then throw it aside. Another five minutes passes, and then finally, finally, you see the van coming, tumbling down the street as it always tumbles down the street: as though it is too heavy, as though it will tip over.*

*You are wearing jeans and Freddie notices this when he gets out of the van to open your door.* You getting married in that? *he asks.* No, *you say.* There's a dress in my bag, *you say.*

*You climb into the van. The only seat available, except for two in the tight back, is the center one in the first row. You have never seen the van so crowded. Not before. Not since. You climb over a woman in the first row who barely moves to let you in. Right in front of you, in the place on the floor where your feet should go, is a huge box, a package you're sure that someone is leaving for a prisoner. In order to fit, you must put your feet up on the package. Your knees press into your chest, and you wonder how you are going to make this long ride. With all the stops in between, it will be nearly four hours from door to door.*

*You arrive at the prison, it is just past nine. The women and children line up to be processed. You do not. You have brought a dress and you want to change into it, fix your makeup, try to look pretty. You wait until the women have been cleared to enter the prison so that you won't be interrupted while you are in the ladies' room, and for about five minutes, you are not bothered. Then, as you are putting on mascara, someone begins to pound manically on the door. You think there's an emergency, a fire, and you rush to unlock the door, but before you get to it, you hear the voice of a woman.*

*The woman on the other side yells* Yo! Somebody in there? *And from the tone in her voice, you realize she just wants to use the toilet. You cannot believe it! You are annoyed that she didn't just use the other bathroom. That bathroom is exactly like the one you're using, except it says* MEN *on the door instead of* WOMEN. *But since men rarely visit anyone in prison, that bathroom is regularly used by women. You yell through the closed door. You say to the woman that you'll be out in a minute, but of course you don't mean exactly a minute. You mean as fast as possible, which you thought was understood, but after a minute goes by, a minute to nearly the exact second, she begins pounding again. This time, you yank open the door and curse her out. You are ready to fight. You indicate this, that you have no problem stepping to your business. You don't know what you look like when you say this but the woman seems to take you seriously. She backs up, mutters, walks away from you, and suddenly you are embarrassed at what this must look like to the police who is standing at the desk to the left of you, waiting to process you.*

*Back in the bathroom, you remember getting dressed for your first wedding. You remember how your mother taped a piece of lapis to you. It was something blue, she said, but also for good energy. You remember your sister helping you on with your dress, and the photographer who captured that moment, the zipping up of the dress, on film. It's all important, your mother had said, about even these most intimate pictures being taken.* You'll cherish this one day, *she'd said. If only she knew.*

*But she doesn't know. You have only told her that there is man, a man who is in prison. You have not told her you're marrying him. You have not told her how much you love him. You are scared to tell her and even more scared to tell your father. You have always been the kind of daughter who suspected that there wasn't much room to make mistakes. Even if there was room, surely it must be gone now, considering all the trouble you caused as a teenager and young adult. You don't want to lose your parents. You decide to tell them nothing. And there is a price for that decision. It is your wedding day, and you cannot remember ever feeling quite so lonely, quite so isolated. You emerge from the bathroom.*

*You hand the police your visitor form. He knows you are getting married.* Sure you want to do this? *he asks. You do not answer.*

*You resent all the intrusions into your feelings by people you don't know, people who don't know you. When you requested permission to get married, there was the counselor who talked with you about Rashid, his crime and his sentence.*

Mr. Rashid has a sentence of twenty years to life for the crime of murder in the second degree. Are you aware of this? (Yes.) This means he will not come up for parole until after he has served a sentence of twenty years. Are you aware of this? (Yes.) Mr. Rashid can only apply for family reunion visits after you've been married for ninety days. After the ninety days, Albany will decide if you're eligible. If you're eligible, you'll be placed on a list to participate. Are you aware of this? (Yes.)

*The counselor had gone on in this way, as though Rashid wasn't sitting there at the table, and finally when he finished and left, you had exploded. You were mad because you thought he was disrespectful to Rashid by not addressing the both of you during his monologue. You were mad because the man had made it seem as though Rashid was not there, and you didn't need one other thing to make it seem as though Rashid was not there. You began to go on, to become consumed by your anger, but Rashid had interrupted you. First he kissed you and then he said,* Don't pay that shit no mind, baby. He's just doing his job. The important thing is that we're getting married. *You agreed. But you were still mad that day.*

*And you are mad right now, weeks and weeks later, as the police asks you that question,* You sure you want to do this? *You want to ask him why he cares what you do, but instead you grimace. You go through the metal detector. You head into the visiting room.*

*In the visiting room the officer assigns you to a special table, one over in the corner and almost hidden behind a pole. He is trying to be nice, to afford you a modicum of privacy. You understand this. You even appreciate the effort, but it does not replace how exposed you feel. You continue to frown as you sit there, waiting for Rashid to arrive.*

*You look at your watch. Rashid is taking longer than normal to get into the visiting room. Frustration begins to build inside of you. You begin to think about running out of the prison with no expla-nation. If you do that and if later Rashid calls to ask what hap-pened, you could say he should have been more timely if he* really *wanted to marry you. You could put the blame on him. You are thinking this as that question*—Are you sure you want to marry him?—*twirls around your head, twirls and jumps and yells and snickers. You begin having a heated argument in your head:*

What kind of stupid question is that, anyway? *You silently demand this, hands on hips, neck going, mouth twisted.* Who can ever be sure of anything? *You continue, even as you know that the argument you are earnestly trying to erect is poor, at best.*

*Another part of you starts rattling on about lots of things that you are sure of during your life. It says that there are lots of things you're sure of right now. Getting married just isn't one of them. The argument is over. No use fighting with the truth. You crumble into defeat but not before cursing the police who asked you the question. You will the tears back behind your eyes, and then you read the list you have made in your head. This is what you're sure of:*

*That you and Rashid need to be alone. Not just for sex, although sex is a big part of it. There are these other important things the two of you have never shared. You have never cooked for Rashid and you want to. You want to make him one of his favorite dishes: vegetable curry and roti (he'll have to handle the roti), banana bread, avo-cado salad with your special secret dressing, honey-pineapple chicken, or else blueberry pancakes, vegetarian sausage, and plan-tains for brunch. This is what you're sure of. This is what you know.*

*You know you want to touch Rashid, your skin against his skin, an hour-long massage. You want to rub his feet, give him a long hot bath, wash his hair, oil it, oil him, let him relax in your arms, let him sleep there while you watch him, this is what you're sure of on the morning of your marriage. You decide it is enough, and you tell Rashid you're ready when he finally walks into the room.*

*He walks in wearing a white shirt, a shirt you've never seen before. He's carrying a bouquet of yellow tissue-paper flowers.* Here, baby, *he says, smile wide as a river.* My friend made these for you. Every bride ought to have a bouquet. Especially my bride. That's why I took a little long to get down here. The stupid police didn't want to let these in. But I figured you didn't have family here, you didn't have friends or a cake or nothing, so you should at least have flowers. Here baby, *Rashid says again.* Take them.

*And you do, you take them. You think they are stunning, more beautiful than the roses from your first wedding, the wedding where your whole family came, the wedding with the expensive printed invitations and four-tiered cake and the open premium bar and the Tattinger Brut de Brut and the live band and your bridesmaids in peach dresses and ushers in tuxedos, and the woman from the Ethical Culture Society who officiated, and the honeymoon in Greece, and all that love and support and hope and approval everywhere, flowing from everyone. Who could have predicted, who could have known, that just ten years later, you'd be here in a prison, with no one, no one there except Rashid and his friend, a man called Natural. Natural, who was also a prisoner, had agreed to witness, to be the best man.*

*He's there, Rashid's friend, when you pick up the flowers, the yellow paper ones. He's there when you try not to cry, but the paper flowers are the evidence of all you have and all you do not have. They are why you cannot help yourself. You begin to weep, to sob, and*

*Rashid doesn't understand. He thinks it is him.* Did I do something, baby? *he implores.*

*It is not him, but you do not say this. You only cry. You cry when the Imam comes and asks both of you if you are truly ready to honor a marriage contract. You cry when you exchange vows in the corner of the visiting room over the sound of change clanging in the vending machine and the argument someone is having over who gets the last microwaveable chicken sandwich.*

*You cry when the guard says,* Okay, folks. Visiting room is closed. *You cry as you leave and Rashid thinks it's him.* Baby, do you think you made a mistake? *he asks, desperate and terrified. You don't think that.* Of course not, *you say. But you say it with less conviction than you should have said it. You know this, but you leave.*

*It is night, your first night as Rashid's wife, but you don't feel any different, since everything looks the same. When you left the prison, the midday spring sun was no brighter than usual. The night moon is no more round, no more golden now. When you get back to New York City, you do what you could do on any night of your life. You meet a girlfriend. She takes you out. You eat a big fattening Italian dinner and a huge dessert. All that food makes you feel sick but you eat anyway. You eat and eat. You get drunk from the food. You tell your friend it's time to go home. You go home. You get in bed. You are alone. It is your wedding night. You are alone. You hope you will dream of Rashid. At least that. At least. You think of him and you think of him. You slide your hand down your body, play with your nipples, open your legs. You imagine Rashid is kissing you. You love the way Rashid kisses you. You can almost feel his tongue, lips, and teeth mixing with your tongue, lips, and teeth. You slip you fingers inside yourself. You raise your hips, and now you can almost see him entering you, first slow, long, and then fast, faster. He is in you. He is you. You can call up the sensation, Rashid in you, Rashid as you. You feel yourself begin to rise in yourself. You hold your breath for several seconds and then you start to come. You come hard. You say Rashid's name out loud. You say it the way you know you will say it when he does finally make love to you. That day will get here. This is what you are praying for and imagining, right before you fall asleep. You fall asleep, but you do not dream.*

# eve

*e*xactly ninety days after the wedding, Rashid applied to the Department of Corrections in Albany for eligibility in the family reunion program. Four weeks later we were given a date. We were informed that we would have our first conjugal visit, what we call a trailer, a reference to the housing on the prison compound in which we will be staying, in less than a month. I received a letter of instruction from the prison, and my life divided into a list of *can do's* and *cannot do's*.

The letter told me that I could bring in my own sheets and towels. What I could not do was bring in my own sheets and towels if they were orange, blue, white, gray, or green.

I could bring in my own shampoo and conditioner, lotion, makeup, and soap. I could not bring in my own shampoo and conditioner, lotion, makeup, and soap if they contained any sort of alcohol.

I could bring in my own packaged foods. I could not bring in my own packaged foods if they were packaged in glass or under pressure, if they contained poppy seeds or alcohol.

The instructions went on and on, and then they went on some more, and for three weeks I spent hundred of dollars on regulation sheets and towels and toiletries and bags and bags of food. I shopped for seasonings I hadn't had to buy in years: salt, black pepper, sugar. By the time I was done, I had bought a near truck-load of packaged foods (*Just in case,* I told Rashid.

*We're not going to have to time to eat,* he responded. *Not that stuff anyway,* he giggled.)

Shampoo bottles, lotions, conditioners, and hair gels, I meticulously read labels that before I'd never even noticed. Every one that I picked up seemed to have alcohol in it. I became overwhelmed with anxiety. I paced aisles in drugstores. I confronted store managers and demanded to know *exactly* why they don't carry nonalcoholic toiletries.

Eventually I found a hodgepodge of what I needed and I began to pack. It was still several days before the visit. I packed. I waited. And it was during that period of waiting, when I only had time to imagine what our trailer visit would be like, that it dawned on me: Rashid was about to see me naked for the first time. Upon that realization, I had a fullblown anxiety attack. My skin got blotchy. My breath tightened. Sitting down, my heart rate stayed above one hundred and twenty beats per minute. I was a mess.

I began to roll back through all of the years and all of the visits I'd spent disguised by pretty dresses, mascara, lipstick, and eyeliner. Now Rashid would wake up with me. As is. Raw. But the idea of us being alone got even scarier. It got even worse.

We were going to make love. We were going to make love after four years that had been marked by small kisses that we held in our mouths and stored behind our teeth. We used to hold our breath, trying to make those kisses last. And they did, those kisses lasted so long, they became our sex, whole and complete.

And now I was terrified. I was terrified that I would never be able to live up to the sexy fantasies that we shared with each other in letters, on the phone. Now that it was time to move past the small caresses Rashid and I had become used to, I was scared I wouldn't know where to go or how to get there. Making love was a new world, and I was worried I wouldn't know how to do anything in the new world, the world of virtual freedom.

I never believed, neither did Rashid, he said this to me, that we were ever going to get to a place past those fast visiting-room kisses. We never expected to marry while Rashid was in prison, but one lonely spring, we'd just done it. It was almost spur-of-the-moment—as much as anything can be spur-of-the-moment in a prison. *I never thought you'd marry me. Not while I was in jail, anyway,* Rashid had said, over and over. *I just didn't think you'd do it,* he'd said, amazed, grinning.

*I didn't think so either,* I responded. *But I couldn't wait anymore. I had to be with you.* I paused for a moment, and then I added, *I hope that you like me.*

*What are you talking about, asha? I love you.*

*I mean sexually.*

*Come on, asha. Don't even go there. It would be impossible for me not to love being with you.*

And I tried, I really did try to believe him. I tried not to sound defensive, but I failed, and Rashid loved to remind me so. Months later, when the sex between us had become easy, fluid, he would tease me. He'd laugh and ask me if I remembered how I was in the beginning, how I'd said,

*Look. You can't touch me when I first get in there. Okay? Because I'm going to be nervous.*

*Okay,* Rashid had said.

*Look, I'm serious. Don't try to pressure me,* I continued.

*I won't.*

*I mean it, Rashid. You better relax.*

*No problem.*

*You're not listening to me. You don't understand how it is when I come in. Those police might treat me any old way. And they might make me be in any kind of mood.*

*What do you mean, honey?*

*You know how stupid these people can be, how they say dumb stuff all the time. They might put me in a bad mood. But besides that, I mean in general, I might feel nervous.*

*I think you said that already.*

*Okay. Well, I'm just trying to make sure my point gets across. You don't have to get an attitude.*

*First of all, I don't have an attitude, because I'm much too happy. But you know what I do think? I think you've been a pretty big talker all this time. So I guess now we see the real deal. The real deal is you want to be on some kind of virgin shit now. Think maybe you can't handle me?*

Rashid could barely contain his laughter.

*Fuck you,* I said.

*Now we talking my language!* Rashid said through laughter, and then the recording came on: *You have one more minute.*

Then Rashid told me he loved me. *I love you, I love you, I love you,* he'd told me for the last time before we were together, almost like other couples: undressed, unmonitored, unrestrained, unrestricted.

# venerated, sanctified

$\boldsymbol{N}$ot just the first time, but whenever the date for a trailer visit comes around, everybody knows it. Friends ask if I will be free on those particular days and of course I say, *No, I'll be with Rashid.* People nod and grin and wink and then they laugh. I know that they don't mean to be insulting, but inside I twist up just a little. From my vantage point what I see is that at last here's my private moment, a moment when finally I can look at the person I love without cameras watching, and still, there's nothing private about it.

People regularly make jokes about what my time with Rashid is going to be like, until eventually I make jokes too. Nobody seems to understand that to me, the time on the trailer is sacred. It's an experience which should be spoken of in hushed and sober voices. Making love should be a holy communion.

It took me years but now I see. Before Rashid I thought making love was something my body did all by itself. My body as this independent thing, separate and distinct from my spirit, my soul. I thought making love was just this physical thing.

But the way Rashid and I would cook together, clean, tell jokes, watch television, pray, dance, stand outside in the rain, stare at each other, bathe together, massage and rock, was what I came to understand as erotica. It was what I came to understand as making love. Our sex was and is a whole thing, a circle that is everywhere present. And it is a land that, from the very first time, Rashid and I would travel to, humble, heads

153

bowed, bearing gifts, confessions readied, and souls laid bare. And each time we have returned, we have returned in this way.

On our first trailer, Rashid picked me up and carried me over the threshold of the trailer. He carried me over to the couch and set me down easy. He did not touch me. Not immediately. He never touches me immediately, or without asking.

So I asked.

*Will you kiss me?*

And he did, his arms tightened around my waist, and his mouth lost itself inside my mouth. And about his hands and mouth? They were these: a river, a sail, a passport, a country, a time. A time venerated and a time sanctified. (Amen. Amen.)

# night

*N*ights on the trailer are unnaturally still and silent. No loud city cars, no singing country crickets. Just a quiet immobility which belies all of those endless emotions, the love and the longing, the rage and the sadness, the desperation and the fear, the starvation and the fantasies which define and color the walls, ceilings, cells, and trailers of correctional facilities. But like everyone else who gets locked on the grounds, I have no choice. I cannot run outside and scream, cannot let my emotions overtake me. And so I do what all of us there do. I accept the unnatural, and finally, see it as normal, average, everyday bread.

The first night we lay together, Rashid and I, entangled, our breath a shared breath, I knew that never in my life had I trusted anyone as I trusted this man. Never in my life had I been naked the way I was naked with him. Naked in the way no clothes, no sheets, nor fullness of night can disguise.

With Rashid, I learned to make love the way I learned to swim. Frightened but determined, dropped into waters where the choice to survive could only be my own.

I wanted to be with Rashid in a way I hadn't ever been with a man. Before we came together, I only knew how to have sex in these two ways: as the girl who was a freak, and as the girl who was frigid. The girl who was the freak was the girl who had been trained, since she was seven years old, to act, crawl, accept, beg, dance, acquiese, stifle her screams, fake her orgasms, shake her titties, plaster a smile, and give in to every madness, at the life-threatening whims of whichever old man towered and then took over so many of her dreams. And it was always an old man. And I was always a girl.

The girl who was frigid was the girl who knew that somewhere inside herself was the capacity for great love. She was the girl who had met men who touched her at her core, but men who she feared might discover what she believed was filth beneath her flesh. She would nearly freeze when those men had touched her because she thought any honest move she made would give away the secrets that discolored her spirit.

To be in this place with Rashid, it had taken three and a half years of steady work, healing rituals, psychological research, burning candles, praying, reading astrology books, doing numerology, talking to friends in the middle of the night, and reminding myself daily that suicide was not an option. It took getting hysterical and it took Rashid accepting my hysteria and loving me back into calm. It took crying the tears my seven and ten, my thirteen and seventeen-year-old selves never could. It took going to the edge of sanity, standing on a cliff with its long drop into the jagged rocks of the crazies. It took making a last-minute parachute out of my own skin, my own bones.

But in the beginning, when I first started confronting the memories, I felt powerful seeing myself as *the victim*. After all of those years of thinking it had been my fault and my fault alone, I appreciated, even enjoyed, not shouldering the blame for the actions and illnesses of grown men.

Loving Rashid, Rashid loving me, made everything change.

I began to grow tired of not trusting or being fully happy. I began to resent the fact that, as a victim, I was expected to be weird, sad, and in need of therapy. I began to feel like I had been set up to be scarred forever, off-balance, angry, and hateful. That I was never supposed to like sex or being touched. That I was supposed to stay drunk or high or fat or addicted to nicotine. I was supposed to be everything I never wanted to be, everything I was never raised to be, and then I was supposed to die, still in pain.

But I knew that I deserved something more. I knew it wasn't fair. I conceded my childhood, my teenage years, and most of my twenties to the abuse, but I told Rashid I needed the rest of my life to belong to me. I told him this just before the first trailer visit. And that's when I knew I needed to be more than the victim I had hidden behind.

The victim was great for a time, safe for a time. She allowed me to forgive myself and allowed me to cry. The victim even gave me an identity, which was something I didn't have for those long years between seven and twenty-seven.

But ultimately, the victim couldn't save me. The victim couldn't help me create a new me, a me who trusts easily, laughs freely, and loves openly. The victim couldn't help me dance my dance, or write my poems, or enjoy my man. The victim couldn't help me tell my story, my whole story, the part of the story that does indeed smile, crack jokes, and relax at the movies. The victim couldn't help me to love kissing. The victim couldn't teach me how to share any intimate spaces. The victim couldn't summon up brand-new colors, spread them across the pages, make a brilliant new-age rainbow, toss it up into the sky, and let it spill royal purple raindrops onto my tongue.

Of course it didn't hurt, all those years when Rashid and I did not have trailers, when we were forced to actually communicate on those six-hour visiting-room dates. We were forced to become friends, best friends, before becoming lovers. Unlike all of my previous relationships, when, halfway through a discussion or disagreement, we could fall into bed, fucking our issues away, Rashid and I had no option but to talk it all through, figure out the roots of our anger and our confusion, and then to uncover our specific, individual needs. And that was how I learned what making love was really meant to be.

By the time we did finally come together, I had found the pieces of myself that had been forgotten, left in corners, swept under rugs. I told Rashid he was the first man who had all of me, the beautiful and the ugly, the perfect parts and the parts which were held together with tape and a prayer. When we entered each other, we entered and then enjoined two worlds that were previously undiscovered.

And within that moment we found home in ourselves, lush and bountiful. We found a place only we could have envisioned and crystallized, a world which pushed forward new life, pushed down old boundaries, and embraced the new moons of its own black and perfect sky.

# home, revisited

*f*or hours after the first trailer, when I found myself back home, alone, I wandered in and out of the rooms in my apartment. I could not believe that Rashid was not with me. I didn't understand how, if I could feel him with me as strongly as I did, why couldn't I see him? I looked and I looked but he didn't turn up. He was not outside the door waiting for me to open up. I opened up the door anyway, checked the hallway, but did not find my husband there. I went back inside and put on an Otis Redding CD. I turned the shower on hot as I could take it, stripped, got under the water, and tried to evaporate, like the steam, like the time, but it did not happen.

For a long time after I got out of the shower, I just stood there, naked and damp. I did not pull a towel around me. I did not reach for the lotion. I did not turn away. I just stared into my reflection in the steamy bathroom mirror and began thinking about how sometimes I had felt as though I was a divorcée from my own body. It was the way I could stand back from it, study it, critique or admire it, and eventually command it. I could be so clinical that some had accused me of being unhealthy, obsessive, or simply strange. But for me, being able to stare at who I am and what I look like is progress.

For so long my body had been this hated thing, this enemy, this betrayer. I had done everything I could to ignore it out of existence. My body was Judas offering me up for shillings and rice every time I walked out the door and dared venture into a world judged by colors and shapes. By far, though, the worst betrayals came when I was fucking.

My body used to try to kill me every time I parted my lips or my legs, willingly or unwilling. It would choke me in this crazy undercover way that no one else ever noticed, but for me, there was no air. Even during the rare occasions that someone actually loved me, when my lover would take his time with me, remember the color of my eyes, even then the passageway to my lungs would sputter and finally lock itself tight into itself. My own body choked me from the inside out, letting me live only for the pleasure of its next attack. It was some wild shit.

And so that evening my eyes studying first my hard brown nipples and approving of them; my eyes moving down and accepting, if not fully satisfied with, my round though not fat stomach; and my stomach with its light-colored stretchmarks and fine line of black hair that begins at my navel and follows a straight line down to my pussy; that evening taking all of this in, taking all of this me in without cringing or critiquing, was indeed progress.

In our four years together, I had come to believe, Rashid had helped me come to believe, that even my stomach is sexy, that I am sexy. It was the way he would become transfixed on some part of me. From my eyes to my ass, he always told me, in blushing detail, how beautiful I was.

*Don't no man want to feel no rock up under him, asha,* he said to me during the trailer visit as we stood in front of a mirror looking at ourselves, examining who together we appeared to be.

*Girl, you're the way a woman supposed to be, sweet and thick. You ain't nobody's fat so get that shit out your head. You just don't* look like them sick-ass white girls from those magazines. And you not supposed to look like that. Shoot. I want a real woman. I want a Black woman. I want a fine woman. And that's what I got.

That first visit Rashid had forced me to look at myself, nude, in the mirror, with all the lights on.

*Look at yourself, Momi,* Rashid had said. *You so god-damn beautiful!*

I had looked because he had made me look, but I felt my pupils try to curl shut. I squinted and strained, wanting to see through myself, to see only the glass of the mirror, but it didn't work. I wanted to see my body as an indistinguishable brown mass, but Rashid refused me my selective blindness.

I watched as he smoothed his hands up my thighs, up my stomach, cupping my breasts from behind. He had run his tongue over his fingertips, and now they played with my nipples, which brought out in me an involuntary moan and then scream, arch and then grind. After all of our years of talking, all of our fantasies poured out to each other, slowly, through whispers or giggles, after all the visits when we talked because we could not touch, he knew me, and he knew that he knew me.

He knew my body, its fears, and its every nerve and yearning. He knew how my face looked when the hunger became too strong to be contained. He knew everything I had ever told him, everything I had never told him, everything I had never even thought about myself. He knew at that moment I was so desperately wet that he could have felt it down the inside of my legs if he wanted to. And he wanted to, but he waited.

He made us both wait as he smiled slightly, noticing the way my tongue and teeth played with my lips, how they reached for something to hold, to suckle, to swallow. I am telling you, I needed that man to fill me everyway and everywhere.

Have you ever loved like that, where there is no part of your lover you do not want to be touched and, finally, filled by? That's how I wanted him, in every opening I had.

Rashid kissed the back of my neck, bit the back of my neck, and whispered,

*What you want, girl?*

*P-P-lease* . . . I managed. *P-P-lease* . . . , I managed again, fearful he didn't hear me the first time.

With one hand on my back he eased me down until I was bent all the way over. My hands balanced me on the floor, his hands steadied him against my hips.

He slipped inside me naturally, with no struggle, no searching. Inside me he was tight, fitted and perfect, and I felt certain, with each sweet, long stroke he made, that I was made, like some cherished encasing, just for him.

And my lungs, they just expanded as I breathed him, as I breathed him and I breathed me, into every one of my open and wanting pores.

# *there are emotions*
# *that have no name*

*i*'ve never thought too often about whether or not Rashid and I should actually be allowed to have trailer visits, but every now and then there will be a talk show on and the subject will be all of the rights that people believe prisoners have. Eventually someone arrives at the issue of conjugal visits.

*Can you believe it?!* someone will yell. *These people go to jail and get to have sex!*

Often the people yelling are crime victims themselves who are in so much pain that the idea of anyone proposing an alternate point of view seems insane. But sometimes I imagine myself as a special guest on the show, one who cannot be interrupted.

In that scenario, I would tell them how conjugal visits are, first of all, not a right, but a privilege which can be taken away at any time. Then I would tell them that most prisoners come back out into society, and in general, the ones who do not re-offend are the ones who were able to get some schooling, learn some marketable skills, participate in alternatives to violence and in antidrug programs, and yes, the ones who were able to maintain family ties through regular and conjugal visits. I would tell them conjugal visits are not paid for with tax money, that they are paid for with various auxillary profits associated with the prison. And I would tell them, I would stress to them, that they should not worry. Despite conjugal visits, I would say, prisons remain painfully sexually repressive environments.

I would tell them how, from the prison administration's point of view, conjugal visits lower tension; people don't want to get into trouble and lose the privilege.

I would never, ever give back the times Rashid and I have spent together on trailers. They have been among the most beautiful times in my life, filled with the most love, passion, peace, and clarity I have ever known. But there is also no question how those visits leave me, how they leave us both, awash in a loneliness and hurt as sharp and unavoidable as the rocks in the white waters of the Delaware. The hurt rushes you like that water. It yanks you unmercifully and barefoot over those rocks. It pauses for no one, and it pauses for nothing. Sometimes it feels even worse than that. It never feels any better.

Leaving Rashid. I prepare for it from the minute I arrive. By the time the clock reads 7:00 on the morning of my departure, Rashid and I are fighting. As much as we try to avoid it, some small disagreement occurs, and instead of ignoring it as I would usually do, I lose my temper. I tell Rashid that I'm glad I'm going.

*I hate being here!* I say to him. I scream it sometimes.

*I know, baby,* Rashid says. He says it every time and then picks me up, brings me over to a chair, sits me in his lap, rocks me, kisses me. *I know, baby,* Rashid says again and again and again and again. *I hate it too.* And we stay like this for the last hour before we hear the gate that surrounds the trailer site being unlocked. I start to get up. *Wait,* Rashid says. *Wait until everybody else is outside. Somebody has to be last. Might as well be us.*

*Okay, baby. Okay,* I whisper, and Rashid holds me tighter. *Let me kiss you one more time,* Rashid says, *while we're still alone.*

*While nobody's watching.* And he kisses me. He goes far, far, deep inside my mouth, and he kisses me. After this I leave. It seems unbelievable how it could happen. But it happens. I stand up. I smooth my dress. I smile. I leave.

*What's it like to be separated like that?* friends have asked. *It's like an enemy tank barreling over the land,* I tell them. *Except that we are the land,* I say. *We are the battleground. We are the after-effects of a scorched-earth policy.*

When a talk show or the news comes on saying how easy prisoners have it, my friends call me up. *You should write a letter,* they say. *You should tell them what it's really like,* they say, but I do not agree. There could be no one single letter to tell what it's like, all of what it's like, from top to bottom, from the inside to the outside.

*There are emotions that have no name.* A friend says this to me, and now I know she is right. I know it when I do sit down one day to write about what leaving the trailer feels like and find I cannot do it. I begin to imagine that I am a dancer instead. If I was a dancer, I could really explain what I felt. If I was a dancer, I think, I would use every ounce of strength I had to leap into the air, leap beyond where anyone could see, and then I would crumble down deep into the floor where I would remain while the music kept playing.

If I was the music itself, I would play in C minor, pianissimo, a concerto written for the solo cello.

And if I was not a writer and not a dancer and not a concerto, if I was still just a child, still unformed and still uninhibited, and a child who could get away with expressing whatever I wanted to, wherever I wanted to, I would just cry. I would cry from my bowels, from the deepest and most remote space inside of me, and I would never feel compelled to stop.

# everywhere without

*N*ot just after a trailer visit, but on random days, it hits, the loneliness. It's like living under the constant threat of terrorism, the loneliness I live with. I never know when, like some secretly planted bomb, it will explode. Where will I be? Will I be injured? If I am injured, will the damage be permanent? Will the injuries kill me? If I am lucky enough to survive one explosion, will another come behind it and finish me off?

This is what the prison has taught me: Loneliness is a terrorist, except it has no righteous cause, no moral foundation, no God. There is no reasoning with it, none.

*I can't imagine the separation,* a girlfriend says to me. *What's it like, being everywhere without Rashid?* she asks.

I tell her about the first time I went to England to do a poetry reading. While I was there I stayed in Brixton, but one afternoon I was riding through central London with a friend, another poet visiting from Brooklyn. He leaned over to me, my friend did, as we rode on the top of a double-decker bus, and said as we entered Piccadilly Circus,

*You know, there are no garbage cans on the street in this part of town.*

*Why not?* I asked.

My friend looked around us, apparently checking to see if anyone could hear us, and then he whispered in my ear,

*Because of bombs.*

*Oh,* I responded. *Right, right.*

It was after this conversation that I noticed the signs posted everywhere warning people to be on the lookout for suspicious bags. Those signs, they do not let you forget that you are never really safe. Afterwards, and despite the fact that no bomb went off during my stay in England, there was this slightly edgy feeling in my stomach the whole time I was there, and every time I've gone back.

I tell my girlfriend that the streets of New York leave me with a similar uncomfortable feeling of impending disaster; not of physical bombs, C-4, dynamite, and such, but of sudden, violent, emotional eruptions. Walking in any given New York neighborhood calls up dangerous fantasies about Rashid and me being together on these streets. We are holding hands, a couple, and it is this image which is the detonator, since for me it is not the memories I have which are haunting. It's the ones which are yet to be made, the ones which I know may never be made.

New York streets and neighborhoods explode regularly in my face. They are shrapnel. They are dumdum bullets. They remind me that, too often, I do not live in the today of my life, but in a yesterday which never was, and a tomorrow which may never be.

In the streets of my New York, there are no real memories for Rashid and me. I cannot say we laughed on this block, and fought on that one, and this is why I make things up. This is why I abandon my own reality, and lose all sorts of time imagining a life that never was. We will never be teenagers together, Rashid and I. He will never save me from the isolation and self-destructiveness of my youth. I will never save him from crime and prison. But I think and think how we could have, *if only*. And I drown in that thought. I sink in it, become lost in it, lose time in it, which I cannot afford. I cannot afford to lose any more time; the prison has taken enough.

To try to defend myself against it, the loneliness, I mean, I take myself on lunch dates, dinner dates. I take myself out to the movies, and I take myself on trips abroad, on trips anywhere. But the distance between what they offer and what I need is a grand canyon. It is the real grand canyon. Whatever I lurch toward in an effort to escape the loneliness always winds up having a huge hole in the middle. It's a hole only Rashid's physical and emotional presence can fill. It's a hole so deep that if you drop anything into it, you'll never hear the landing. And it's a hole so wide that made me finally understand this thing for what it was: a worldwide organization. Loneliness. Wherever I went, whatever streets, whatever city, it had set up camp. It was always there, waiting for me.

*During its reigns of terror was when I thought of her most, the widow, the murdered man's wife. What did she look like? I never knew. Rashid didn't either. The only face I knew was the one I imagined her to have. Not in the moment she learned her husband had been killed; no, that face I cannot conjure. But the one she is wearing when she turns to say something to him,* Honey, would you please help me . . . , *and then it comes back, the memory, and she says, out loud to anyone and to no one,* Oh my God, he's not here. Who am I talking to?

*It's that face I think I may know, not entirely, but in part. Maybe just around the eyes. I think I know it like the nightmare that repeats itself every so often: violence and separation. It's always the same frightening dream, and I cannot wake myself from it, nor predict it, nor stop it, finally. Please, can't somebody just make it stop?*

# two weeks later

**t**wo weeks afer the trailer visit, I began to feel sick. Everything smelled terrible and made me nauseous. No matter how much rest I got, I was tired and weak. I started watching the days on the calender. My cycle was off and I told Rashid. Two days afterwards, I told him what I had confirmed as true: I was pregnant. We were on the phone and I told Rashid just like that, with no buildup. I went right to the heart of the matter. *I am pregnant,* I said.

≈

I never thought it could happen to me. This is where I have to begin. Rashid and I didn't use protection because I never thought I could get pregnant.

*I don't think I can get pregnant. I've never ever gotten pregnant, even when I was young and careless.* I said this to Rashid before we had our trailer visit. I said it and I believed it with the whole of my heart. *We don't need to use any protection,* I said.

*Okay, baby,* Rashid said, and when the time came, he entered me and entered me, and once I even joked with him. Exhausted, I said, *Whew! Now that was some baby-making sex!* Rashid agreed and we laughed. We laughed and we did it again and again.

≈

Pregnant, I went to friends for help. I had no idea what I should do. My finances were at an all-time low, and I was on unemployment. I had just found a school willing to accept most of my credits. I matriculated and was less than a year away from finally finishing my Bachelor's degree. My days were spent going to classes, writing poetry, letters, and essays, running, and waiting for grants to come in. In no way did I feel prepared to bring a child into the world. Nevertheless, when I remember that time, I remember that I have never felt quite so necessary in the world as I did when I carried the baby Rashid and I had made.

One afternoon, a woman I am no longer friends with said, after learning I was conflicted about having the baby, that she felt powerful after she had an abortion. She told me her story in a Washington, D.C., restaurant where we were having lunch together.

*You know, I was raped when I was student,* she told me. *Well, the man got me pregnant and so I had an abortion. After I got rid of it, I felt so powerful, so in control of my body.*

And when she said this, I was so stunned by her comparison—me being impregnated by the man I love, her by a rapist—that I was silent. I was rigidly silent. I wanted to talk, though. I wanted to tell her that if I did have the baby I *knew* it would be a girl. *I can just feel that,* I wanted to say, but did not. I would have a summer-born girl, a Cancerian like me, a possible painter or poet, a dancer or doctor. *A baby really is like having a second chance,* I wanted to say. Me, except minus everything that ever went wrong. But I never said this to the woman that day. I never said it to anyone while I was pregnant.

Soon after the rape comment I left the restaurant, and when I did I massaged the place on my belly where I thought my baby was. I massaged it with more passion than I ever had before. That woman and I never did go back to being friends again. We spoke off and on, but after a few months had passed, we came completely apart. We did it without explanation or battle. We just came apart, but I know that the fissure began on that day in Washington, D.C.

*I loved my baby. This is what I am trying to say.*

❦

There were so many obstacles. I simply could not have the baby. That was the decision I would come to and finally present to Rashid. He did not agree, however, and for the first and only time in our relationship, we became adversaries. Rashid said he felt we should go ahead. *We should have the baby,* Rashid said firmly.

*We? What we are you talking about? I'm the one who's going to have to raise the baby and I'm the one who has no money,* I answered.

*Most Black women have no money,* he argued back.

*It's not the right time. I have nothing to offer a baby. Not a decent home or stable income. Nothing.*

*You have love. That's what children need. God knows it's what I needed when I was a child.*

*Look, I am not ready. Why can't you understand that?* I insisted this. I insisted it as mean as I could, as mean and as adamant. But Rashid pushed through my anger. He leaned close to me, the midday sun in his eyes, sweat on his brow. His voice was low.

*My mother told me once that I was supposed to be an abortion, but it was 1962 and she couldn't. She told me it had been just a year since she'd had my brother, and she and my father had split up already. She told me she was only twenty-two, and I was supposed to be an abortion. But I wasn't. By the grace of Allah.* Rashid said this and then sat back. He breathed in long and deep.

And although I was shocked by this information, and although I got a fast horrible flash of what my life might have been like had Rashid never been born, I also suspected he was trying to make me feel guilty. I crunched my face at Rashid and said, *Well, she shouldn't have told you that, but it doesn't change our situation. That information doesn't make me any more prepared to be a mother.*

Rashid looked surprised at the lack of sympathy in my response. He implored, *asha, don't you want to have our baby?* And that infuriated me. I covered my mouth with my hands to keep from screaming *I hate you!*

*Rashid, don't you want to be home to raise at least one of your babies?* I countered sarcastically, and when I did, Rashid pulled back from me. His eyes turned sad, and I knew I had said the wrong thing. I knew that despite his incarceration, Rashid had done everything in his power to be a force in his child's life. He has always sent his son whatever money he could, and he has asked his family to please help, to support not just the boy, but also Dawn, the young mother who was left there at eighteen with a baby but no boyfriend.

Rashid had gone to prison one month after his boy was born. He was lucky, I told him this over and over, that his son's mother was a bright woman, a hardworking, honest woman, who never let the child be hungry, and who never interferred with Rashid having a relationship with his son.

*I'm sorry,* I said to Rashid. *I shouldn't have said that. About your son.*

During the time of the pregnancy, our control over our emotions spun wildly out and away from us. They spun away from me and they spun away from Rashid, and all of our visits, phone calls, and letters seemed to all spiral downward into these devastating fights. It was a horrible clash of our wills, and both of us, practiced in the art of debating, pulled out every emotional dirty trick we could to prevail over the other.

In the end, it was me. My arguments prevailed and Rashid said, *Okay, asha, you win.* I called a clinic and scheduled an appointment, and as soon as I did I knew only one thing was true: that I was a winner of nothing. I was, in fact, feeling more like I was about to lose everything.

≈

There are things Rashid has never told me about that time. Not even now. Once when I asked him, *Who supported you when I was pregnant? Who did you talk to?* He just said quietly, *It's not the kind of thing you can talk about in prison.*

*What did you feel then?* I pushed.

*I can't remember that time. Between the baby and our fights, it's all an ugly blur,* Rashid said. *What about you?* Rashid asked me. *What did you feel? I mean besides the—you know—besides that and how bad it was, what did you feel then, asha?*

*I felt guilty,* I said, *and profoundly sad. And afraid. I was afraid I didn't have the thing it takes to be a good mother.*

*How could you say that?* Rashid exclaimed. He sat back in his chair and looked completely confused.

I hesitated and tried to figure out how to explain myself.

Just say how it was, I thought, and then began, slowly, speaking. *You know what they say about people who've been abused.* I waited for a reaction, but Rashid was just staring at me. I continued, *I was scared. I thought I might be bad for the baby. I thought I could hurt the baby.*

*You would never hurt our baby,* Rashid said finally. *Never.*

*I know that now. But when I got pregnant, I began thinking about the abuse every day. Like when the memories first came,* I explained. *It was that bad. I don't know why. When I was pregnant, the abuse informed every one of my days. Whatever else I was thinking about, I was also thinking about that. It was there, behind every story, behind every time I cried, no matter why I said I was crying. It was that, the thing. It was there.*

*I wish you would have told me that. You never told me that.*

*I couldn't tell you. Even though I wasn't raised to believe like this, I can't help it. I have this association: motherhood and womanhood. And I was thinking about Dawn and how she brought your son up so well, and she was this standard, and she was eighteen, I was almost thirty, and even still I couldn't see doing what she had done. I couldn't see being a good single mother, raising a child you could be proud of, the way you're proud of your son. I could only see damage.* I paused for moment, and then I said, *I was afraid you wouldn't want me anymore.*

*That could never happen,* Rashid said. *Never. I wish you would have told me all this stuff back then. We could have gotten rid of it back then.*

*I wish I had told you too. But you and I both know how it was then. How we were.*

Rashid nodded, and for a moment I thought I saw it again, the particular pain he wore during the time of the abortion. For a moment it seemed as though it was all there again like an avenging ghost, hovering alongside us, howling. When I saw it, I thought if only there had been some way to have known how our emotions would have run during the time of the abortion, I would have prepared myself and I would have prepared Rashid.

I could have suggested that I stay away from him, or that we limit our phone calls. I could have reread one of my books on conflict resolution. I could have found a mediator. But I didn't know better back then, and neither did Rashid, and so we fussed constantly, fought bitterly. We were no help to one another in the time of the abortion. We were only exhausted, Rashid and I. The two of us were losers. I see that now. But then I could only see and understand my own pain. Now I know that both of us had laid out our womb on a steel gurney in a mid-Manhattan clinic.

In that time, though, we would go reeling toward the very edge of the ugliest kinds of arguments, the kinds that can break a couple apart, the kinds that you cannot commit to memory, because if you did, you would just have to leave. You would have to go away forever. At least I would have had to go away. I am certain of this.

If only I had known better, though, I would have found a way to peel back all the pain, Rashid's and my own. I would have recalled the necessity of our touch. And our touch beyond the usual walls and barriers. I would have pressed us together, full and tight, flesh upon flesh, one body, one breath, synchronized and steady.

# hush, little baby

*t*he night before the abortion, Rashid called to tell me he was sorry. *Baby, you know if I could be with you I would be. I'm so sorry you have to go through this,* Rashid said as his voice split in two.

*Okay,* I responded, disconnecting myself from myself.

*Please don't be mad at me, asha.*

*I'm not mad.*

*You're something.*

*I'm nothing.*

*Don't say that, asha. Listen. I'm going to call you tomorrow. Will you talk to me? Will you tell me what happened?*

*Yeah.*

*Baby. You have to know I'm going to be there with you tomorrow.*

*No you won't. You're never there. You're in jail.* I said this and then nothing else. We were silent for what seemed like an interminable amount of time, until Rashid took a deep breath. His voice was low, gentle.

*I love you, asha. I will always love you. Always, always.*

*I love you more,* I said, and our conversation ended there, like that, and I closed my eyes. I burrowed my head into my pillow and tried to imagine what I would feel like after my baby was gone. I tried to prepare myself.

There was no way to prepare myself. This is what I would say to Rashid when he called me after the abortion. *My sister tried to warn me,* I told him, *but I didn't listen.*

*Those places are like factories,* she'd said to me one morning on the phone. While I was pregnant my sister called me from her home in Los Angeles nearly every morning. *You have to be prepared for that,* she'd warned me in one of our final conversations before the procedure.

The day it happened was a Thursday and it was November and it was cold, not bitter, but unpleasant outside, very much so. I wrapped up all the way, head, neck, and hands, and took a taxi to the clinic in Manhattan. When I arrived there, I saw two people, a Black woman and a white man. They had set up a table and displayed two horrible pictures. I was sure that the pictures were of dead fetuses, but I did not look. I could not look. I stepped toward the building where the clinic is located and the couple at the table started screaming: *Don't kill your baby! PLEASE! Don't kill your baby.*

Their screams grabbed on to the hem of my coat and dragged behind me, nearly keeping me from making it through the double glass doors of the building, through the corridor and onto the elevator. I did make it, but it was a struggle. I pressed the number of the floor I'd been given, and the door closed and I began to rise. The elevator was slow. It shook. I did too. But we got there, and immediately I began to record everything, every color in that place, every scent. I knew I had to remember exactly how it was so that I could go home, write it in my journal, and later, read it to Rashid.

The elevator at the clinic opened right into a waiting room. I looked around and wondered why the the color scheme was so dark, why the decor was so synthetic. The walls were a stubborn brown, which surprised me. I did not expect something bright, no yellows or oranges, but perhaps blue, a color to soothe, to soften.

I noticed that there was nothing made of wood. There were no plants. There were only folding metal chairs, with seats cushioned in foam and black plastic. There were rows and rows of them. I started counting them. How many women can come here in a single day? Nine in the first row, seven on the side, another nine behind the seven, and then I lost track. I stopped counting and walked over to the painted gray steel counter where there were two receptionists.

*Good morning,* I said through a smile I had been practicing all morning.

Neither receptionist answered me. My smile faded. *I have an 8:00 appointment,* I continued.

*Sign in over there,* one of the women mumbled. She motioned with her eyes to a place on the counter I tried to, but could not find.

*Where do you mean?* I asked, still trying to be polite.

*Right there,* she pronounced, clearly annoyed. I signed in, and now I had an attitude as well.

For about ten minutes I sat alone in a corner of the waiting room, and then an old girlfriend of mine walked in. She took a seat next to me, hugged me, held my hand. A week before the abortion she'd called. *What's wrong?* she'd asked, *You sound terrible,* she said. I had paused for a moment and then said it, blunt, the way I'd said it to Rashid.

*I'm pregnant. I'm going to get an abortion next week.*

*I'll be there,* she'd offered with no hesitation, *since Rashid can't, I will. Don't worry.*

In all of the years that I had been with Rashid, through all of our dramas, our fights, and our marriage, I always thought I could make it alone. Prison is so isolating that you get used to handling any problems and all the pain it creates by yourself. But this abortion was Goliath, and I was no David. I could not do this alone. I accepted any love I could get. I needed every kindness I could get, every warmth. My sister and my friends, the few who knew, rose to the occasion. They called and they wrote and they listened to me. I looked at Talibah, my girl-friend from college. I held her hand tightly in mine, and then I thanked God for her. I thanked God again and again.

After thirty minutes passed, a nurse came out and called me into the back area. The woman did not say hello and she did not introduce herself. She just explained what was about to happen to me. She said,

*We're doing a sonogram. Pull down your pants and underpants and lay on the table.* Her voice never changed its volume or tone. I did as I was told. The unidentified woman slapped cold grease on my stomach, but she did it without saying why. For several minutes she pressed her fingers down hard onto my abdomen. It hurt and when I could not take it any longer, I said to her,

*That hurts. What are we doing now?*

*Oh,* she responded without feeling or apology. *We've got to try to get a clear picture of the size of the pregnancy so we can determine the exact age.*

*You can see my*—I cut myself off. What do I say now, I wondered? What noun to use? Could I still say, as I'd been saying for the last two months, my baby? Is she still my baby?

*Yes. You can see it right here.* She pointed to the monitor. I looked. I squinted, but I saw nothing distinguishable.

*How big?* I asked, meaning the pregnancy.

*Well, it's hard to say . . .* the nurse began.

*How big?* I pressed, my voice raised slightly by determination.

*It's about one and a quarter millimeters, eight weeks.*

And when she said this, suddenly my pregnancy became even more real to me than it had ever been before. It was, for me, the first time and only place that I had publicly been seen and confirmed as this: a woman with child. All those days on the train, walking down the street, going to school, visiting the prison, no one knew I was pregnant. There was no way for anyone to know I was pregnant, and when the pain of the situation began to march up toward me, I would trick it away. If no one around me knew what was happening to me, and if even I denied what was happening to me, was it really happening to me?

Of course that trick could not work here. Here I had no defenses. I began to cry. I cried long heaving sobs, and the nurse looked at me. Her expression did not change, but she did say, *I'm sorry.* She handed me a tissue, and then she told me we were done. She told me to go back out into the waiting room. I got up off the table, pulled my pants up, and walked back out into the room. The room with folding chairs, the brown walls, and forty or fifty women I did not know, but who would see me as many of my friends have never seen me: emotions laid completely bare, no shield, no armour.

After half an hour, a voice called me to the lab along with three other women. *It is time to take blood,* we were informed. We made fists. We stuck our arms out like some sort of strange wave. We got syringed on the assembly line. We were sent back to the waiting room.

Fifteen minutes later, someone called my name again. I was told that it was time for my counseling session, which was being handled by a woman I only ever came to know as "The

Supervisor." We sat down without greeting or introduction and began a rote process:

*Social Security number?* she began. I gave my number to her, and she continued, *Are you aware of other choices, adoption, foster care?*

*They're not options for me,* I said.

*Okay, then please read and sign the release papers.*

The release papers described all of the things that could possibly go wrong with the procedure. They could fail to remove the entire pregnancy, it said. I could even die. At the bottom of the page, it said that the clinic is not liable if anything happens to me. *What is your responsibility to me?* I asked. *Can I get that in writing too?*

*That's not our policy,* the Supervisor said. *But don't worry,* she continued almost smiling, *we've been around for years. We're licensed and regulated by the Department of Health.* Her voice glowed, and as she started telling me about the abortion itself, about what would happen when I went in for mine, I started thinking about how easy it had always been for me to be pro-choice. I started thinking about how I always believed that the idea of the government determining when a woman had to start a family was insane.

And even though I still held these beliefs as I sat there in that counseling session, something visceral, something at the very core of me, felt shaken, out of place, wrong, when it was me about to have *one and one quarter millimeters* of my womb scraped out and left in a hazardous waste material bag. It was going to be scraped out and I was going to call it freedom but I didn't feel free and I didn't feel good. I felt confused and terrified and I wondered if she could understand that. I wondered if she knew she was looking at a mother in mourning. Her voice pinched on in the background of my thoughts. I faded in and out of what she was saying: . . . *A hundred women we service every day* . . . , and, *over before you know it* . . . My teeth began to grind, my fists tightened. Eventually I signed the papers and got sent to another reception area, one closer to the operation room.

Only one other woman was there waiting alongside me. She was tiny, except for her belly. Later I learned she was five and a half months pregnant. Later I learned she was getting an abortion too, but while mine took between five and fifteen minutes, hers took place over a three-day period. I tried not to stare at her swelling. I thought about how babies were often born prematurely, my God, at six months. In only two months from then, a girlfriend of mine would in fact give birth to her baby, a beautiful girl, who was born after only a five-month pregnancy.

But I pushed my negative thoughts away. I did not want to judge the woman sitting next me. I did not know the specifics of her story, why she was there on that Thursday in November. What I did know was that she was in a lot of pain. Water was squeezing out from every part of her. Her breath was chopped into tiny pieces. She begged for painkillers and a nurse with a voice as rough and hard as a prizefighter's hands said,

*Honey, I just gave you one. You're fine!* And then she disappeared through a door. I moved next to the small woman with the big stomach. I took her hand in mine. I took it as gently as I could. *Come on,* I whispered, *I'll do deep breathing with you. It'll help. Inhale as deep as you can,* I said, *Like this,* and I breathed through my nose, sucked the air down to my diaphragm, and exhaled through my mouth. I did it the way I had learned to do in yoga class. The woman tried her best and together we breathed and together we prayed. *Please, God, let the pain go away. Or at least go down. Please, God, please.* It was me who said this. *Amen,* the woman whispered. *Amen,* she whispered again, and we continued holding hands, but we said nothing else. Not even when the nurse came to get me. We did not even say good-bye when I rose to leave. We said nothing at all. We did not need to.

The nurse took me up in an elevator, up into a room where another woman, not a nurse, told me to *Strip all the way down, honey, like you takin' a shower.* I stripped and put on the hospital robe they provided me with. An air conditioner blew cold air on my back, but I did not feel cold. I did not feel anything. Another nurse appeared in another doorway and told me to follow her. She brought me into a tiny room with big bright lights and a steel gurney in it. In the corner of the room was the hazardous waste material bag, my baby's humble coffin. It was red, the bag, and I stared at it as another nurse walked in and began to rattle off instructions:

*Sit down on the table, slide down to the end, lie back.*

I did as she asked while tears and hysteria began to redefine my face. I did not even try to calm down. The anesthetician came in. He was cheerful and bouncy. He said,

*Hi, honey. I need your arm. But listen, you've got to stop crying. It'll impair your breathing. Okay? Can you go ahead and do that for me?*

Then the nurse said softly, *Don't be scared, you're going to be fine. It'll be over before you know it.*

The doctor entered and introduced himself. In the four

hours I spent in that clinic, that was the first and only time I learned someone's name. I tried to introduce myself as well, but the crying slashed my words. It ripped them down incomprehensibly. I babbled and the doctor continued,

*Hey, what you crying for? I haven't even touched you yet.*

My legs were strapped into stirrups. *That was the last thing I remember,* I said to Rashid a day and a half later, *before waking up in the recovery area.* I told him that when I woke, I tried to sit up immediately, but still slightly dressed, fell back. I could not run out, but I wanted to. I just lay there. I looked around me. I was surrounded by women, perhaps twenty of them. They were in hospital beds like mine, in robes like mine. I thought that yesterday we all were pregnant, today not one of us is. Today, not a single baby among us. A recovery room nurse came over to me. *Hello,* she said, in a voice so kind I thought my heart would shatter.

*Please don't leave me,* I whispered, I begged. *I don't want to be alone. Please,* I said again and again, *Please.*

I told Rashid how the nurse was nice, how she was the first really nice person I'd met at the clinic, and I told him how I was crying but no water was coming out of my eyes and how this made me panic, how I thought maybe my whole body had become dysfunctional, useless, worn-out, upside-down, wrong-side-out. *That's not true, that's not true,* Rashid said when I told him these things. *We will have beautiful babies one day, asha. This was the wrong time. But you are the right woman. To be with me, to have my babies. You always have been the right woman. You always will be the right woman,* Rashid said.

After he said this I was quiet for a moment, and then, out of meanness and pain, *Still feel like you were there with me? In spirit and all?*

*Please don't do that, asha,* Rashid said. *I can't fight with you. I just cannot do it. Anyway, the important thing is whether or not you felt like I was there.*

And although I was hurting and angry and empty, my womb was empty anyway, I refused to lie to Rashid. I would not withhold the truth from him. *Yes,* I whispered, *I did, baby. I really felt like you were there,* I said. I paused for a few seconds and then said, *Rashid?*

*Yes, baby?*

*Did I tell you that I felt hated in that place? Did I tell you I didn't understand how I could have felt so hated there?*

*It's a clinic, baby. People get under pressure and forget how to act. But they didn't hate you. asha?* Rashid asked.

*Yes?*

*Do you know I love you, girl? I love you so much. You have to know I love you so much. We're going to get past this. I promise you that.* And then the computerized operator came on. *You have one more minute,* it says, and we say good-bye. We got off the phone and I crawled into bed. I pulled the covers around me, put my hand between my legs and held it there. I held it like I was trying to keep anything else from falling out of me. Falling out or being pulled or cut or scraped out. *Good night,* I said out loud from under my covers. *Good night, my baby.*

And my eyes searched the room for some sign from the baby who will never be mine. I wanted a breeze to push through the room. I wanted my candle to flicker out and then back on again. I wanted the branch on the tree outside my window to move. I wanted something to fall off the wall, a lightbulb to go out, but none of this happened.

My room was entirely still. The baby that could have been, but never would be mine, was gone. And that's all there was.

Nothing else. No more to say or think or hope for or imagine. She was just gone, my baby. I repeated that just under my breath. *She's gone,* I said aloud so I could make myself believe it. I chanted it and I chanted it. The last two months were real. There could be no denial. They did happen, and the baby did happen, and the baby did not happen. I chanted so I would remember everything. I chanted so I would never ever return to this place. *She's gone, she's gone,* I said and I said. And then finally I became still, and I became quiet. For the next few hours I lay in bed and I did not speak, and I did not sleep, and I did not move.

# after

*a*lmost three weeks after the abortion, I was sitting one morning in the visiting room sipping on bad vending-machine coffee. Inside, I felt something which had been foreign to me for so long. I felt at peace. I felt easy with myself. *This is it,* I thought, *my life,* with all its burdens, but also with all of its blessings.

I began to see those blessings again, all the love in my life, the creativity, the hopes and possibilities, the friends and the family. I saw the blessings and they were the lighted roads I had been seeking. The ones which send me, protected, over and over, out into the world. The ones which bring me back home again.

On that morning of peace in the visiting room, Rashid asked me to put the coffee aside, and I did. As he often does when he is about to be serious with me, he took my face in his hands. We were so close that I could not see him, but I felt him, breath, skin, sweat, and pulse.

*Welcome back,* he said to me.

*Excuse me?*

*You haven't been yourself since this whole thing, but I noticed the last two times on the phone and this morning even, you're back to being my asha. Smiling asha. Silly asha. Laughing and sweet asha. It was really lonely without you here. So, welcome back.*

I put my arms around Rashid, and I draped both of my legs over his legs. I checked to see if the police noticed how we were sitting—me practically in my husband's lap, straddling him. We were lucky. If the police did notice us, for some reason they did not come over and repeat the rules:

*Excuse me, Mr. Rashid, please tell your wife to keep her feet flat on the floor and her chair and her person on her side of the table at all times.*

Uninterrupted by rules, I continued, *I never even considered having any man's baby until you,* I whispered. *But this wasn't the right time, was it, honey?*

Rashid shook his head slowly, and then looked at me. He said nothing. He just held me. He held our emotions, our hurt, and all of our hope in his arms. He held me and it was a brilliant morning. Even the visiting room with its shaded windows and lifeless colors could not mask it. It was a brilliant morning and my beloved was holding me. He was holding me so thoroughly that I could tell him anything, deny him nothing, give him everything.

Whenever I have thought I could not love Rashid more, and whenever I have thought I could not be more naked with him, he will say something to me, or he will do something for me, or else he will just touch me in this way that makes me want to find a part of myself that I have somehow forgotten about and turn it over to him.

This was what I was thinking that morning and I began to fidget slightly in Rashid's arms. He asked me what was wrong. *Aren't you comfortable?* he asked me.

*Yes,* I said. *Of course,* I said. *It's just that I want to tell you something.*

*What is it, baby?*

I turned to face Rashid and kiss him. *Come here,* I said, *so I can whisper to you.* He leaned toward my mouth. I kissed his ear and then said softly, *I can't wait to one day have your baby. If I ever get pregnant again, even if it's before you come home, I'm going to have your baby.*

And when I said this, Rashid held me tighter and the police did not bother us and the sun pushed through the thick glass and shades and rested on our backs and we were still, my beloved and I. We were completely at peace, and we remained that way, still and at peace, calm and resolved, without words, and without movement, and without tears, for a very, very, very long time.

# *no strings attached*

**W**e were in the dead of winter, a winter with neither relief nor pause, except that at last we had been given our second trailer. I was a little scared. I wanted to make love with Rashid, but sex was no longer this thing to simply fantasize about and enjoy. Sex was this thing which could produce life. I went to see my husband armed with a diaphragm, spermicide, warnings, and condoms.

After waiting to be processed for three hours in the room that had no chairs, no water fountain, no vending machines, nothing, we were walked into the facility. The site holds four trailers, and as soon as the guard unlocked the gate, our husbands and sons came rushing out to us. Rashid always leads the group and always greets me with a big smile and a bigger hug.

*Let me take that for you, baby,* he said on the afternoon that our second trailer visit began. He took my garment bag off of my shoulder. With his other hand he lead me over to our trailer. When we got to the door he said, *Wait a second, honey.*

Rashid placed the bag down, just inside the trailer. As he had done on the first visit, he picked me up and carried me over to the couch. He sat beside me. We held each other, in a sense no differently than when we are in the visiting room, but somehow it was completely different. Boundaries were gone, well, temporarily set aside.

*Can I kiss you?* Rashid asked, moving, kneeling over me.

*Yes,* I said, and arched my body upward to receive him.

Rashid eased into our kiss, memorizing first my lips, and

then my tongue, and then behind my teeth. He kissed me as though I could disappear if he did it wrong. He kissed me as though I could break. He kissed me as though he could break.

I pulled Rashid on top me, deep into my breast. Beard, tears, and flesh, we were all one entity seeking air, comfort, life-affirming touch. *Has anyone else ever seen you like this?* I wondered, holding him tight as my arms would allow.

I looked at Rashid, past his skin, pores, sinew and lines. I peeled away his thirty-four years until once again he was tiny, a boy of only nine, maybe even seven. *Did anyone love you then as a child is supposed to be loved, unconditionally, thoroughly, no strings attached?* I thought this, but I did not say it. *Do I love you like that now?*

What I knew was that I loved my husband as best as I possibly could. But within the bizarre reality of our monitored life, would my best ever be good enough to erase this stark landscape or his demons? Would my best be good enough to cleanse his open sores and help him create wholeness out of the charred and scattered pieces of himself? What *has* Rashid lost along his own particular trail of tears, from Guyana to the South Bronx, from the South Bronx to Rikers, from Rikers to almost every maximum-security correctional facility in New York State? Small remains of who he is and was and hopes to be: How were we to gather them all up, keep what's necessary, discard what's not?

*Momi,* Rashid said to me bravely, *I just don't know that it's fair to you, I mean, keeping you here. I feel selfish. You could own the world, and look. You're here in a trailer on a prison ground. I feel like I hold you back, but I need you, Momi. Please never hate me. I love you so much.*

My tongue played over the light tears on his face. I caressed

Rashid with my lips. I felt it was the best response I could give at the moment. Had I actually spoken, what would I have said? My head was telling me he was selfish. That he should let go. That he never should have brought me here. He should have been a dog, uncommunicative, irresponsible, abusive, *a typical man*. A man I couldn't love.

But my body, heart, and spirit stood in defiant and diametric opposition to my head. I felt more than love for Rashid. I believed in, respected, and *enjoyed* getting lost in him. Over the years, his love had been enough to make me withstand being a woman who went home every night of every day to dinner for one and an empty bed. The fullness of his love allowed phone-call fantasies to replace an evening on the town.

I let the warmth and wet of my body disguise my ambivalence and fears and all of my hurtings. *Make love to me, Momi,* Rashid pleaded, hushed and hungry. I did not hesistate. We have these forty-four hours together every three to five months. I knew and he knew there was not a second to spare. I knew and he knew exactly what we have always searched for. We knew where it was. We knew how to get there.

I removed what little clothing Rashid still had on and asked him to step back, to let me look at him. It had been over three months since the first and only time that I saw my husband naked. I stared at the faint scar on his abdomen. I touched it. My fingers tried to recall a memory my eyes could not. Had this scar been here before? It had to have been. It was an old mark. It looked like a childhood mark, faded and comfortable in its place. I stared and stared but the memory did not come. Right then, had I made the attempt, I could have convinced myself that this was the first time that I ever saw my husband nude.

My arms circled Rashid around his hips. My mouth moved toward his close, closer. I began to taste him down his stomach, down the inside of each thigh. I swallowed part and then all of him, until he screamed, moaned, arched, begged me to ride him. I moved him down to the couch and slipped on top of him. My hands were flat, spread across his chest. The ride began. Slowly at first. We didn't want to rush. We wanted to keep things as they were, in perfect balance.

I tilted my head toward the ceiling and just above my head I saw our dreams beginning to paint the air. Our bodies coasted. They became a multicolored magic carpet. They were a deep purple uptown Cadillac, a black horse with wings that could fly us out of this madness.

Rashid pulled me until I was down on his face. My nose to his nose. My lips against his lips. And my nipples against his nipples. Our sweat was the holy water our throats had craved forever. *Don't move, baby . . . let me hold you,* Rashid said, pressing his hands into the small of my back. *Let me do this, Momi,* he continued, pumping upward and into me.

*This is what they say, baby . . . in those books . . . to feel like you're one person with your lover . . . I . . . feel like we're one,* Rashid panted. And we were. We were in tune, intuitive, indefatigable, inexorable.

And then the phone rang. Right there, right then, unbelievably, the phone rang. It was a guard. It could only be a guard. The phones on trailers are one-way phones. They allow police to call and check on us whenever necessary. Rashid slid out from beneath me, picked up the receiver, and a voice was so loud that even I, several feet away, could hear it. It was time for the count.

Rashid pulled on his state green pants, black boots, and

white sweatshirt. He inhaled deeply, opened the door, and stepped outside. He stood there waiting for the guard to come around and verify his presence. This check happens seven or eight times during every visit.

After it was determined that Rashid and the three other men who were having a trailer visit were exactly where they were supposed to be, the guard yelled into a walkie-talkie that the count was clear. My husband came back inside.

Back inside he found me where he left me, only now I was wrapped up tight inside the blankets and sheets we had previously discarded. When Rashid had opened that door, when he had stepped outside, I'd become desperately cold. Desperately cold and suddenly alone, I had pulled the blankets around me and watched him as he had gone through the door.

Rashid has said that when we are old, we will remember little of this time. *No room for bad memories, because we're going to crowd our lives with good ones.* My husband is an optimistic man. He always has been. For as long as I've known him. But I know that when I am old and these years are a long time past us, despite any good memories we may one day create, what I will always remember about the prison experience is how it was being on trailers. The two of us there, always together, always alone.

# the prisoner's wife

*b*ave I said how almost every prisoner I have ever known has told me when I asked that he's coming home in just one minute? *One minute.* Not ten minutes, not fifteen, but one minute. Even the brothers I've met who are doing thirty years with life on the back. *When you coming home, Pa?* I'll ask. *I'll be home in a minute, girl,* he'll say to me, and mean it. And I would look into his face wet with sincerity, and think, okay, sure. Whatever you say. And as though the brother could read my doubts, he would inevitably and with considerable passion add, *You'll see, girl. I'm going to be home in one minute. Yeah. In one minute.*

Have I said that Rashid told me that he would be home in one minute as well? He said it like this, over and over: *Mama,* he would begin, *Mama, I got this. I'm telling you, baby. I'm going to get some rhythm with the feds. I knew in the state courts my issues weren't as clear. I never really expected to win an appeal in the state. But I had to go through them to get to the feds. Remember? I explained all that to you. Remember? I told you when you first got with me.*

*I remember, baby.*

*But the feds are different, asha. I know I got the law on my side with them.*

*Really, baby?*

*I'm telling you, girl. I got this.*

Have I said that I've worked around legislators in my life, that I have some idea about how they think, what influences how they vote? And have I said that I listen to people, average,

195

everyday people, in hair salons and on airplanes, when I go to get my nails done, when I go to the gym? I hear the rage and the unwillingness to talk, to discuss crime and criminals, transformation and mercy. When Rashid talked about his appeal, I talked about the social and political climate in which he was making that appeal. *That ain't got nothing to do with the law,* Rashid said.

*What does, then?* I asked.

*Look, the law is the law, baby. It's already on the books and it's on my side.* Rashid said this, with his back straight, his smile wide.

Have I said how Rashid can argue the law, argue it like a seasoned attorney, perhaps even better, because it's his own life he's fighting for? And how Rashid can write a brief that you would never guess wasn't written by a lawyer, which is why I couldn't fight him when he said he was going to win the appeal. The law was his territory, Rashid used to say that. He would say it and then back it up by quoting cases and precedents.

*Writing's your territory,* Rashid has said to me, *but the law is mine. I wouldn't question you if you told me that a letter or article I wrote was all messed up, and I think you should trust me when I tell you things about the law. I wouldn't tell you law I wasn't certain about. You have to have some faith in what I know, baby. You have to have some faith in me.*

*Okay,* I said. I said it because I did have faith in him. Because I would never have been in that prison for a single second if I didn't have faith in my husband, a big, ever-growing faith. And this is why I resigned. I took Rashid's hand in my hand. I looked at him directly, and I said, *You're right. You're right. I believe you, honey.* I gave in to his arguments, each one of them. Have I said that? How I gave in of my own free will? I gave in and all the while knew I was ignoring the voice inside myself that warned me to keep my defenses up. The voice that admonished me to balance faith with reality. But I ignored it at every turn. I just listened to my husband and became a believer. I believed because I wanted to believe. I wanted to believe whatever he said about the law and his case and the appeal and how he would get a time cut and how he would be home in the next two years and how no matter what, there was just no way the state was going to keep him for all that time. I believed this. I did. I did.

Have I said how often somebody will look at me, flush with concern, place their hand on my shoulder, wrinkle their brow, and ask in a whisper, *So, asha, when is Rashid coming home, anyway? How much longer do you all have to go?*

*A minute,* I say to them. *Rashid will be home in just a minute,* I repeat, and then I disappear inside myself. I disappear inside my prayers. I concentrate. I meditate. I summon up faith enough for a hundred women, maybe even more, and I begin to pray. But I do not pray to just any God. I pray to every God I have ever heard of. I call out whatever name, in whatever manner of worship. I am loud and I speak in tongues. I am soft and I whisper just below my breath. I sob and then I am stoic. But no matter how I go to meet God, two things never change. Every time I go, I go begging and I go ready to deal.

*Sweet Jesus (Mary? Joseph? Peter or Paul?), Allah, Jah, Yemaja, Ra, Obatala. Buddha, Kali Ma, Oh Great Spirit, You, You whose name cannot be known or spoken. Look, look. Can you see me, arms out, reaching into the four winds? Jesus, here I am, here, here, genuflecting at the altar, swallowing bread and wine. Allah, I'm facing the* Ka'ba *on my knees. My forehead is to the ground. Can you see me, Obatala, Yemaja, Ellegba? I'm here at the crossroads stand-*

*ing in need of direction, a signpost, a tiny clue, a piece torn from a map. Where am I? Am I as lost as I think I am? Am I close, am I far? Am I hot, am I cold? Can you see me, who can see me? Can you hear me, who can hear me? Who's willing to come bargain with the prisoner's wife?*

*Listen. I have already given up cigarettes and wine, and after today I will stop cursing. I'll leave short tight dresses in the back of my closet. I'll cover my hair. I'll stop eating sugar. I'll stop drinking coffee. Is there more, do you want more? That's no problem. I'll drop my fast, mean judging of people. I'll be more patient. I will never tell another lie. I'll never stretch the truth again. I will grow more love in my heart. Can You see me trying, Lord? You have to see how hard I am trying. Were you there when I went to the park at six o'clock that Sunday morning surrounded by six of the people closest to me? We washed our hands, feet, and faces. We lit black and red candles in the wind. We stood in the presence of You and of our ancestors. We synchronized our prayers, and the six of us called on You. Did You hear us? Our voices rising into one voice. Can You just tell me if You heard us? If You or even one of Your angels heard us that morning, or later when I was home alone, praying out loud, trying to lean against my own shadows, imploring them for support. They did not support me, my shadows. They were too busy dancing. Did You see that, how my shadows abandoned me to go dance on the wall? They danced on the wall where Rashid's picture is hanging. I was jealous of how my own shadows could dance with Rashid. I wanted to dance with him. I wanted to dance for him and I said so that night. I said it out loud. I want to dance with and for my husband. Did You hear me when I said it? Did anyone hear me? Anyone at all? Anyone? Anyone?*

Have I said what it sounds like when a heart breaks inside a prison? It doesn't sound like a crash, and it doesn't sound like a shatter. When a heart breaks inside a prison, if it sounds like anything at all, then it sounds like a scream that's trapped in a building caught on fire. It sounds like a scream that is not female and that is not male. It is just human, the scream, human and desperate, and it tries to throw itself high, up and over the hysterical pitch of the sirens, and the greedy chomping of the flames. It tries but it does not succeed.

It does not succeed and finally, exhausted, it falls back where it gets vanished into a bigger, meaner orchestra of screams that comes from the fire and that comes from the sirens. The little human scream gets surrounded, enveloped, and then neutralized. My scream, or her scream, or her scream, or his, are turned, without mercy, into ashes and soot. They are turned into ashes and soot and are then left behind to be rinsed or washed away forever.

Have I said that prison is a fire that seems to always be able to roar the loudest, to spread the furtherest, to swallow the most, and to spare the least?

# *slipping*

**W**e lose the appeal. It is July, the month of my birth, and Rashid tells me the news one hot afternoon when I am visiting him. We are standing outside. Not outside exactly, but in a cage that is attached to the visiting room. The ceiling of the cage is nearly open, but the air is blocked by the crisscrossing razor wire. Still it is better somehow than being indoors, we pretend it is, and in fact, a tiny wind hangs between us and cools itself along our foreheads.

Rashid tells me that we have lost, and I nod my head. *Yes, yes,* I say, although I do not know why. I am certainly not affirming the decision, but perhaps it is a response to the question Rashid does not ask me, the one that I know is lurking behind the bad news: *(You going to stay with me, baby)*?

*Yes. Yes,* I say it again and then fade for a moment into the pain, the loss, the reality of it. *Okay,* I say, and pull my husband toward me. I try to comfort him. I hug him, but not very hard because I do not have the strength to hug him very hard. My strength lies between us on the floor. I see it there, splattered and useless.

My arms are closed weakly around Rashid's waist. I nod my head again. Nod because I keep hearing the bad news in my head. I hear it in stereo. I hear it like a gun being fired just past my ear. *We lost the appeal! We LOST the appeal!! WE LOST, WE LOST, WE LOST, WE LOST!!* The words are an automatic loaded with dumdum bullets, an Uzi hung out a car window, spitting death into the tree-lined street.

And for two months afterward, I will negotiate my days as

though I am in mourning. I am functional in life, but not passionate about it. The only time I allow any emotion to roam freely is when I am with Rashid. When I am with him, I allow his needs, his desire, his unbelievable optimism to fill the gutted rooms inside me. With Rashid, I laugh, I tease. With Rashid I am sexy and warm and driven by his faith. With Rashid I can lay visions onto the concrete walls around us and over and over I can say, *Yes, yes. (I'm going to stay with you, baby.)*

And then something starts to shift, not shift so much as fall flat, as flat as the words which begin to fill the journal I write in each morning, dull, starched, ironed-down, burned, unusable words. No matter how hard I try, and I do, I try for weeks and weeks, I lose the language, and then the desire to pretty the situation up. Even with Rashid, I am limp. All I can think about is what decor can I hang upon another seven years locked down, away? What ornaments, what trinkets, what bright lights, what color paint? And when I begin to ask these questions, there is nothing Rashid can say, no comfort he can offer, no possible solution, no new vision that can snatch me back into dreaming with him. I become consumed with anger.

I go back and back and back and back. What did Rashid say and when did he say it? What arguments had he erected, what promises had he made? In a fit of hysteria one night, I storm through my apartment and pull boxes of his letters out of the closets. I scour them for the hope Rashid sent me again and again and again. I read letters that cited cases, letters that talked about time cuts. Letters that said, *When I come home, which will be sooner than you think . . .*

I sit for hours one evening in the middle of my room surrounded by hundreds of letters. I think if I can gather them up, show Rashid where he promised me, maybe things will be all right again. Maybe he will fix it so we do win the appeal. For the whole of our relationship, Rashid has always been an honest man. If only I can confront him with his own words I know he will turn things around. Rashid, the strong. Rashid, the honest. Rashid, the beautiful. He cannot, fast as night, become Rashid, the liar. Rashid, the terrible. Rashid, the enemy.

Of course this does not happen. I confront Rashid and he can only apologize, can only say,

*Baby, I told you what I believed was true.*

But his sincere beliefs are not good enough for me. I return to my anger and I return to it silently, without warning. I just go back, and eventually Rashid notices, but I admit nothing, deny everything. Rashid pushes. He interrogates me about the way I have suddenly become too tired to hold up my end of the conversation, and what about how I have become too busy to come and have a visit with him? Rashid asks me these questions again and again, but I am resilient. Even the way I say hello, Rashid declares one day, even then, I sound different. I listen but only say,

*Really?*

*What's wrong, baby? You have to tell me. Don't keep your feelings all to yourself.*

Yet this is exactly what I want to do. My feelings are all I have, all that I can keep and control, all that won't change unless *I* so determine it. Besides this, I know he will only tell me the two things I want least to hear. He will tell me things are going to be all right, but he will not say how, and he will not say when. After, he will tell me I knew what I was getting into when I fell in love with him. He will say this confidently as though there was some manual in existence, some workbook. And he will say this as though on that first visit or second, he had warned me, *Listen, asha, there will be many nights when you will be lonely, and frustrated, and feel defeated.*

We live with this, my tight silence, for weeks. It seems that in those weeks we relive every long year already gone to the prison.

Yet, there are moments when I lurch toward disclosure, toward explaining how I feel and why. During phone conversations, there are a number of times when Rashid's insistent warmth and love overwhelm me. And I know if we were together, I would yield beneath his touch, beneath the very hint of it, but we are apart. We are apart and I am not visiting him very much, and this forces us to grasp at one another across telephone wires. With that barrier in place, the need to protect myself proves greater. It snatches me back one time, two times, three times, four.

And then one night I have a dream. I'm not usually the one who remembers dreams, that's Rashid's specialty, but this one is so clear that I wake up with a new vision. I pick up my journal and in it I begin to write my husband a letter.

*I feel myself slipping.* This is how I begin the letter to Rashid, the letter in the journal. The letter about my dream.

*I am slipping,* I write, *but not in the way you would think, as though the ground has suddenly turned slick, like black ice in winter. But slipping as if I have been dropped down a great, deep well. This was the dream, but the dream is alive, the dream is my life.* I say this in the letter.

*I am in the well and I am screaming to get out, screaming but nobody can hear me, and finally my voice fails.*

*My hands, then, I think, and I pound and I pound with them against the stone walls of my cage, and at last I am heard. It is you (Rashid) and you turn your arms into a thick, rough rope. You lower the rope that is your arm and I reach it, but only when I stand on the very tips of my toes. I grab on but the rope burns, and this is when the slipping begins again, slipping now from the burning, slipping from the fire. The rope that is your arm is cutting into me, and it is going one way, and I am going the other way. You know it, I know it.*

*Come on,* you say to me, *comeon comeon comeon.*

*I'm trying,* I yell up to you, *but my hands are burning.*

*Stay with me, asha,* you plead. *Stay with me, baby. You can do this. We can do this. Come on. Comeoncomeoncomeon.*

In my dream Rashid's voice is a drum, although not a beat above me, and not a beat beside me. It is a beat inside me, his voice, inside me like the music of my childhood used to be inside me, the music of my teenage dancing years, the music which had been the one consistent joy during those years.

Back then, songs organized all of my movements. They determined who I was friends with, what I did on weekends, everything. But as I grew older, I tried to gain control over my life, and I stopped drinking and hanging out and going to clubs, and fusing all those Friday nights into Saturdays on flashing, heated, dance floors. And when I let all of it go, I let the music go too. I did not understand how the song and the beat were not the problem.

But it forgave me, my lost music did, and now it had returned to me. I could hear it and I could also see it. My music had returned in a dream, not with the lights, and not the crowds, but the beat inside was back again in the voice of my beloved. It carries me, that voice, that drum, and suddenly I become weightless. Suddenly my hands do not burn. In the dream, I begin to feel myself being lifted out of the well.

*How did you do it?* I want to know this from Rashid as soon as my body edges up over the top of the dream-well. *How, how?* Rashid's arms are around me. He is sitting, I crawl into his lap.

*I don't know what I did,* he says. *I don't know.*

I want Rashid to tell me something! To explain how he got me from down there, to back on top, and the whole time, no magic, no rescue squad, no fancy technology. I question and I question, but finally, there is only us, Rashid and me, there, alone, and the dream ends. I wake up and make myself a cup of coffee and pull out my journal and begin to write:

*The pain of our separation is a vise and we pull on it, and we pull on it, until it gives. It opens up, that vise, never completely, but enough so that we are able to move. We are able to declare that it has lost in the end, to you, and to me, and to the people we are, and to the people we are trying to become.*

# a difficult monologue

*t*here came a Saturday morning, late in the autumn after Rashid lost the appeal, when I was on my way upstate to the prison. Everything seemed the same. The van pulled into the South Bronx to pick up the last few passengers, and I got out of the van to go get a cup of coffee, but the usual sense of excitement I felt because I was about to see my husband had been replaced by exhaustion and frustration. I felt especially crowded and discomforted by the normal early Saturday city noises and movements: the car radios pumping Biggie and R. Kelly, the school-age children and their frantic mothers crying and whining, and all the fly girls who had just left the after-hours spot chattering over the barking and bravado of the men who flank them.

It was not yet seven o'clock, yet all this life was walking and rushing beside and then past me. It astonished me. It nearly staggered me, and then it stilled me. I watched and watched and the more I watched, the more I became immersed in a sense of isolation. Where did I fit in, here in the messy, loose, late-night, early-morning, smeared-makeup, cacophonous world? And as I was wondering this and feeling sorry for myself, Freddie the van driver came over. He told me to get on the van, which was really not a van. He was using a minibus to accommodate an increased number of passengers. Freddie laughed and said, *Come on, asha. Aren't you ready to see your husband?*

*Yes,* I nodded and dragged myself and all of my emotions onto the minibus where I found that the double seat which I had occupied alone before I went outside now contained a pretty young woman.

*Excuse me,* I said to her and slid into my seat. *Good morning,* I said to her and hoped she was pleasant.

*Good morning!* she chirped, which made me notice her for real, because it is a rare thing to meet someone on the way to a prison who chirps at you.

I smiled at the young woman and thought she could not be any older than twenty-one. Later I would find out that I was right. I would find out that this young woman who was talkative and bright was nineteen years old. I would find out that she was Dominican, that her name was Elisabeth, and that her man was doing twenty-five to life on a felony murder conviction. She would tell me these things without my prompting. She would tell me because she needed to talk as much as I needed to connect with someone. There was no one in her family, the young woman would explain to me, to whom she could really talk. They didn't understand why she stayed with Tony, her boyfriend, after he was convicted, and her friends didn't really understand either, she would tell me.

*I understand,* I said.

The nineteen-year-old woman beside me named Elisabeth was pretty, with wide, bright brown eyes, long, curly hair that she had not tried to manage, and red, red lips. She told me she met Tony while they were in high school and that she had always loved him. *From the beginning,* she told me. *I loved him right away and I've never stopped,* she told me.

*I understand that too,* I said.

Elisabeth told me about the crime, a story about a robbery gone bad and how no one was supposed to die, but the cashier who also turned out to be the owner reached for his own pistol, and out of fear and nervousness, Tony squeezed the trigger. *Just once,* the young woman said, as though this was a justification. *He never meant to kill nobody. His best friend was in the car waiting, and at the trial that's who testified against my boyfriend, and all the lawyer could do was say sorry, but you know, he still took the last installment check. Even though nothing he promised came true, that man just took the money and Tony's mother is not a rich woman. She had pulled together every piece of money she ever had. She borrowed money and she sold stuff to save her son because the lawyer had promised her. He looked her dead up in the eye and said the only evidence was the best friend's testimony but he could get that knocked out. But he was wrong. My man got twenty-five to life. Did I tell you that? Twenty-five to life!*

*Yes,* I said. *You told me.*

*Tony already did two years on Rikers. That's where he's coming from now. This is my first time upstate,* she said, and then paused and then added, *You know, he was a good student in school. Not as good as me, but he got mostly B's. Sometimes C's. But mostly B's. I got mostly A's.*

Elisabeth would tell me again how people in her family wanted her to get on with her life and how sometimes, just sometimes, even she thought she should get on with her life, but, she told me, she had no idea how to leave, loving him the way she did. *I know,* I said. *I really, really know that feeling,* I emphasized. And then Elisabeth concluded her story. She said, *Anyway. I know he's coming on home kind of soon because of the appeal.*

*The appeal?* I asked.

*Yeah,* she said. *Everybody knows for sure that he got an unfair trial,* she said, as I looked at her, trying not to betray my feelings, trying to keep my gaze steady, my face from twisting up.

I turned my body away from hers as naturally as I could. I

sat straight back in my seat. I closed my eyes and did not tell her that everybody did not know for sure that he got an unfair trial. I did not tell her that even if they did know for sure, it still might not make a difference, and I did not tell her what I did know for sure.

I did not say that she, *for sure,* should not count on her man coming home on appeal. That, *for sure,* the chances of that happening were very, very slim. At best. I did not say that if she stayed, she was, *for sure,* in for a terrifically long, lonely ride, the kind of ride that makes you begin talking to yourself, and that whatever she was predicting for her tomorrows ought to be turned loose right now. I did not tell her how six years ago I believed in things that today I cannot even comprehend. I just listened to this young woman because maybe. Maybe things would be different for her. Maybe she would never look up, as I have looked up, and realize how much prisons defined her life. Maybe she would never come back from a correctional facility as I have come back from a correctional facility, and stood there motionless in front of my own door for many, many seconds, nearly a minute, waiting for a policeman behind a bullet-proof glass to buzz me in, before I am aware of what I am doing, and then scramble to put my own key in my own lock. Maybe she would never meet someone whose man is doing ten years or fifteen and think, *Wow, that's all? They're lucky.* I have thought that. I have thought that more than once.

And maybe she would never look down at her her wrists, as I have looked down at my wrists, and thought she saw red welts on them, as though it had been her, not him, who had been yanked out of a car, thrown down on the concrete, legs kicked open, arms pulled almost out of their sockets, hands cuffed extra-tight behind her back. Maybe she would never have to say out loud to herself, as I have had to say out loud to myself, that it was he not she who did the crime. It was he not she who was in prison, that all she had ever been guilty of was loving someone.

I looked back over at Elisabeth and for a moment I wanted to say all of these things. I wanted to warn her because no one had warned me, and somebody should have. Somebody should have sat me down and said how their life became. They should have shown me their before and after pictures, but no one did, and I wanted to prepare this young girl, and at one point I even took a deep breath. I took the kind of breath you take just before you lapse into a difficult monologue, but the minibus pulled into the first prison complex where she had to get off but I had to stay on, because I don't get off until the third and final complex in that poor, broken-down, winding fifteen-mile region of prisons. She had to leave right then, and so all I said was, *Have a great visit!*

And later, in the afternoon, when our visits were over and we were sad and exhausted and falling into and out of sleep, it seemed out of place. It seemed like it would have been salt in the wound to say, *This is just the beginning. You're about to feel like this for a very long time. You're about to feel even worse than you do right now. More lonely. More isolated.* In the hours after leaving our partners, I feel like we should have the right to honor silence. We should have the right to hold the last taste of our visits under our tongues. I didn't say a word.

But that night when I was home, I began to feel consumed by the need to talk, to tell what I'd come to know over these years, to tell what I'd seen. I wanted to tell for Elisabeth, but mostly I wanted to tell for me, because it was true what she said, that so many of our family and friends don't understand and so we stop trying to explain, but still there are all these stories in us. Even though so many of us shut down, and become pretenders, and say defensively that *We don't care if nobody knows him because my business is my business.* Even then, we have stories to tell, experiences to share. I have heard so many of them. They get whispered on the vans in the time before and just past the dawn.

They get whispered by the women who, away from the prison, often say to coworkers and acquaintances that they are not married. And by the women who will lie about where they are going every weekend when they hoist themselves and their children and their packages together onto a van before seven in the morning. The stories get whispered by the women who are silent about husbands and lovers at family gatherings. Family gatherings where everybody knows, but nobody says, which is the way it is in my family, and which is why at significant moments in my life, I began to feel like a huge part of myself didn't really exist. Part of me didn't exist because during those times with my family when I should have felt open and unguarded, there was no Rashid. There was no discussion of Rashid, no picture of him, no questions, no arguments, nothing. Rashid had been secreted away as though I was ashamed of him. I am not ashamed of him. I thought about that the night after the day when I met Elisabeth.

And I thought about how, when Elisabeth spoke of her sense of isolation, it underscored my own sense of isolation, and it would have been so easy right then to disappear into the pain, into the insanity, of prisons. And I couldn't let that happen. After all these years I knew I owed myself and I owed Rashid and I owed our relationship more than disappearing. In the very least, even if from that day forward, I never went up into a prison again, if I never saw Rashid again, I owed us the truth. The whole, entire, out-loud, in-public truth, which meant I had to admit that despite all of the losses and all of the hurt, there were these moments in Rashid's arms that were a luxury of bliss. There were these times when we shared an absolute embarrassment of love. There were days that had set a standard for days.

And because of those moments and days, I knew that I also owed to us to proclaim as loudly as I'd cried after we lost the appeal, after everything that had ever cut me or cut Rashid these last seven years, that at the end of the twentieth century, when there were some people who, more than anything else, wanted the stock market to keep booming, and some who wanted to lose another fifteen pounds, and some who wanted to become big stars in small films, and some who wanted brand-new sports utility vehicles, and some who wanted Clinton impeached, and some who wanted to rock Hilfiger gear daily, and some who wanted to write rhymes and make phat beats, and some who wanted their next ten-dollar bag of whatever they could sniff or shoot or smoke away, and in a time when most of us wanted cures for AIDS and cancer and a realistic way to keep our blood pressure down, the greatest of my own personal needs was for my husband to come home to me.

To come home to me healthy and to come home whole, right then, in the very second that I was wishing for it. I realized that I wanted Rashid home more than I wanted to write the next line or poem, and more than I wanted to run the next mile, because at the core of me I felt certain I could always write and I could always run, but what I could not do was beg or borrow or broker or bribe back time. And to my great surprise, this realization did not plunge me into a greater sadness. It did not make me think about all that I was missing. It made me think about all that I had. It made me think I was blessed. To want someone like that. To be wanted by someone like that.

And in my room that night, sitting cross-legged on my bed, watching the first coat of night drape over the trees and garage outside my window, I began to smile and I began to cry, because all at once I could remember how full I felt when I did no more than hold Rashid's hand, and I could also remember how nullified I felt when I had to leave. But those memories weren't what was important. What was important was that while I was going up and back over good memories and bad ones, I did not feel alone, although surely I was alone in that room. It did not matter. For the very first time, I did not feel it to be so. I felt Rashid was right there, beside me. I could not see him, but I could smell the oil he wears. It was there, that particular scent, on the inside of my hands. And I could imagine his touch. I closed my eyes. My flesh reacted. It twitched. It went flush, and when the heat eased, I opened my eyes and reached for my journal and waited.

I waited for my emotions to transform themselves into language, into something that would remind me and Rashid in our very worst and most difficult times, when we are in some visiting room thinking that all there is to see are the towers and the guns and the razor wires that circle everywhere above us like vultures arrived too soon, that we are alive. Despite how much harder the bid has gotten since Rashid lost the appeal. Despite all the anger and anguish and quivering faith and rushing confusion, we are alive and somehow together. And we might not have been.

There might have been another story to tell, for Rashid and for me, and it might have been a horror story and it might have been a tragic story, and mostly it might have been a separate story. Rashid's in one book, mine in another. But the story we have written, the one which is bigger and more defining than all the other stories, was the one which would begin with the words I finally wrote late that night. I wrote five words over and over that two years later became this book, but when I started, the only thing I could think to say, the only thing I thought I needed to say, was that this is a love story. That's what I wrote, all down one page and then down another. This is a love story. This is a love story.

*28 July*

Beloved,

Here is the base of night where I can meet you. I can always meet you, here, where the day has ended, and the dark has come like a reverent lover, to carry me back to myself, to give me back to my prayers. I meet you here in silence every night of my life, Rashid. Have I told you this before? I know I'm not supposed to write you a letter like this.

I said I wouldn't write you a letter like this, given the state of things between us. Yesterday I read a card that you gave me once at the end of a trailer visit. The card said sometimes it's good to leave, to wrap yourself in the cloak of quiet, to sit alone, to reacquaint yourself with your dreams. Of course you are my dreams and of course the prison is my nightmare. How do I separate the two, Rashid? When we began you said you were sure I would get used to things, that with time, the pain would become more manageable. It never did.

I have to confess something to you, beloved. I am praying that you will call me tonight. I know I was the one who said we should limit our contact but I am praying each time the phone rings that it's you. I want you to call me tonight, and I also wanted you to call me last night, and I also wanted you to call me the night before that. You have always asked of me this one thing: to make a decision and to stick to it. I'm trying to, Rashid. I know I said I needed some time away, and I remember how I struggled to get you to understand, and I know I'm not doing very well. Have I said yet that I love you? Have I said how loving you keeps complicating the picture, obscuring my escape route out of this prison life?

Sometimes I wonder if you know how much I think about you. I could spend every hour of every day lost in the memories *of how we are together. Maybe that's why I wrote this book. So I could legitimize daydreaming about us being together. Remember the last time we were on a trailer and I asked, Can I look at you, Rashid? Before we make love, I asked, can you step back and can I look at you? And you said yes and took off everything, and stood there before me and let my fingers trace your scars and veins and sinew.*

*You are the most beautiful man I have ever seen. You are the most beautiful man I could ever hope to see. Did I say that then? That your beauty overwhelms me. It distracts me. Sometimes I have to look away from you in order to talk to you, and sometimes I have to forget what you look like, and sometimes I have to forget everything. Sometimes I have to leave everything we are and have been in a closet, all packed up and hidden, so that I can move from one hour into the next.*

*Memory can be such a tease, a stripper disappearing behind the fast dark curtain with a smile. You can look but you can't touch. What happens when you need to touch and there's only the air and the air is hot and tight and does not serve you?*

*Last night when it was late, I took a taxi home. The name on the driver's license was the same as your family name, and as we bumped through the streets of Manhattan, and over the Brooklyn Bridge, and up Atlantic and then Washington Avenues, I fantasized that the driver was you and that we had a conversation that started out about politics but ended up with us falling in love. Only this time you came home with me. You came home with me right then in the very moment we fell in love. This time no walls, no police, no doors without keys, no vans, no visiting rooms, no dress codes, no state-issue green pants, no kissing on the clock, no stolen touches, no loneliness, no leaving. Maybe it was a silly thing to do, but hunger breeds a strange appetite, and besides it made the ride go quickly.*

*You keep asking, How can I go away from you? I never know what to say when you ask. I could never really leave you, Rashid. I just can't face the prison anymore. That's not true. I can face the prison. What I can't face is turning my back another time and walking alone, out of that door, looking once over my shoulder to see if you are watching me. You always are.*

*Anyway, the truth is that I don't believe this separation will be forever. I can stay away now because I look into tomorrow and see you there. I see the sky seduce its own self with its own colors and then turn into a sweet, thick dusk with stars galloping in the background. That's where you are, in the starbright distance walking toward me, smiling the way you always manage to smile, even when everything inside you feels like it's being quartered, and then quartered once more. I know you felt this way the last time we saw each other. I swear it took all the courage I had to look past your brave front. I didn't want to see how much I was hurting you. I wanted so much to believe that you were really doing fine, but we have never lied to each other. I had to look.*

*Rashid, I want you to know something I did not tell you the last time we saw each other when I said that I had no idea how I was going to make it through the next three hours on the visit, let alone the next five years on the bid. You looked at me so soberly I could feel myself tremble. You asked, What do you want me to do, asha? Tell me and I'll do it. Do you want me to figure out some way to be up out of here?*

*And when you said that, my heart skipped. I began to panic, and I almost screamed No! No! I said they would kill*

*you, and you, in the same sober voice, said, Listen to me, asha.
If I am killed trying to get to you, it would be the most noble
death I could die. Do you remember that?*

*And do you remember how afterwards I was so quiet? For the
rest of the visit, I was so quiet and I just stared at you. I know
you wondered why and I know I didn't explain. I couldn't. I was
an incomprehensible maze of emotion then. But if I could
have, I would have told you how much I wanted to be noble for
you too. I would have said that you deserve that. You deserve that
from me. And if I had had it in me to speak that day I would
have told you that in some small way, this book I have written
about us has been my attempt at being noble.*

*I have never told you how terrified I am of taking our love
and placing it out on a public dais to be viewed and scrutinized, but Audre Lorde said if we could learn to work when we
were tired, then we could learn to work when we were afraid.
And when I thought about that, I wondered, What if you are
tired and afraid at the same time? I've been tired and afraid
at the same time, but I realize that you have been too, and so I
figured if you could keep loving me then in the complete way
you've been loving me, then I could keep writing with the same
vigor. That was the bottom line, and that was how I wrote
every single word I wrote. That was how I wrote even when the
memory that those words contained nearly broke me down.
That's how I did it.*

*I have so much work to finish right now, but I don't want to
stop writing you this letter. I wish we were talking, that you
were here in front of me, but I would even settle for the phone.
Did I tell you that I've been praying you would call me
tonight, and that I prayed the same thing last night, and the
same thing the night before that? I miss your voice so badly. I*

*keep trying to hear it in my head, like a favorite song or great speech, but all I hear are snatches. I can't hear the whole verse, never a whole quote. My God, I miss your voice. I miss everything about you. I miss the way you nod your head when you're listening to me. You have always made me feel brilliant.*

*I miss the way you can look like a seven-year-old boy and a big grown man all in the same instant. I miss the way you look at me when you want me. I miss your hunger. I miss your passion for life and for justice and for young people and for Islam. And for me. I miss your passion for me. I miss that most of all. It's what I always wanted. It's what I never had. Until you. I miss you. In my eyes, in my ears, on my skin, on my legs, on my stomach, and face. I miss you in my mouth, behind my teeth, under my tongue, on the very tips of my fingers. My hands have become less useful, not touching you.*

*You might think this is, Rashid, but this is not a good-bye letter. I'm just writing down my heart for you so you can always go back to it and know how I feel. Isn't there a song that goes: Don't say good-bye, always say see you later? I do not say good-bye in this letter, because good-bye is meaningless between people who have loved each other with all the clarity and precision with which we have loved each other. I do not say good-bye, Rashid. I just say see you in a minute, baby. See you in a minute.*

*The Girl Hunters*

# BY MICKEY SPILLANE

# The
# Girl Hunters

### By

## MICKEY SPILLANE

1962

NEW YORK: E. P. DUTTON & CO., INC.

This one is for Elliott Graham
who sweated more waiting for Mike
than he did as a dogface waiting for us
brown-shoes fly-boys to give him aerial cover.
So here we go again, E.G., with more to come. But
this one is for you.

*The Girl Hunters*

# CHAPTER 1

They found me in the gutter. The night was the only thing I had left and not much of it at that. I heard the car stop, the doors open and shut and the two voices talking. A pair of arms jerked me to my feet and held me there.

"Drunk," the cop said.

The other one turned me around into the light. "He don't smell bad. That cut on his head didn't come from a fall either."

"Mugged?"

"Maybe."

I didn't give a damn which way they called it. They were both wrong anyhow. Two hours ago I was drunk. Not now. Two hours ago I was a roaring lion. Then the bottle sailed across the room. No lion left now.

Now was a time when I wasn't anything. Nothing was left inside except the feeling a ship must have when it's torpedoed, sinks and hits bottom.

A hand twisted into my chin and lifted my face up. "Ah, the guy's a bum. Somebody messed him up a little bit."

"You'll never make sergeant, son. That's a hundred-buck suit and it fits too good to be anything but his own. The dirt is fresh, not worn on."

"Okay, Daddy, let's check his wallet, see who he is and run him in."

The cop with the deep voice chuckled, patted me down and came up with my wallet. "Empty," he said.

Hell, there had been two bills in it when I started out. It must have been a pretty good night. Two hundred bucks' worth of night.

I heard the cop whistle between his teeth. "We got ourselves a real fish."

"Society boy? He don't look so good for a society boy. Not with his face. He's been splashed."

"Uh-uh. Michael Hammer, it says here on the card. He's a private jingle who gets around."

"So he gets tossed in the can and he won't get around so much."

The arm under mine hoisted me a little straighter and steered me toward the car. My feet moved; lumps on the end of a string that swung like pendulums.

"You're only joking," the cop said. "There are certain people who wouldn't like you to make such noises with your mouth."

"Like who?"

"Captain Chambers."

It was the other cop's turn to whistle.

"I told you this jingle was a fish," my pal said. "Go buzz the station. Ask what we should do with him. And use a phone—we don't want this on the air."

The cop grunted something and left. I felt hands easing me into the squad car, then shoving me upright against the seat. The hands went down and dragged my feet in, propping them against the floorboard. The door shut and the one on the other side opened. A heavy body climbed in under the wheel and a tendril of smoke drifted across my face. It made me feel a little sick.

The other cop came back and got in beside me. "The captain wants us to take him up to his house," he said. "He told me thanks."

"Good enough. A favor to a captain is like money in the bank, I always say."

"Then how come you ain't wearing plainclothes then?"

"Maybe I'm not the type, son. I'll leave it to you young guys."

The car started up. I tried to open my eyes but it took too much effort and I let them stay closed.

*You can stay dead only so long. Where first there was nothing, the pieces all come drifting back together like a movie of an exploding shell run in reverse. The fragments come back slowly, grating together as they seek a matching part and painfully jar into place. You're whole again, finally, but the scars and the worn places are all there to remind you that once you were dead. There's life once more and, with it, a dull pain that pulsates at regular intervals, a light that's too bright to look into and sound that's more than you can stand. The flesh is weak and crawly, slack from the disuse that is the death, sensitive with the agonizing fire that is life. There's memory that makes you want to crawl back into the void but the life is too vital to let you go.*

The terrible shattered feeling was inside me, the pieces

having a hard time trying to come together. My throat was still raw and cottony; constricted, somehow, from the tensed-up muscles at the back of my neck.

When I looked up Pat was holding out his cigarettes to me. "Smoke?"

I shook my head.

His voice had a callous edge to it when he said, "You quit?"

"Yeah."

I felt his shrug. "When?"

"When I ran out of loot. Now knock it off."

"You had loot enough to drink with." His voice had a real dirty tone now.

There are times when you can't take anything at all, no jokes, no rubs—nothing. Like the man said, you want nothing from nobody never. I propped my hands on the arms of the chair and pushed myself to my feet. The inside of my thighs quivered with the effort.

"Pat—I don't know what the hell you're pulling. I don't give a damn either. Whatever it is, I don't appreciate it. Just keep off my back, old buddy."

A flat expression drifted across his face before the hardness came back. "We stopped being buddies a long time ago, Mike."

"Good. Let's keep it like that. Now where the hell's my clothes?"

He spit a stream of smoke at my face and if I didn't have to hold the back of the chair to stand up I would have belted him one. "In the garbage," he said. "It's where you belong too but this time you're lucky."

"You son of a bitch."

I got another faceful of smoke and choked on it.

"You used to look a lot bigger to me, Mike. Once I couldn't

have taken you. But now you call me things like that and I'll belt you silly."

"You son of a bitch," I said.

I saw it coming but couldn't move, a blurred white open-handed smash that took me right off my feet into the chair that turned over and left me in a sprawled lump against the wall. There was no pain to it, just a taut sickness in the belly that turned into a wrenching dry heave that tasted of blood from the cut inside my mouth. I could feel myself twitching spasmodically with every contraction of my stomach and when it was over I lay there with relief so great I thought I was dead.

He let me get up by myself and half fall into the chair. When I could focus again, I said, "Thanks, buddy. I'll keep it in mind."

Pat shrugged noncommittally and held out a glass. "Water. It'll settle your stomach."

"Drop dead."

He put the glass down on an end table as the bell rang. When he came back he threw a box down on the sofa and pointed to it. "New clothes. Get dressed."

"I don't have any new clothes."

"You have now. You can pay me later."

"I'll pay you up the guzukus later."

He walked over, seemingly balancing on the balls of his feet. Very quietly he said, "You can get yourself another belt in the kisser without trying hard, mister."

I couldn't let it go. I tried to swing coming up out of the chair and like the last time I could see it coming but couldn't get out of the way. All I heard was a meaty smash that had a familiar sound to it and my stomach tried to heave again but it was too late. The beautiful black had come again.

My jaws hurt. My neck hurt. My whole side felt like it was coming out. But most of all my jaws hurt. Each tooth was an independent source of silent agony while the pain in my head seemed to center just behind each ear. My tongue was too thick to talk and when I got my eyes open I had to squint them shut again to make out the checkerboard pattern of the ceiling.

When the fuzziness went away I sat up, trying to remember what happened. I was on the couch this time, dressed in a navy blue suit. The shirt was clean and white, the top button open and the black knitted tie hanging down loose. Even the shoes were new and in the open part of my mind it was like the simple wonder of a child discovering the new and strange world of the ants when he turns over a rock.

"You awake?"

I looked up and Pat was standing in the archway, another guy behind him carrying a small black bag.

When I didn't answer Pat said, "Take a look at him, Larry."

The one he spoke to pulled a stethoscope from his pocket and hung it around his neck. Then everything started coming back again. I said, "I'm all right. You don't hit that hard."

"I wasn't half trying, wise guy."

"Then why the medic?"

"General principles. This is Larry Snyder. He's a friend of mine."

"So what?" The doc had the stethoscope against my chest but I couldn't stop him even if I had wanted to. The examination was quick, but pretty thorough. When he finished he stood up and pulled out a prescription pad.

Pat asked, "Well?"

"He's been around. Fairly well marked out. Fist fights, couple of bullet scars—"

"He's had them."

"Fist marks are recent. Other bruises made by some blunt instrument. One rib—"

"Shoes," I interrupted. "I got stomped."

"Typical alcoholic condition," he continued. "From all external signs I'd say he isn't too far from total. You know how they are."

"Damn it," I said, "quit talking about me in the third person."

Pat grunted something under his breath and turned to Larry. "Any suggestions?"

"What can you do with them?" the doctor laughed. "They hit the road again as soon as you let them out of your sight. Like him—you buy him new clothes and as soon as he's near a swap shop he'll turn them in on rags with cash to boot and pitch a big one. They go back harder than ever once they're off awhile."

"Meanwhile I can cool him for a day."

"Sure. He's okay now. Depends upon personal supervision."

Pat let out a terse laugh. "I don't care what he does when I let him loose. I want him sober for one hour. I need him."

When I glanced up I saw the doctor looking at Pat strangely, then me. "Wait a minute. This is that guy you were telling me about one time?"

Pat nodded. "That's right."

"I thought you were friends."

"We were at one time, but nobody's friends with a damn drunken bum. He's nothing but a lousy lush and I'd as soon throw his can in the tank as I would any other lush. Being

friends once doesn't mean anything to me. Friends can wear
out pretty fast sometimes. He wore out. Now he's part of a
job. For old times' sake I throw in a few favors on the side
but they're strictly for old times' sake and only happen once.
Just once. After that he stays bum and I stay cop. I catch him
out of line and he's had it."

Larry laughed gently and patted him on the shoulder.
Pat's face was all tight in a mean grimace and it was a way I
had never seen him before. "Relax," Larry told him. "Don't
*you* get wound up."

"So I hate slobs," he said.

"You want a prescription too? There are economy-sized
bottles of tranquilizers nowadays."

Pat sucked in his breath and a grin pulled at his mouth.
"That's all I need is a problem." He waved a thumb at me.
"Like him."

Larry looked down at me like he would at any specimen.
"He doesn't look like a problem type. He probably plain
likes the sauce."

"No, he's got a problem, right?"

"Shut up," I said.

"Tell the man what your problem is, Mikey boy."

Larry said, "Pat—"

He shoved his hand away from his arm. "No, go ahead and
tell him, Mike. I'd like to hear it again myself."

"You son of a bitch," I said.

He smiled then. His teeth were shiny and white under
tight lips and the two steps he took toward me were stiff-
kneed. "I told you what I'd do if you got big-mouthed again."

For once I was ready. I wasn't able to get up, so I kicked
him right smack in the crotch and once in the mouth when
he started to fold up and I would have gotten one more in

if the damn doctor hadn't laid me out with a single swipe of his bag that almost took my head off.

It was an hour before either one of us was any good, but from now on I wasn't going to get another chance to lay Pat up with a sucker trick. He was waiting for me to try it and if I did he'd have my guts all over the floor.

The doctor had gone and come, getting his own prescriptions filled. I got two pills and a shot. Pat had a fistful of aspirins, but he needed a couple of leeches along the side of his face where he was all black and blue.

But yet he sat there with the disgust and sarcasm still on his face whenever he looked at me and once more he said, "You didn't tell the doctor your problem, Mike."

I just looked at him.

Larry waved his hand for him to cut it out and finished repacking his kit.

Pat wasn't going to let it alone, though. He said, "Mike lost his girl. A real nice kid. They were going to get married."

That great big place in my chest started to open up again, a huge hole that could grow until there was nothing left of me, only that huge hole. "Shut up, Pat."

"He likes to think she ran off, but he knows all the time she's dead. He sent her out on too hot a job and she never came back, right, Mikey boy? She's dead."

"Maybe you'd better forget it, Pat," Larry told him softly.

"Why forget it? She was my friend too. She had no business playing guns with hoods. But no, wise guy here sends her out. His secretary. She has a P.I. ticket and a gun, but she's nothing but a girl and she never comes back. You know where she probably is, Doc? At the bottom of the river someplace, that's where."

And now the hole was all I had left. I was all nothing, a

hole that could twist and scorch my mind with such incredible pain that even relief was inconceivable because there was no room for anything except that pain. Out of it all I could feel some movement. I knew I was watching Pat and I could hear his voice but nothing made sense at all.

His voice was far away saying, "Look at him, Larry. His eyes are all gone. And look at his hand. You know what he's doing. He's trying to kill me. He's going after a gun that isn't there anymore because he hasn't got a license to carry one. He lost that and his business and everything else when he shot up the people he thought got Velda. Oh, he knocked off some goodies and got away with it because they were all hoods caught in the middle of an armed robbery. But that was it for our tough boy there. Then what does he do? He cries his soul out into a whiskey bottle. Damn—look at his hand. He's pointing a gun at me he doesn't even have anymore and his finger's pulling the trigger. Damn, he'd kill me right where I sit."

Then I lost sight of Pat entirely because my head was going from side to side and the hole was being filled in again from the doctor's wide-fingered slaps until once more I could see and feel as much as I could in the half life that was left in me.

This time the doctor had lost his disdainful smirk. He pulled the skin down under my eyes, stared at my pupils, felt my pulse and did things to my earlobe with his fingernail that I could barely feel. He stopped, stood up and turned his back to me. "This guy is shot down, Pat."

"It couldn't've happened to a better guy."

"I'm not kidding. He's a case. What do you expect to get out of him?"

"Nothing. Why?"

"Because I'd say he couldn't stay rational. That little exhibition was a beauty. I'd hate to see it if he was pressed further."

"Then stick around. I'll press him good, the punk."

"You're asking for trouble. Somebody like him can go off the deep end anytime. For a minute there I thought he'd flipped. When it happens they don't come back very easily. What is it you wanted him to do?"

I was listening now. Not because I wanted to, but because it was something buried too far in my nature to ignore. It was something from away back like a hunger that can't be ignored.

Pat said, "I want him to interrogate a prisoner."

For a moment there was silence, then: "You can't be serious."

"The hell I'm not. The guy won't talk to anybody else *but* him."

"Come off it, Pat. You have ways to make a person talk."

"Sure, under the right circumstances, but not when they're in the hospital with doctors and nurses hovering over them."

"Oh?"

"The guy's been shot. He's only holding on so he can talk to this slob. The doctors can't say what keeps him alive except his determination to make this contact."

"But—"

"But nuts, Larry!" His voice started to rise with suppressed rage. "We use any means we can when the chips are down. This guy was shot and we want the one who pulled the trigger. It's going to be a murder rap any minute and if there's a lead we'll damn well get it. I don't care what it takes to make this punk sober, but that's the way he's going to be and I don't care if the effort kills him, he's going to do it."

"Okay, Pat. It's your show. Run it. Just remember that there are plenty of ways of killing a guy."

I felt Pat's eyes reach out for me. "For him I don't give a damn."

Somehow I managed a grin and felt around for the words. I couldn't get a real punch line across, but to me they sounded good enough.

Just two words.

# CHAPTER 2

Pat had arranged everything with his usual methodical care. The years hadn't changed him a bit. The great arranger. Mr. Go, Go, Go himself. I felt the silly grin come back that really had no meaning, and someplace in the back of my mind a clinical voice told me softly that it could be a symptom of incipient hysteria. The grin got sillier and I couldn't help it.

Larry and Pat blocked me in on either side, a hand under each arm keeping me upright and forcing me forward. As far as anybody was concerned I was another sick one coming in the emergency entrance and if he looked close enough he could even smell the hundred-proof sickness.

I made them take me to the men's room so I could vomit again, and when I sluiced down in frigid water I felt a small bit better. Enough so I could wipe off the grin. I was glad there was no mirror over the basin. It had been a long time since I had looked at myself and I didn't want to start now.

Behind me the door opened and there was some hurried medical chatter between Larry and a white-coated intern who had come in with a plainclothesman. Pat finally said, "How is he?"

"Going fast," Larry said. "He won't let them operate either. He knows he's had it and doesn't want to die under ether before he sees your friend here."

"Damn it, don't call him my friend."

The intern glanced at me critically, running his eyes up and down then doing a quickie around my face. His fingers flicked out to spread my eyelids open for a look into my pupils and I batted them away.

"Keep your hands off me, sonny," I said.

Pat waved him down. "Let him be miserable, Doctor. Don't try to help him."

The intern shrugged, but kept looking anyway. I had suddenly become an interesting psychological study for him.

"You'd better get him up there. The guy hasn't long to live. Minutes at the most."

Pat looked at me. "You ready?"

"You asking?" I said.

"Not really. You don't have a choice."

"No?"

Larry said, "Mike—go ahead and do it."

I nodded. "Sure, why not. I always did have to do half his work for him anyway." Pat's mouth went tight and I grinned again. "Clue me on what you want to know."

There were fine white lines around Pat's nostrils and his lips were tight and thin. "Who shot him. Ask him that."

"What's the connection?"

Now Pat's eyes went half closed, hating my guts for beginning to think again. After a moment he said, "One bullet almost went through him. They took it out yesterday. A ballistics check showed it to be from the same gun that killed

Senator Knapp. If this punk upstairs dies we can lose our lead to a murderer. Understand? You find out who shot him."

"Okay," I said. "Anything for a friend. Only first I want a drink."

"No drink."

"So drop dead."

"Bring him a shot," Larry told the intern.

The guy nodded, went out and came back a few seconds later with a big double in a water glass. I took it in a hand that had the shakes real bad, lifted it and said, "Cheers."

The guy on the bed heard us come in and turned his head on the pillow. His face was drawn, pinched with pain and the early glaze of death was in his eyes.

I stepped forward and before I could talk he said, "Mike? You're—Mike Hammer?"

"That's right."

He squinted at me, hesitating. "You're not like—"

I knew what he was thinking. I said, "I've been sick."

From someplace in back Pat sucked in his breath disgustedly.

The guy noticed them for the first time. "Out. Get them out."

I waved my thumb over my shoulder without turning around. I knew Larry was pushing Pat out the door over his whispered protestations, but you don't argue long with a medic in his own hospital.

When the door clicked shut I said, "Okay, buddy, you wanted to see me and since you're on the way out it has to be important. Just let me get some facts straight. I never saw you before. Who are you?"

"Richie Cole."

"Good. Now who shot you?"

"Guy they call . . . The Dragon. No name . . . I don't know his name."

"Look . . ."

Somehow he got one hand up and waved it feebly. "Let me talk."

I nodded, pulled up a chair and sat on the arm. My guts were all knotted up again and beginning to hurt. They were crying out for some bottle love again and I had to rub the back of my hand across my mouth to take the thought away.

The guy made a wry face and shook his head. "You'll . . . never do it."

My tongue ran over my lips without moistening them. "Do what?"

"Get her in time."

"Who?"

"The woman." His eyes closed and for a moment his face relaxed. "The woman Velda."

*I sat there as if I were paralyzed; for a second totally immobilized, a suddenly frozen mind and body that had solidified into one great silent scream at the mention of a name I had long ago consigned to a grave somewhere. Then the terrible cold was drenched with an even more terrible wash of heat and I sat there with my hands bunched into fists to keep them from shaking.*

*Velda.*

He was watching me closely, the glaze in his eyes momentarily gone. He saw what had happened to me when he said the name and there was a peculiar expression of approval in his face.

Finally I said, "You knew her?"

He barely nodded. "I *know* her."

And again that feeling happened to me, worse this time because I knew he wasn't lying and that she was alive someplace. *Alive!*

I kept a deliberate control over my voice. "Where is she?"

"Safe for . . . the moment. But she'll be killed unless . . . you find her. The one called The Dragon . . . he's looking for her too. You'll have to find her first."

I was damn near breathless. *"Where?"* I wanted to reach over and shake it out of him but he was too close to the edge of the big night to touch.

Cole managed a crooked smile. He was having a hard time to talk and it was almost over. "I gave . . . an envelope to Old Dewey. Newsy on Lexington by the Clover Bar . . . for you."

"Damn it, where is she, Cole?"

"No . . . you find The Dragon . . . before he gets her."

"Why me, Cole? Why that way? You had the cops?"

The smile still held on. "Need someone . . . ruthless. Someone very terrible." His eyes fixed on mine, shiny bright, mirroring one last effort to stay alive. "She said . . . you could . . . if someone could find you. You had been missing . . . long time." He was fighting hard now. He only had seconds. "No police . . . unless necessary. You'll see . . . why."

"Cole . . ."

His eyes closed, then opened and he said, "Hurry." He never closed them again. The gray film came and his stare was a lifeless one, hiding things I would have given an arm to know.

I sat there beside the bed looking at the dead man, my thoughts groping for a hold in a brain still soggy from too many bouts in too many bars. I couldn't think, so I simply looked and wondered where and when someone like him had found someone like her.

Cole had been a big man. His face, relaxed in death, had hard planes to it, a solid jaw line blue with beard and a nose that had been broken high on the bridge. There was a scar beside one eye running into the hairline that could have been made by a knife. Cole had been a hard man, all right. In a way a good-looking hardcase whose business was trouble.

His hand lay outside the sheet, the fingers big and the wrist thick. The knuckles were scarred, but none of the scars was fresh. They were old scars from old fights. The incongruous part was the nails. They were thick and square, but well cared for. They reflected all the care a manicurist could give with a treatment once a week.

The door opened and Pat and Larry came in. Together they looked at the body and stood there waiting. Then they looked at me and whatever they saw made them both go expressionless at once.

Larry made a brief inspection of the body on the bed, picked up a phone and relayed the message to someone on the other end. Within seconds another doctor was there with a pair of nurses verifying the situation, recording it all on a clipboard.

When he turned around he stared at me with a peculiar expression and said, "You feel all right?"

"I'm all right," I repeated. My voice seemed to come from someone else.

"Want another drink?"

"No."

"You'd better have one," Larry said.

"I don't want it."

Pat said, "The hell with him." His fingers slid under my arm. "Outside, Mike. Let's go outside and talk."

I wanted to tell him what he could do with his talk, but the numbness was there still, a frozen feeling that restricted thought and movement, painless but effective. So I let him steer me to the small waiting room down the hall and took the seat he pointed out.

There is no way to describe the immediate aftermath of a sudden shock. If it had come at another time in another year it would have been different, but now the stalk of despondency was withered and brittle, refusing to bend before a wind of elation.

All I could do was sit there, bringing back his words, the tone of his voice, the way his face crinkled as he saw me. Somehow he had expected something different. He wasn't looking for a guy who had the earmarks of the Bowery and every slop chute along the avenues etched into his skin.

I said, "Who was he, Pat?" in a voice soggy and hollow.

Pat didn't bother to answer my question. I could feel his eyes crawl over me until he asked, "What did he tell you?"

I shook my head. Just once. My way could be final too.

With a calm, indifferent sincerity Pat said, "You'll tell me. You'll get worked on until talking won't even be an effort. It will come out of you because there won't be a nerve ending left to stop it. You know that."

I heard Larry's strained voice say, "Come off it, Pat. He can't take much."

"Who cares. He's no good to anybody. He's a louse, a stinking, drinking louse. Now he's got something I have to have. You think I'm going to worry about him? Larry, buddy, you just don't know me very well anymore."

I said, "Who was he?"

The wall in front of me was a friendly pale green. It was blank from one end to the other. It was a vast, meadowlike area, totally unspoiled. There were no foreign markings, no distracting pictures. Unsympathetic. Antiseptic.

I felt Pat's shrug and his fingers bit into my arm once more. "Okay, wise guy. Now we'll do it my way."

"I told you, Pat—"

"Damn it, Larry, you knock it off. This bum is a lead to a killer. He learned something from that guy and I'm going to get it out of him. Don't hand me any pious crap or medical junk about what can happen. I know guys like this. I've been dealing with them all my life. They go on getting banged around from saloon to saloon, hit by cars, rolled by muggers and all they ever come up with are fresh scars. I can beat hell out of him and maybe he'll talk. Maybe he won't, but man, let me tell you this—I'm going to have my crack at him and when I'm through the medics can pick up the pieces for their go. Only first me, understand?"

Larry didn't answer him for a moment, then he said quietly. "Sure, I understand. Maybe you could use a little medical help yourself."

I heard Pat's breath hiss in softly. Like a snake. His hand relaxed on my arm and without looking I knew what his face was like. I had seen him go like that before and a second later he had shot a guy.

And this time it was me he listened to when I said, "He's right, old buddy. You're real sick."

I knew it would come and there wouldn't be any way of getting away from it. It was quick, it was hard, but it didn't hurt a bit. It was like flying away to never-never land where all is quiet and peaceful and awakening is under protest because then it will really hurt and you don't want that to happen.

Larry said, "How do you feel now?"

It was a silly question. I closed my eyes again.

"We kept you here in the hospital."

"Don't do me any more favors," I told him.

"No trouble. You're a public charge. You're on the books as an acute alcoholic with a D and D to boot and if you're real careful you might talk your way out on the street again. However, I have my doubts about it. Captain Chambers is pushing you hard."

"The hell with him."

"He's not the only one."

"So what's new?" My voice was raspy, almost gone.

"The D.A., his assistant and some unidentified personnel from higher headquarters are interested in whatever statement you'd care to make."

"The hell with them too."

"It could be instrumental in getting you out of here."

"Nuts. It's the first time I've been to bed in a long time. I like it here."

"Mike—" His voice had changed. There was something there now that wasn't that of the professional medic at a bedside. It was worried and urgent and I let my eyes slit open and looked at him.

"I don't like what's happening to Pat."

"Tough."

"A good word, but don't apply it to him. You're the tough one. You're not like him at all."

"He's tough."

"In a sense. He's a pro. He's been trained and can perform

certain skills most men can't. He's a policeman and most men aren't that. Pat is a normal sensitive human. At least he was. I met him after you went to pot. I heard a lot about you, mister. I watched Pat change character day by day and what caused the change was you and what you did to Velda."

*The name again. In one second I lived every day the name was alive and with me. Big, Valkyrian and with hair as black as night.*

"Why should he care?"

"He says she was his friend."

Very slowly I squeezed my eyes open. "You know what she was to me?"

"I think so."

"Okay."

"But it could be he was in love with her too," he said.

I couldn't laugh like I wanted to. "She was in love with me, Doc."

"Nevertheless, *he* was in love with *her*. Maybe you never realized it, but that's the impression I got. He's still a bachelor, you know."

"Ah! He's in love with his job. I know him."

"Do you?"

I thought back to that night ago and couldn't help the grin that tried to climb up my face. "Maybe not, Doc, maybe not. But it's an interesting thought. It explains a lot of things."

"He's after you now. To him, you killed her. His whole personality, his entire character has changed. You're the focal point. Until now he's never had a way to get to you to make you pay for what happened. Now he has you in a nice tight bind and, believe me, you're going to be racked back first class."

"That's G.I. talk, Doc."

"I was in the same war, buddy."

I looked at him again. His face was drawn, his eyes searching and serious. "What am I supposed to do?"

"He never told me and I never bothered to push the issue, but since I'm his friend rather than yours, I'm more interested in him personally than you."

"Lousy bedside manner, Doc."

"Maybe so, but he's my friend."

"He used to be mine."

"No more."

"So?"

"What happened?"

"What would you believe coming from an acute alcoholic and a D and D?"

For the first time he laughed and it was for real. "I hear you used to weigh in at two-o-five?"

"Thereabouts."

"You're down to one-sixty-eight, dehydrated, undernourished. A bum, you know?"

"You don't have to remind me."

"That isn't the point. You missed it."

"No I didn't."

"Oh?"

"Medics don't talk seriously to D and D's. I know what I was. Now *there* is a choice of words if you can figure it out."

He laughed again. *"Was.* I caught it."

"Then talk."

"Okay. You're a loused-up character. There's nothing to you anymore. Physically, I mean. Something happened and you tried to drink yourself down the drain."

"I'm a weak person."

"Guilt complex. Something you couldn't handle. It happens to the hardest nuts I've seen. They can take care of anything until the irrevocable happens and then they blow. Completely."

"Like me?"

"Like you."

"Keep talking."

"You were a lush."

"So are a lot of people. I even know some doctors who—"

"You came out of it pretty fast."

"At ease, Doc."

"I'm not prying," he reminded me.

"Then talk right."

"Sure," he said. "Tell me about Velda."

# CHAPTER 3

"It was a long time ago," I said.

And when I had said it I wished I hadn't because it was something I never wanted to speak about. It was over. You can't beat time. Let the dead stay dead. If they can. But was she dead? Maybe if I told it just once I could be sure.

"Tell me," Larry asked.

"Pat ever say anything?"

"Nothing."

So I told him.

"It was a routine job," I said.

"Yes?"

"A Mr. Rudolph Civac contacted me. He was from Chicago, had plenty of rocks and married a widow named Marta Singleton who inherited some kind of machine-manufacturing fortune. Real social in Chicago. Anyway, they came to New York where she wanted to be social too and introduce her new husband around."

"Typical," Larry said.

"Rich-bitches."

"Don't hold it against them," he told me.

"Not me, kid," I said.

"Then go on."

I said, "She was going to sport all the gems her dead husband gave her which were considerable and a prime target for anybody in the field and her husband wanted protection."

Larry made a motion with his hand. "A natural thought."

"Sure. So he brought me in. Big party. He wanted to cover the gems."

"Any special reason?"

"Don't be a jerk. They were worth a half a million. Most of my business is made of stuff like that."

"Trivialities."

"Sure, Doc, like unnecessary appendectomies."

"Touché."

"Think nothing of it."

He stopped then. He waited seconds and seconds and watched and waited, then: "A peculiar attitude."

"You're the psychologist, Doc, not me."

"Why?"

"You're thinking that frivolity is peculiar for a D and D."

"So go on with the story."

"Doc," I said, "later I'm going to paste you right in the mouth. You know this?"

"Sure."

"That's *my* word."

"So sure."

"Okay, Doc, ask for it. Anyway, it was a routine job. The target was a dame. At that time a lot of parties were being tapped by a fat squad who saw loot going to waste around the neck of a big broad who never needed it—but this was a classic. At least in our business."

"How?"

"Never mind. At least she called us in. I figured it would be better if we changed our routine. That night I was on a homicide case. Strictly insurance, but the company was paying off and there would be another grand in the kitty. I figured it would be a better move to let Velda cover the affair since she'd be able to stay with the client at all times, even into the ladies' room."

Larry interrupted with a wave of his hand. "Mind a rough question?"

"No."

"Was this angle important or were you thinking, rather, of the profit end—like splitting your team up between two cases."

I knew I had started to shake and pressed my hands against my sides hard. After a few seconds the shakes went away and I could answer him without wanting to tear his head off. "It was an important angle," I said. "I had two heists pulled under my nose when they happened in a powder room."

"And—the woman. How did she feel about it?"

"Velda was a pro. She carried a gun and had her own P.I. ticket."

"And she could handle any situation?"

I nodded. "Any we presumed could happen here."

"You were a little too presumptuous, weren't you?"

The words almost choked me when I said, "You know, Doc, you're asking to get killed."

He shook his head and grinned. "Not you, Mike. You aren't like you used to be. I could take you just as easy as Pat did. Almost anybody could."

I tried to get up, but he laid a hand on my chest and shoved me back and I couldn't fight against him. Every nerve in me started to jangle and my head turned into one big round blob of pain.

Larry said, "You want a drink?"

"No."

"You'd better have one."

"Stuff it."

"All right, suffer. You want to talk some more or shall I take off?"

"I'll finish the story. Then you can work on Pat. When I get out of here I'm going to make a project of rapping you and Pat right in the mouth."

"Good. You have something to look forward to. Now talk."

I waited a minute, thinking back years and putting the pieces in slots so familiar they were worn smooth at the edges. Finally I said, "At eleven o'clock Velda called me at a prearranged number. Everything was going smoothly. There was nothing unusual, the guests were all persons of character and money, there were no suspicious or unknown persons present including the household staff. At that time they were holding dinner awaiting the arrival of Mr. Rudolph Civac. That was my last connection with Velda."

"There was a police report?"

"Sure. At 11:15 Mr. Civac came in and after saying hello to the guests, went upstairs with his wife for a minute to wash up. Velda went along. When they didn't appear an hour and a half later a maid went up to see if anything was wrong and found the place empty. She didn't call the police, thinking that they had argued or something, then went out the private entrance to the rear of the estate. She served dinner with a lame excuse for the host's absence, sent the guests home and cleaned up with the others.

"The next day Marta Civac was found in the river, shot in the head, her jewels gone and neither her husband nor Velda was ever seen again."

I had to stop there. I didn't want to think on the next part anymore. I was hoping it would be enough for him, but when I looked up he was frowning with thought, digesting it a little at a time like he was diagnosing a disease, and I knew it wasn't finished yet.

He said, "They were abducted for the purpose of stealing those gems?"

"It was the only logical way they could do it. There were too many people. One scream would bring them running. They probably threatened the three of them, told them to move on out quietly where the theft could be done without interruption and allow the thieves to get away."

"Would Velda have gone along with them?"

"If they threatened the client that's the best way. It's better to give up insured gems than get killed. Even a rap on the head can kill if it isn't done right and, generally speaking, jewel thieves aren't killers unless they're pushed."

I felt a shudder go through my shoulders. "No. The body— showed why." I paused and he sat patiently, waiting. "Marta was a pudgy dame with thick fingers. She had crammed on three rings worth a hundred grand combined and they weren't about to come off normally. To get the rings they had severed the fingers."

Softly, he remarked, "I see."

"It was lousy."

"What do you think happened, Mike?"

I was going to hate to tell him, but it had been inside too long. I said, "Velda advised them to go along thinking it would be a heist without any physical complications. Probably when they started to take the rings off the hard way the woman started to scream and was shot. Then her husband and Velda tried to help her and that was it."

"Was what?"

I stared at the ceiling. Before it had been so plain, so simple. Totally believable because it had been so totally terrible. For all those years I had conditioned myself to think only one way because in my job you got to know which answers were right.

Now, suddenly, maybe they weren't right anymore.

Larry asked, "So they killed the man and Velda too and their bodies went out to sea and were never found?"

My tired tone was convincing. I said, "That's how the report read."

"So Pat took it all out on you."

"Looks that way."

"Uh-huh. You let her go on a job you should have handled yourself."

"It didn't seem that way at first."

"Perhaps, but you've been taking it out on yourself too. It just took that one thing to make you a bum."

"Hard words, friend."

"You realize what happened to Pat?"

I glanced at him briefly and nodded. "I found out."

"The hard way."

"So I didn't think he cared."

"You probably never would have known if that didn't happen."

"Kismet, buddy. Like your getting punched in the mouth."

"But there's a subtle difference now, Mikey boy, isn't there?"

"Like how?" I turned my head and watched him. He was the type who could hide his thoughts almost completely, even to a busted-up pro like me, but it didn't quite come off. I knew what he was getting to.

"Something new has been added, Mike."

"Oh?"

"You were a sick man not many hours ago."

"I'm hurting right now."

"You know what I'm talking about. You were a drunk just a little while back."

"So I kicked the habit."

"Why?"

"Seeing old friends helped."

He smiled at me, leaned forward and crossed his arms. "What did that guy tell you?"

"Nothing," I lied.

"I think I know. I think I know the only reason that would turn you from an acute alcoholic to a deadly sober man in a matter of minutes."

I had to be sure. I had to see what he knew. I said, "Tell me, Doc."

Larry stared at me a moment, smiled smugly and sat back, enjoying every second of the scene. When he thought my reaction would be just right he told me, "That guy mentioned the name of the killer."

So he couldn't see my face I turned my head. When I looked at him again he was still smiling, so I looked at the ceiling without answering and let him think what he pleased.

Larry said, "Now you're going out on your own, just like in the old days Pat used to tell me about."

"I haven't decided yet."

"Want some advice?"

"No."

"Nevertheless, you'd better spill it to Pat. He wants the same one."

"Pat can go drop."

"Maybe."

This time there was a peculiar intonation in his voice. I half turned and looked up at him. "Now what's bugging you?"

"Don't you think Pat knows you have something?"

"Like the man said, frankly, buddy, I don't give a damn."

"You won't tell me about it then?"

"You can believe it."

"Pat's going to lay charges on you."

"Good for him. When you clear out I'm going to have a lawyer ready who'll tear Pat apart. So maybe you'd better tell him."

"I will. But for your own sake, reconsider. It might be good for both of you."

Larry stood up and fingered the edge of his hat. A change came over his face and he grinned a little bit.

"Tell you something, Mike. I've heard so much about you it's like we're old friends. Just understand something. I'm really trying to help. Sometimes it's hard to be a doctor and a friend."

I held out my hand and grinned back. "Sure, I know. Forget that business about a paste in the mouth. You'd probably tear my head off."

He laughed and nodded, squeezed my hand and walked out. Before he reached the end of the corridor I was asleep again.

They make them patient in the government agencies. There was no telling how long he had been there. A small man, quiet, plain-looking—no indication of toughness unless you knew how to read it in his eyes. He just sat there as if he had all the time in the world and nothing to do except study me.

At least he had manners. He waited until I was completely awake before he reached for the little leather folder, opened it and said, "Art Rickerby, Federal Bureau of Investigation."

"No," I said sarcastically.

"You've been sleeping quite a while."

"What time is it?"

Without consulting his watch he said, "Five after four."

"It's pretty late."

Rickerby shrugged noncommittally without taking his eyes from my face. "Not for people like us," he told me. "It's never too late, is it?" He was smiling a small smile, but behind his glasses his eyes weren't smiling at all.

"Make your point, friend," I said.

He nodded thoughtfully, never losing his small smile. "Are you—let's say, capable of coherent discussion?"

"You've been reading my chart?"

"That's right. I spoke to your doctor friend too."

"Okay," I said, "forget the AA tag. I've had it, you know?"

"I know."

"Then what do we need the Feds in for? I've been out of action for how many years?"

"Seven."

"Long time, Art, long time, feller. I got no ticket, no rod. I haven't even crossed the state line in all that time. For seven years I cool myself off the way I want to and then all of a sudden I have a Fed on my neck." I squinted at him, trying to find the reason in his face. "Why?"

"Cole, Richie Cole."

"What about him?"

"Suppose you tell me, Mr. Hammer. He asked for you, you came and he spoke to you. I want to know what he said."

I reached way back and found a grin I thought I had forgotten how to make. "Everybody wants to know that, Rickey-back."

"Rickerby."

"So sorry." A laugh got in behind the grin. "Why all the curiosity?"

"Never mind why, just tell me what he said."

"Nuts, buddy."

He didn't react at all. He sat there with all the inbred patience of years of this sort of thing and simply looked at me tolerantly because I was in a bed in the funny ward and it might possibly be an excuse for anything I had to say or do.

Finally he said, "You *can* discuss this, can't you?"

I nodded. "But I won't."

"Why not?"

"I don't like anxious people. I've been kicked around, dragged into places I didn't especially want to go, kicked on my can by a cop who used to be a friend and suddenly faced with the prospects of formal charges because I object to the police version of the hard sell."

"Supposing I can offer you a certain amount of immunity?"

After a few moments I said, "This is beginning to get interesting."

Rickerby reached for words, feeling them out one at a time. "A long while ago you killed a woman, Mike. She shot a friend of yours and you said no matter who it was, no matter where, that killer would die. You shot her."

"Shut up, man," I said.

*He was right. It was a very long time ago. But it could have been yesterday. I could see her face, the golden tan of her skin, the incredible whiteness of her hair and eyes that could taste and devour you with one glance. Yet, Charlotte was there still. But dead now.*

"Hurt, Mike?"

There was no sense trying to fool him. I nodded abruptly. "I try not to think of it." Then I felt that funny sensation in my back and saw what he was getting at. His face was tight and the little lines around his eyes had deepened so that they stood out in relief, etched into his face.

I said, "You knew Cole?"

It was hard to tell what color his eyes were now. "He was one of us," he said.

I couldn't answer him. He had been waiting patiently a long time to say what he had to say and now it was going to come out. "We were close, Hammer. I trained him. I never had a son and he was as close as I was ever going to get to having one. Maybe now you know exactly why I brought up your past. It's mine who's dead now and it's me who has to find who did it. This should make sense to you. It should also tell you something else. Like you, I'll go to any extremes to catch the one who did it. I've made promises of my own, Mr. Hammer, and I'm sure you know what I'm talking about. Nothing is going to stop me and you are my starting point." He paused, took his glasses off, wiped them, put them back on and said, "You understand this?"

"I get the point."

"Are you sure?" And now his tone had changed. Very subtly, but changed nevertheless. "Because as I said, there are no extremes to which I won't go."

When he stopped I watched him and in the way he sat, the way he looked, the studied casualness became the poised kill-crouch of a cat, all cleverly disguised by clothes and the innocent aspect of rimless bifocals.

Now he was deadly. All too often people have the preconceived notion that a deadly person is a big one, wide in the shoulders with a face full of hard angles and thick-set teeth and a jawline that would be a challenge too great for anyone to dare. They'd be wrong. Deadly people aren't all like that. Deadly people are determined people who will stop at nothing at all, and those who are practiced in the arts of the kill are the most deadly of all. Art Rickerby was one of those.

"That's not a very official attitude," I said.

"I'm just trying to impress you," he suggested.

I nodded. "Okay, kid, I'm impressed."

"Then what about Cole?"

"There's another angle."

"Not with me there isn't."

"Easy, Art, I'm not that impressed. I'm a big one too."

"No more, Hammer."

"Then you drop dead, too."

Like a large gray cat, he stood up, still pleasant, still deadly, and said, "I suppose we leave it here?"

"You pushed me, friend."

"It's a device you should be familiar with."

I was getting tired again, but I grinned a little at him. "Cops. Damn cops."

"You were one once."

After a while I said, "I never stopped being one."

"Then cooperate."

This time I turned my head and looked at him. "The facts are all bollixed up. I need one day and one other little thing you might be able to supply."

"Go ahead."

"Get me the hell out of here and get me that day."

"Then what?"

"Maybe I'll tell you something, maybe I won't. Just don't do me any outsized favors because if you don't bust me out of here I'll go out on my own. You can just make it easier. One way or another, I don't care. Take your pick."

Rickerby smiled. "I'll get you out," he said. "It won't be hard. And you can have your day."

"Thanks."

"Then come to me so I won't have to start looking for you."

"Sure, buddy," I said. "Leave your number at the desk."

He said something I didn't quite catch because I was falling asleep again, and when the welcome darkness came in I reached for it eagerly and wrapped it around me like a soft, dark suit of armor.

# CHAPTER 4

He let me stay there three days before he moved. He let me have the endless bowls of soup and the bed rest and shot series before the tall thin man showed up with my clothes and a worried nurse whose orders had been countermanded somehow by an authority she neither understood nor could refuse.

When I was dressed he led me downstairs and outside to an unmarked black Ford and I got in without talking. He asked, "Where to?" and I told him anyplace midtown and in fifteen minutes he dropped me in front of the Taft. As I was getting out his hand closed on my arm and very quietly he said, "You have one day. No more."

I nodded. "Tell Rickerby thanks."

He handed me a card then, a simple business thing giving the address and phone of Peerage Brokers located on Broadway only two blocks off. "You tell him," he said, then pulled away from the curb into traffic.

For a few minutes I waited there, looking at the city in a strange sort of light I hadn't seen for too long. It was morning, and quiet because it was Sunday. Overhead, the sun forced its way through a haze that had rain behind it, making the day sulky, like a woman in a pout.

The first cabby in line glanced up once, ran his eyes up and down me, then went back to his paper. Great picture, I thought. I sure must cut a figure. I grinned, even though nothing was funny, and shoved my hands in my jacket pockets. In the right-hand one somebody had stuck five tens, neatly folded and I said, "Thanks, Art Rickerby, old buddy," silently, and waved for the cab first in line to come over.

He didn't like it, but he came, asked me where to in a surly voice and when I let him simmer a little bit I told him Lex and Forty-ninth. When he dropped me there I let him change the ten, gave him two bits and waited some more to see if anyone had been behind me.

No one had. If Pat or anyone else had been notified I had been released, he wasn't bothering to stick with me. I gave it another five minutes then turned and walked north.

Old Dewey had held the same corner down for twenty years. During the war, servicemen got their paper free, which was about as much as he could do for the war effort, but there were those of us who never forgot and Old Dewey was a friend we saw often so that we were friends rather than customers. He was in his eighties now and he had to squint through his glasses to make out a face. But the faces of friends, their voices and their few minutes' conversation were things he treasured and looked forward to. Me? Hell, we were old friends from long ago, and back in the big days I never missed a night picking up my pink editions of the *News* and *Mirror* from Old Dewey, even when I had to go out of my way to do it. And there were times when I was in business that he made a good intermediary. He was always there, always dependable, never took a day off, never was on the take for a buck.

But he wasn't there now.

Duck-Duck Jones, who was an occasional swamper in the Clover Bar, sat inside the booth picking his teeth while he read the latest *Cavalier* magazine and it was only after I stood there a half minute that he looked up, scowled, then half-recognized me and said, "Oh, hello, Mike."

I said, "Hello, Duck-Duck. What are you doing here?"

He made a big shrug under his sweater and pulled his eyebrows up. "I help Old Dewey out alla time. Like when he eats. You know?"

"Where's he now?"

Once again, he went into an eloquent shrug. "So he don't show up yesterday. I take the key and open up for him. Today the same thing."

"Since when does Old Dewey miss a day?"

"Look, Mike, the guy's gettin' old. I take over maybe one day every week when he gets checked. Doc says he got something inside him, like. All this year he's been hurtin'."

"You keep the key?"

"Sure. We been friends a long time. He pays good. Better'n swabbing out the bar every night. This ain't so bad. Plenty of books with pictures. Even got a battery radio."

"He ever miss two days running?"

Duck-Duck made a face, thought a second and shook his head. "Like this is the first time. You know Old Dewey. He don't wanna miss nothin'. Nothin' at all."

"You check his flop?"

"Nah. You think I should? Like he could be sick or somethin'?"

"I'll do it myself."

"Sure, Mike. He lives right off Second by the diner, third place down in the basement. You got to—"

I nodded curtly. "I've been there."

"Look, Mike, if he don't feel good and wants me to stay on a bit I'll do it. I won't clip nothin'. You can tell him that."

"Okay, Duck."

I started to walk away and his voice caught me. "Hey, Mike."

"What?"

He was grinning through broken teeth, but his eyes were frankly puzzled. "You look funny, man. Like different from when I seen you last down at the Chink's. You off the hop?"

I grinned back at him. "Like for good," I said.

"Man, here we go again," he laughed.

"Like for sure," I told him.

Old Dewey owned the building. It wasn't much, but that and the newsstand were his insurance against the terrible thought of public support, a sure bulwark against the despised welfare plans of city and state. A second-rate beauty shop was on the ground floor and the top two were occupied by families who had businesses in the neighborhood. Old Dewey lived in humble quarters in the basement, needing only a single room in which to cook and sleep.

I tried his door, but the lock was secure. The only windows were those facing the street, the protective iron bars imbedded in the brickwork since the building had been erected. I knocked again, louder this time, and called out, but nobody answered.

Then again I had that funny feeling I had learned not to

ignore, but it had been so long since I had felt it that it was almost new and once more I realized just how long it had been since I was in a dark place with a kill on my hands.

Back then it had been different. I had the gun. I was big.

Now was—how many years later? There was no gun. I wasn't big anymore.

I was what was left over from being a damn drunken bum, and if there were anything left at all it was sheer reflex and nothing else.

So I called on the reflex and opened the door with the card the tall thin man gave me because it was an old lock with a wide gap in the doorframe. I shoved it back until it hit the door, standing there where anybody inside could target me easily, but knowing that it was safe because I had been close to death too many times not to recognize the immediate sound of silence it makes.

He was on the floor face down, arms outstretched, legs spread, his head turned to one side so that he stared at one wall with the universal expression of the dead. He lay there in a pool of soup made from his own blood that had gouted forth from the great slash in his throat. The blood had long ago congealed and seeped into the cracks in the flooring, the coloring changed from scarlet to brown and already starting to smell.

Somebody had already searched the room. It hadn't taken long, but the job had been thorough. The signs of the expert were there, the one who had time and experience, who knew every possible hiding place and who had overlooked none. The search had gone around the room and come back to the body on the floor. The seams of the coat were carefully torn open, the pockets turned inside out, the shoes ripped apart.

But the door had been locked and this was not the sign of someone who had found what he wanted. Instead, it was the sign of he who hadn't and wanted time to think on it—or wait it out—or possibly study who else was looking for the same thing.

I said, "Don't worry, Dewey, I'll find him," and my voice was strangely hushed like it came from years ago. I wiped off the light switch, the knob, then closed the door and left it like I found it and felt my way to the back through the labyrinth of alleys that is New York over on that side and pretty soon I came out on the street again and it had started to rain.

His name was Nat Drutman. He owned the Hackard Building where I used to have my office and now, seven years later, he was just the same—only a little grayer and a little wiser around the eyes and when he glanced up at me from his desk it was as if he had seen me only yesterday.

"Hello, Mike."

"Nat."

"Good to see you."

"Thanks," I said.

This time his eyes stayed on me and he smiled, a gentle smile that had hope in it. "It has been a long time."

"Much too long."

"I know." He watched me expectantly.

I said, "You sell the junk from my office?"

"No."

"Store it?"

He shook his head, just once. "No."

"No games, kid," I said.

He made the Lower East Side gesture with his shoulders and let his smile stay pat. "It's still there, Mike."

"Not after seven years, kid," I told him.

"That's so long?"

"For somebody who wants their loot it is."

"So who needs loot?"

"Nat—"

"Yes, Mike?"

His smile was hard to understand.

"No games."

"You still got a key?" he asked.

"No I left to stay. No key. No nothing anymore."

He held out his hand, offering me a shiny piece of brass. I took it automatically and looked at the number stamped into it, a fat 808. "I had it made special," he said.

As best I could, I tried to be nasty. "Come off it, Nat."

He wouldn't accept the act. "Don't thank me. I knew you'd be back."

I said, "Shit."

There was a hurt look on his face. It barely touched his eyes and the corners of his mouth, but I knew I had hurt him.

"Seven years, Nat. That's a lot of rent."

He wouldn't argue. I got that shrug again and the funny look that went with it. "So for you I dropped the rent to a dollar a year while you were gone."

I looked at the key, feeling my shoulders tighten. "Nat—"

"Please—don't talk. Just take. Remember when you gave? Remember Bernie and those men? Remember—"

"Okay, Nat."

The sudden tension left his face and he smiled again. I said, "Thanks, kid. You'll never know."

A small laugh left his lips and he said, "Oh I'll know, all right. That'll be seven dollars. Seven years, seven dollars."

I took out another ten and laid it on his desk. With complete seriousness he gave me back three ones, a receipt, then said, "You got a phone too, Mike. Same number. No 'thank yous,' Mike. Augie Strickland came in with the six hundred he owed you and left it with me so I paid the phone bill from it. You still got maybe a couple bucks coming back if we figure close."

"Save it for service charges," I said.

"Good to see you, Mike."

"Good to see you, Nat."

"You look pretty bad. Is everything going to be like before, Mike?"

"It can never be like before. Let's hope it's better."

"Sure, Mike."

"And thanks anyway, kid."

"My pleasure, Mike."

I looked at the key, folded it in my fist and started out. When I reached the door Nat said, "Mike—"

I turned around.

"Velda . . . ?"

He watched my eyes closely.

"That's why you're back?"

"Why?"

"I hear many stories, Mike. Twice I even saw you. Things I know that nobody else knows. I know why you left. I know why you came back. I even waited because I knew someday you'd come. So you're back. You don't look like you did except for your eyes. They never change. Now you're all beat up and skinny and far behind. Except for your eyes, and that's the worst part."

"Is it?"

He nodded. "For somebody," he said.

I put the key in the lock and turned the knob. It was like coming back to the place where you had been born, remembering, yet without a full recollection of all the details. It was a drawing, wanting power that made me swing the door open because I wanted to see how it used to be and how it might have been.

Her desk was there in the anteroom, the typewriter still covered, letters from years ago stacked in a neat pile waiting to be answered, the last note she had left for me still there beside the phone some itinerant spider had draped in a nightgown of cobwebs.

The wastebasket was where I had kicked it, dented almost double from my foot; the two captain's chairs and antique bench we used for clients were still overturned against the wall where I had thrown them. The door to my office swung open, tendrils of webbing seeming to tie it to the frame. Behind it I could see my desk and chair outlined in the gray shaft of light that was all that was left of the day.

I walked in, waving the cobwebs apart, and sat down in the chair. There was dust, and silence, and I was back to seven years ago, all of a sudden. Outside the window was another New York—not the one I had left, because the old one had been torn down and rebuilt since I had looked out that window last. But below on the street the sounds hadn't changed a bit, nor had the people. Death and destruction were still there, the grand overseers of life toward the great abyss, some slowly, some quickly, but always along the same road.

For a few minutes I just sat there swinging in the chair, recalling the feel and the sound of it. I made a casual inspection of the desk drawers, not remembering what was there, yet enjoying a sense of familiarity with old things. It was an old desk, almost antique, a relic from some solid, conservative corporation that supplied its executives with the best.

When you pulled the top drawer all the way out there was a niche built into the massive framework, and when I felt in the shallow recess the other relic was still there.

Calibre .45, Colt Automatic, U.S. Army model, vintage of 1914. Inside the plastic wrapper it was still oiled, and when I checked the action it was like a thing alive, a deadly thing that had but a single fundamental purpose.

I put it back where it was beside the box of shells, inserted the drawer and slid it shut. The day of the guns was back there seven years ago. Not now.

Now I was one of the nothing people. One mistake and Pat had me, and where I was going, one mistake and *they* would have me.

Pat. The slob really took off after me. I wondered if Larry had been right when he said Pat had been in love with Velda too?

I nodded absently, because he had changed. And there was more to it, besides. In seven years Pat should have moved up the ladder. By now he should have been an Inspector. Maybe whatever it was he had crawling around in his guts got out of hand and he never made the big try for promotion, or, if he did, he loused up.

The hell with him, I thought. Now he was going wide open to nail a killer and a big one. Whoever killed Richie Cole had killed Senator Knapp in all probability, and in all probability, too, had killed Old Dewey. Well, I was one up on Pat.

He'd have another kill in his lap, all right, but only I could connect Dewey and the others.

Which put me in the middle all around.

*So okay, Hammer, I said. You've been a patsy before. See what you'll do with this one and do it right. Someplace she's alive. Alive! But for how long? And where? There are killers loose and she must be on the list.*

Absently, I reached for the phone, grinned when I heard the dial tone, then fingered the card the thin man gave me from my pocket and called Peerage Brokers.

He was there waiting and when I asked, "Rickerby?" a switch clicked.

Art answered, "You still have a little more time."

"I don't need time. I need now. I think we should talk."

"Where are you?"

"My own office through courtesy of a friend. The Hackard Building."

"Stay there. I'll be up in ten minutes."

"Sure. Bring me a sandwich."

"A drink too?"

"None of that. Maybe a couple of Blue Ribbons, but nothing else."

Without answering, he hung up. I glanced at my wrist, but there was no watch there anymore. Somehow, I vaguely remembered hocking it somewhere and called myself a nut because it was a good Rollex and I probably drank up the loot in half a day. Or got rolled for it.

Damn!

From the window I could see the clock on the Paramount Building and it was twenty past six. The street was slick from the drizzle that had finally started to fall and the crosstown traffic was like a giant worm trying to eat into the belly of

the city. I opened the window and got supper smells in ten
languages from the restaurants below and for the first time
in a long time it smelled good. Then I switched on the desk
lamp and sat back again.

Rickerby came in, put a wrapped sandwich and two cans
of Blue Ribbon in front of me and sat down with a weary
smile. It was a very peculiar smile, not of friendliness, but of
anticipation. It was one you didn't smile back at, but rather
waited out.

And I made him wait until I had finished the sandwich and
a can of beer, then I said, "Thanks for everything."

Once again, he smiled. "Was it worth it?"

His eyes had that flat calm that was nearly impenetrable.
I said, "Possibly. I don't know. Not yet."

"Suppose we discuss it."

I smiled some too. The way his face changed I wondered
what I looked like. "It's all right with me, Rickety."

"Rickerby."

"Sorry," I said. "But let's do it question-and-answer style.
Only I want to go first."

"You're not exactly in a position to dictate terms."

"I think I am. I've been put upon. You know?"

He shrugged, and looked at me again, still patient. "It
really doesn't matter. Ask me what you want to."

"Are you officially on this case?"

Rickerby didn't take too long putting it in its proper
category. It would be easy enough to plot out if you knew
how, so he simply made a vague motion with his shoulders.
"No. Richie's death is at this moment a local police matter."

"Do they know who he was?"

"By now, I assume so."

"And your department won't press the matter?"

He smiled, nothing more.

I said, "Suppose I put it this way—if his death resulted in the line of duty he was pursuing—because of the case he was on, then your department would be interested."

Rickerby looked at me, his silence acknowledging my statement.

"However," I continued, "if he was the victim of circumstances that could hit anybody, it would remain a local police matter and his other identity would remain concealed from everyone possible. True?"

"You seem familiar enough with the machinations of our department, so draw your own conclusions," Rickerby told me.

"I will. I'd say that presently it's up in the air. You're on detached duty because of a personal interest in this thing. You couldn't be ordered off it, otherwise you'd resign and pursue it yourself."

"You know, Mike, for someone who was an alcoholic such a short time ago, your mind is awfully lucid." He took his glasses off and wiped them carefully before putting them back on. "I'm beginning to be very interested in this aspect of your personality."

"Let me clue you, buddy. It was shock. I was brought back to my own house fast, and suddenly meeting death in a sober condition really rocked me."

"I'm not so sure of that," he said. "Nevertheless, get on with your questions."

"What was Richie Cole's job?"

After a moment's pause he said, "Don't be silly. I certainly don't know. If I did I wouldn't reveal it."

"Okay, what was his cover?"

All he did was shake his head and smile.

I said, "You told me you'd do anything to get the one who killed him."

This time a full minute passed before he glanced down at his hands, then back to me again. In that time he had done some rapid mental calculations. "I—don't see how it could matter now," he said. When he paused a sadness creased his mouth momentarily, then he went on. "Richie worked as a seaman."

"Union man?"

"That's right. He held a full card."

# CHAPTER 5

The elevator operator in the Trib Building looked at me kind of funny like when I told him I wanted to find Hy. But maybe Hy had all kinds of hooples looking for him at odd hours. At one time the guy would never have asked questions, but now was now. The old Mike wasn't quite there any more.

In gold, the letters said, HY GARDNER. I knocked, opened the door and there he was, staring until recognition came, and with a subtle restraint he said, "Mike—" It was almost a question.

"A long time, Hy."

But always the nice guy, this one. Never picking, never choosing. He said, "Been too long. I've been wondering."

"So have a lot of people."

"But not for the same reasons."

We shook hands, a couple of old friends saying hello from a long while back; we had both been big, but while he had gone ahead and I had faded, yet still friends and good ones.

He tried to cover the grand hiatus of so many years with a

60

cigar stuck in the middle of a smile and made it all the way, without words telling me that nothing had really changed at all since the first time we had played bullets in a bar and he had made a column out of it the next day.

Hell, you've read his stuff. You know us.

I sat down, waved the crazy blonde bouffant he used as a secretary now out of the room and leaned back enjoying myself. After seven years it was a long time to enjoy anything. Friends.

I still had them.

"You look lousy," Hy said.

"So I've been told."

"True what I hear about you and Pat?"

"Word gets around fast."

"You know this business, Mike."

"Sure, so don't bother being kind."

"You're a nut," he laughed.

"Aren't we all. One kind or another."

"Sure, but you're on top. You know the word that's out right now?"

"I can imagine."

"The hell you can. You don't even know. What comes in this office you couldn't imagine. When they picked you up I heard about it. When you were in Pat's house I knew where you were. If you really want to know, whenever you were in the drunk tank, unidentified, I knew about it."

"Cripes, why didn't you get me out?"

"Mike," he laughed around the stogie, "I got problems of my own. When you can't solve yours, who can solve anything? Besides, I thought it would be a good experience for you."

"Thanks."

"No bother." He shifted the cigar from one side to the other. "But I was worried."

"Well, that's nice anyway," I said.

"Now it's worse."

Hy took the cigar away, studied me intently, stuffed the smoke out in a tray and pulled his eyes up to mine.

"Mike—"

"Say it, Hy."

He was honest. He pulled no punches. It was like time had never been at all and we were squaring away for the first time. "You're poison, Mike. The word's out."

"To you?"

"No." He shook his head. "They don't touch the Fifth Estate, you know that. They tried it with Joe Ungermach and Victor Reisel and look what happened to them. So don't worry about me."

"You worried about me?"

Hy grunted, lit another cigar and grinned at me. He had his glasses up on his head and you'd never think he could be anything but an innocuous slob, but then you'd be wrong. When he had it lit, he said, "I gave up worrying about you a long time ago. Now what did you want from me? It has to be big after seven years."

"Senator Knapp," I said.

*Sure,* he was thinking, *after seven years who the hell would think you'd come back with a little one? Mike Hammer chasing ambulances? Mike Hammer suddenly a reformer or coming up with a civic problem? Hell, anybody would have guessed. The Mike doesn't come back without a big one going. This a kill, Mike? What's the scoop? Story there, isn't there? You have a killer lined up just like in the old days and don't lie to me because I've seen those tiger eyes before. If*

*they were blue or brown like anybody else's maybe I couldn't*
*tell, but you got tiger eyes, friend, and they glint. So tell me.*
*Tell me hard. Tell me now.*

He didn't have to say it. Every word was there in his face,
like when he had read it out to me before. I didn't have to
hear it now. Just looking at him was enough.

I said, "Senator Knapp. He died when I was—away."

Quietly, Hy reminded me, "He didn't die. He was killed."

"Okay. The libraries were closed and besides, I forgot my
card."

"He's been dead three years."

"More."

"First why?"

"Because."

"You come on strong, man."

"You know another way?"

"Not for you."

"So how about the Senator?"

"Are we square?" he asked me. "It can be my story?"

"All yours, Hy. I don't make a buck telling columns."

"Got a few minutes?"

"All right," I said.

He didn't even have to consult the files. All he had to do
was light that damn cigar again and sit back in his chair, then
he sucked his mouth full of smoke and said, "Leo Knapp was
another McCarthy. He was a Commie-hunter but he had more
prestige and more power. He was on the right committee and,
to top it off, he was this country's missile man."

"That's what they called him, the *Missile Man*. Mr.
America. He pulled hard against the crap we put up with
like the Cape Canaveral strikes when the entire program was
held up by stupid jerks who went all that way for unionism

and—hell, read *True* or the factual accounts and see what
happened. The Reds are running us blind. Anyway, Knapp
was the missile pusher."

"Big," I said.

Hy nodded. "Then some louse shoots him. A simple bur-
glary and he gets killed in the process."

"You sure?"

Hy looked at me, the cigar hard in his teeth. "You know
me, Mike, I'm a reporter. I'm a Commie-hater. You think I
didn't take this one right into the ground?"

"I can imagine what you did."

"Now fill me in."

"Can you keep your mouth shut?"

He took the cigar away and frowned, like I had hurt him.
"Mike—"

"Look," I said, "I know, I know. But I may feed you a hot
one and I have to be sure. Until it's ended, it can't come out.
There's something here too big to mess with and I won't even
take a little chance on it."

"So tell me. I know what you're angling for. Your old contacts are gone or poisoned and you want me to shill for you."

"Natch."

"So I'll shill. Hell, we've done it before. It won't be like it's
a new experience."

"And keep Marilyn out of it. To her you're a new husband
and a father and she doesn't want you going down bullet alley
anymore."

"Aw, shut up and tell me what's on your mind."

I did.

I sat back and told it all out and let somebody else help
carry the big lid. I gave it to him in detail from seven years
ago and left out nothing. I watched his face go through all the

changes, watched him let the cigar burn itself out against the lip of the ashtray, watched him come alive with the crazy possibilities that were inherent in this one impossibility and when I finished I watched him sit back, light another cigar and regain his usual composure.

When he had it back again he said, "What do you want from me?"

"I don't know. It could be anything."

Like always, Hy nodded. "Okay, Mike. When it's ready to blow let me light the fuse. Hell, maybe we can do an interview with the about-to-be-deceased on the TV show ahead of time."

"No jokes, kid."

"Ah, cheer up. Things could be worse."

"I know," I quoted, " 'So I cheered up and sure enough things got worse.' "

Hy grinned and knocked the ash off the stogie. "Right now —anything you need?"

"Senator Knapp—"

"Right now his widow is at her summer place upstate in Phoenicia. That's where the Senator was shot."

"You'd think she'd move out."

Hy shrugged gently. "That's foolishness, in a way. It was the Senator's favorite home and she keeps it up. The rest of the year she stays at the residence in Washington. In fact, Laura is still one of the capital's favorite hostesses. Quite a doll."

"Oh?"

He nodded sagely, the cigar at an authoritative tilt. "The Senator was all man and what he picked was all woman. They were a great combination. It'll be a long time before you see one like that again."

"Tough."

"That's the way it goes. Look, if you want the details, I'll have a package run out from the morgue."

"I'd appreciate that."

Two minutes after he made his call a boy came through with a thick Manila envelope and laid it on the desk. Hy hefted it, handed it over and said: "This'll give you all the background on the murder. It made quite a story."

"Later there will be more."

"Sure," he agreed, "I know how you work."

I got up and put on my hat. "Thanks."

"No trouble, Mike." He leaned back in his chair and pulled his glasses down. "Be careful, Mike. You look lousy."

"Don't worry."

"Just the same, don't stick your neck out. Things can change in a few years. You're not like you were. A lot of people would like to catch up with you right now."

I grinned back at him. "I think most already have."


You drive up the New York Thruway, get off at Kingston and take the mountain route through some of the most beautiful country in the world. At Phoenicia you turn off to the north for five or six miles until you come to The Willows and there is the chalet nestling in the upcurve of the mountain, tended by blue spruces forty feet high and nursed by a living stream that dances its way in front of it.

It was huge and white and very senatorial, yet there was a lived-in look that took away any pretentiousness. It was a money house and it should have been because the Senator had been a money man. He had made it himself and had spent it the way he liked and this had been a pet project.

I went up through the gentle curve of the drive and shut off the motor in front of the house. When I touched the bell I could hear it chime inside, and after a minute of standing there, I touched it again. Still no one answered.

Just to be sure, I came down off the open porch, skirted the house on a flagstone walk that led to the rear and followed the S turns through the shrubbery arrangement that effectively blocked off all view of the back until you were almost on top of it.

There was a pool on one side and a tennis court on the other. Nestling between them was a green-roofed cottage with outside shower stalls that was obviously a dressing house.

At first I thought it was deserted here too, then very faintly I heard the distance-muffled sound of music. A hedgerow screened the southeast corner of the pool and in the corner of it the multicolor top of a table umbrella showed through the interlocking branches.

I stood there a few seconds, just looking down at her. Her hands were cradled behind her head, her eyes were closed and she was stretched out to the sun in taut repose. The top of the two-piece bathing suit was filled to overflowing with a matured ripeness that was breathtaking; the bottom half turned down well below her dimpled navel in a bikini effect, exposing the startling whiteness of untanned flesh against that which had been sun-kissed. Her breathing shallowed her stomach, then swelled it gently, and she turned slightly, stretching, pointing her toes so that a sinuous ripple of muscles played along her thighs.

I said, "Hello."

Her eyes came open, focused sleepily and she smiled at me. "Oh." Her smile broadened and it was like throwing a handful of beauty in her face. "Oh, hello."

Without being asked I handed her the terry-cloth robe that

was thrown across the tabletop. She took it, smiled again and threw it around her shoulders. "Thank you."

"Isn't it a little cold for that sort of thing?"

"Not in the sun." She waved to the deck chair beside her. "Please?" When I sat down she rearranged her lounge into a chair and settled back in it. "Now, Mr.—"

"Hammer. Michael Hammer." I tried on a smile for her too. "And you are Laura Knapp?"

"Yes. Do I know you from somewhere, Mr. Hammer?"

"We've never met."

"But there's something familiar about you."

"I used to get in the papers a lot."

"Oh?" It was a full-sized question.

"I was a private investigator at one time."

She frowned, studying me, her teeth white against the lushness of her lip as she nibbled at it. "There was an affair with a Washington agency at one time—"

I nodded.

"I remember it well. My husband was on a committee that was affected by it." She paused. "So you're Mike Hammer." Her frown deepened.

"You expected something more?"

Her smile was mischievous. "I don't quite know. Perhaps."

"I've been sick," I said, grinning.

"Yes," she told me, "I can believe that. Now, the question is, what are you doing here? Is this part of your work?"

There was no sense lying to her. I said, "No, but there's a possibility you can help me."

"How?"

"Do you mind going over the details of your husband's murder, or is it too touchy a subject?"

This time her smile took on a wry note. "You're very blunt,

Mr. Hammer. However, it's something in the past and I'm not afraid to discuss it. You could have examined the records of the incident if you wanted to. Wouldn't that have been easier?"

I let my eyes travel over her and let out a laugh. "I'm glad I came now."

Laura Knapp laughed back. "Well, thank you."

"But in case you're wondering, I did go over the clips on the case."

"And that wasn't enough?"

I shrugged. "I don't know. I'd rather hear it firsthand."

"May I ask why?"

"Sure," I said. "Something has come up that might tie in your husband's killer with another murder."

Laura shook her head slowly. "I don't understand—"

"It's a wild supposition, that's all, a probability I'm trying to chase down. Another man was killed with the same gun that shot your husband. Details that seemed unimportant then might have some bearing now."

"I see." She came away from the chair, leaning toward me with her hands hugging her knees, a new light of interest in her eyes. "But why aren't the police here instead of you?"

"They will be. Right now it's a matter of jurisdiction. Very shortly you'll be seeing a New York City officer, probably accompanied by the locals, who will go over the same ground. I don't have any legal paperwork to go through so I got here first."

Once again she started a slow smile and let it play around her mouth a moment before she spoke. "And if I don't talk— will you belt me one?"

"Hell," I said, "I never hit dames."

Her eyebrows went up in mock surprise.

"I always kick 'em."

The laugh she let out was pleasant and throaty and it was easy to see why she was still queen of the crazy social whirl at the capital. Age never seemed to have touched her, though she was in the loveliest early forties. Her hair shimmered with easy blond highlights, a perfect shade to go with the velvety sheen of her skin.

"I'll talk," she laughed, "but do I get a reward if I do?"

"Sure, I won't kick you."

"Sounds enticing. What do you want to know?"

"Tell me what happened."

She reflected a moment. It was evident that the details were there, stark as ever in her mind, though the thought didn't bring the pain back any longer. She finally said, "It was a little after two in the morning. I heard Leo get up but didn't pay any attention to it since he often went down for night-time snacks. The next thing I heard was his voice shouting at someone, then a single shot. I got up, ran downstairs and there he was on the floor, dying."

"Did he say anything?"

"No—he called out my name twice, then he died." She looked down at her feet, then glanced up. "I called the police. Not immediately. I was—stunned."

"It happens."

She chewed at her lip again. "The police were inclined to—well, they were annoyed. They figured the person had time to get away." Her eyes clouded, then drifted back in time. "But it couldn't have been more than a few minutes. No more. In fact, there could have been no time at all before I called. It's just that I don't remember those first few moments."

"Forget it anyway," I said. "That part doesn't count any more."

Laura paused, then nodded in agreement. "You're right, of course. Well, then the police came, but there was nothing they could do. Whoever it was had gone through the French windows in the den, then had run across the yard, gone through the gate and driven away. There were no tire tracks and the footprints he left were of no consequence."

"What about the house?"

She wrinkled her forehead as she looked over at me. "The safe was open and empty. The police believe Leo either surprised the burglar after he opened the safe or the burglar made him open the safe and when Leo went for him, killed him. There were no marks on the safe at all. It had been opened by using the combination."

"How many people knew the combination?"

"Just Leo, as far as I know."

I said, "The papers stated that nothing of importance was in the safe."

"That's right. There couldn't have been over a few hundred dollars in cash, a couple of account books, Leo's insurance policies, some legal papers and some jewelry of mine. The books and legal papers were on the floor intact so—"

"What jewelry?" I interrupted.

"It was junk."

"The papers quoted you as saying about a thousand dollars' worth."

She didn't hesitate and there was no evasion in her manner. "That's right, a thousand dollars' worth of paste. They were replicas of the genuine pieces I keep in a vault. That value is almost a hundred thousand dollars."

"A false premise is as good a reason for robbery as any."

Her eyes said she didn't agree with me. "Nobody knew I kept that paste jewelry in there."

"Two people did."

"Oh?"

I said, "Your husband and his killer."

The implication of it finally came to her. "He wouldn't have mentioned it to anyone. No, you're wrong there. It wasn't that important to him at all."

"Then why put it in the safe?"

"It's a natural place for it. Besides, as you mentioned, it could be a strong come-on to one who didn't know any better."

"Why didn't you have the combination?"

"I didn't need it. It was the only safe in the house, in Leo's private study—and, concerning his affairs, I stayed out completely."

"Servants?"

"At that time we had two. Both were very old and both have since died. I don't think they ever suspected that there were two sets of jewels anyway."

"Were they trustworthy?"

"They had been with Leo all his life. Yes, they were trustworthy."

I leaned back in the chair, reaching hard for any possibility now. "Could anything else have been in that safe? Something you didn't know about?"

"Certainly."

I edged forward now, waiting.

"Leo *could* have kept anything there, but I doubt that he did. I believe you're thinking of what could be termed state secrets?"

"It's happened before. The Senator was a man pretty high in the machinery of government."

"And a smart one," she countered. "His papers that had

governmental importance were all intact in his safe-deposit box and were recovered immediately after his death by the FBI, according to a memo he left with his office." She waited a moment then, watching me try to fasten on some obscure piece of information. Then she asked, "May I know what you're trying to get at?"

This time there was no answer. Very simply the whole thing broke down to a not unusual coincidence. One gun had been used for two kills. It happens often enough. These kills had been years apart, and from all the facts, totally unrelated.

I said, "It was a try, that's all. Nothing seems to match."

Quietly, she stated, "I'm sorry."

"Couldn't be helped." I stood up, not quite wanting to terminate our discussion. "It might have been the jewels, but a real pro would have made sure of what he was going after, and this isn't exactly the kind of place an amateur would hit."

Laura held out her hand and I took it, pulling her to her feet. It was like an unwinding, like a large fireside cat coming erect, yet so naturally that you were never aware of any artifice, but only the similarity. "Are you sure there's nothing further . . . ?"

"Maybe one thing," I said. "Can I see the den?"

She nodded, reaching out to touch my arm. "Whatever you want."

While she changed she left me alone in the room. It was a man's place, where only a man could be comfortable, a place designed and used by a man used to living. The desk was an oversized piece of deep-colored wood, almost antique in style, offset by dark leather chairs and original oil seascapes. The walnut paneling was hand carved, years old and well polished, matching the worn oriental rug that must have come over on a Yankee clipper ship.

The wall safe was a small circular affair that nestled behind a two-by-three-foot picture, the single modern touch in the room. Laura had opened the desk drawer, extracted a card containing the combination and handed it to me. Alone, I dialed the seven numbers and swung the safe out. It was empty.

That I had expected. What I hadn't expected was the safe itself. It was a Grissom 914A and was not the type you installed to keep junk jewelry or inconsequential papers in. This safe was more than a fireproof receptacle and simple safeguard for trivia. This job had been designed to be burglar-proof and had a built-in safety factor on the third number that would have been hooked into the local police PBX at the very least. I closed it, dialed it once again using the secondary number, opened it and waited.

Before Laura came down the cops were there, two excited young fellows in a battered Ford who came to the door with Police Specials out and ready, holding them at my gut when I let them in and looking able to use them.

The taller of the pair went around me while the other looked at me carefully and said, "Who're you?"

"I'm the one who tuned you in."

"Don't get smart."

"I was testing the wall safe out."

His grin had a wicked edge to it. "You don't test it like that, buddy."

"Sorry. I should have called first."

He went to answer, but his partner called in from the front room and he waved me ahead with the nose of the .38. Laura and the cop were there, both looking puzzled.

Laura had changed into a belted black dress that accented the sweeping curves of her body and when she stepped across the room toward me it was with the lithe grace of an athlete. "Mike—do you know what—"

"Your safe had an alarm number built into it. I checked it to see if it worked. Apparently it did."

"That right, Mrs. Knapp?" the tall cop asked.

"Well, yes. I let Mr. Hammer inspect the safe. I didn't realize it had an alarm on it."

"It's the only house around here that has that system, Mrs. Knapp. It's more or less on a commercial setup."

Beside me the cop holstered his gun with a shrug. "That's that," he said. "It was a good try."

The other one nodded, adjusted his cap and looked across at me. "We'd appreciate your calling first if it happens again."

"Sure thing. Mind a question?"

"Nope."

"Were you on the force when the Senator was killed?"

"We both were."

"Did the alarm go off then?"

The cop gave me a long, deliberate look, his face wary, then, "No, it didn't."

"Then if the killer opened the safe he knew the right combination."

"Or else," the cop reminded me, "he forced the Senator to open it, and knowing there was nothing of real value in there, and not willing to jeopardize his own or his wife's life by sudden interference, the Senator didn't use the alarm number."

"But he was killed anyway," I reminded him.

"If you had known the Senator you could see why."

"Okay, why?" I asked him.

Softly, the cop said: "If he was under a gun he'd stay there, but given one chance to jump the guy and he'd have jumped.

Apparently he thought he saw the chance and went for the guy after the safe was open and just wasn't fast enough."

"Or else surprised the guy when the safe was already opened."

"That's the way it still reads." He smiled indulgently. "We had those angles figured out too, you know. Now do you mind telling me where you fit in the picture?"

"Obscurely. A friend of mine was killed by a bullet from the same gun."

The two cops exchanged glances. The one beside me said, "We didn't hear about that part yet."

"Then you will shortly. You'll be speaking to a Captain Chambers from New York sometime soon."

"That doesn't explain you."

I shrugged. "The guy was a friend."

"Do you represent a legal investigation agency?"

"No longer," I told him. "There was a time when I did."

"Then maybe you ought to leave the investigation up to authorized personnel."

His meaning was obvious. If I hadn't been cleared by Laura Knapp and tentatively accepted as her friend, we'd be doing our talking in the local precinct house. It was a large Keep Off sign he was pointing out and he wasn't kidding about it. I made a motion with my hand to let him know I got the message, watched them tip their caps to Laura and walk out.

When they had pulled away Laura said, "Now what was *that* all about?" She stood balanced on one foot, her hands on her hips in an easy, yet provocative manner, frowning slightly as she tried to sift through the situation.

I said, "Didn't you know there was an alarm system built into that box?"

She thought for a moment, then threw a glance toward the

wall. "Yes, now that you mention it, but that safe hasn't been opened since—then, and I simply remember the police discussing an alarm system. I didn't know how it worked at all."

"Did your husband always keep that combination card in his desk?"

"No, the lawyer found it in his effects. I kept it in the desk just in case I ever wanted to use the safe again. However, that never happened." She paused, took a step toward me and laid a hand on my arm. "Is there some significance to all this?"

I shook my head. "I don't know. It was a thought and not a very new one. Like I told you, this was only a wild supposition at best. All I can say is that it might have established an M.O."

"What?"

"A technique of operation," I explained. "Your husband's killer really could have gone after those jewels. The other man he killed was operating—well, was a small-time jewel smuggler. There's a common point here."

For a moment I was far away in thought. I was back in the hospital with a dying man, remembering the reason why I wanted to find that link so badly. I could feel claws pulling at my insides and a fierce tension ready to burst apart like an overwound spring.

It was the steady insistence of her voice that dragged me back to the present, her "Mike—Mike—please, Mike."

When I looked down I saw my fingers biting into her forearm and the quiet pain in her eyes. I let her go and sucked air deep into my lungs. "Sorry," I said.

She rubbed her arm and smiled gently. "That's all right. You left me there for a minute, didn't you?"

I nodded.

"Can I help?"

"No. I don't think there's anything more here for me."

Once again, her hand touched me. "I don't like finalities like that, Mike."

It was my turn to grin my thanks. "I'm not all that sick. But I appreciate the thought."

"You're lonely, Mike. That's a sickness."

"Is it?"

"I've had it so long I can recognize it in others."

"You loved him very much, didn't you?"

Her eyes changed momentarily, seeming to shine a little brighter, then she replied, "As much as you loved her, Mike, whoever she was." Her fingers tightened slightly. "It's a big hurt. I eased mine by all the social activity I could crowd in a day."

"I used a bottle. It was a hell of a seven years."

"And now it's over. I can still see the signs, but I can tell it's over."

"It's over. A few days ago I was a drunken bum. I'm still a bum but at least I'm sober." I reached for my hat, feeling her hand fall away from my arm. She walked me to the door and held it open. When I stuck out my hand she took it, her fingers firm and cool inside mine. "Thanks for letting me take up your time, Mrs. Knapp."

"Please—make it Laura."

"Sure."

"And can you return the favor?"

"My pleasure."

"I told you I didn't like finalities. Will you come back one day?"

"I'm nothing to want back Laura."

"Maybe not to some. You're big. You have a strange face.

You're very hard to define. Still, I hope you'll come back, if only to tell me how you're making out."

I pulled her toward me gently. She didn't resist. Her head tilted up, she watched me, she kissed me as I kissed her, easily and warm in a manner that said hello rather than goodbye, and that one touch awakened things I thought had died long ago.

She stood there watching me as I drove away. She was still there when I turned out of sight at the roadway.

# CHAPTER 6

The quiet voice at Peerage Brokers told me I would be able to meet with Mr. Rickerby in twenty minutes at the Automat on Sixth and Forty-fifth. When I walked in he was off to the side, coffee in front of him, a patient little gray man who seemingly had all the time in the world.

I put down my own coffee, sat opposite him and said, "You have wild office hours."

He smiled meaninglessly, a studied, yet unconscious gesture that was for anyone watching. But there was no patience in his eyes. They seemed to live by themselves, being held in check by some obscure force. The late edition of the *News* was folded back to the center spread where a small photo gave an angular view of Old Dewey dead on the floor. The cops had blamed it on terrorists in the neighborhood.

Rickerby waited me out until I said, "I saw Laura Knapp today," then he nodded.

"We covered that angle pretty thoroughly."

"Did you know about the safe? It had an alarm system."

Once again, he nodded. "For your information, I'll tell you this. No connection has been made by any department between Senator Knapp's death and that of Richie. If you're assuming any state papers were in that safe you're wrong. Knapp had duplicate listings of every paper he had in his possession and we recovered everything."

"There were those paste jewels," I said.

"I know. I doubt if they establish anything, even in view of Richie's cover. It seems pretty definite that the gun was simply used in different jobs. As a matter of fact, Los Angeles has since come up with another murder in which the same gun was used. This was a year ago and the victim was a used-car dealer."

"So it wasn't a great idea."

"Nor original." He put down his coffee and stared at me across the table. "Nor am I interested in others besides Richie." He paused, let a few seconds pass, then added, "Have you decided to tell me what Richie really told you?"

"No."

"At least I won't have to call you a liar again."

"Knock it off."

Rickerby's little smile faded slowly and he shrugged. "Make your point then."

"Cole. I want to know about him."

"I told you once—"

"Okay, so it's secret. But now he's dead. You want a killer, I want a killer and if we don't get together someplace nobody gets nothing. You know?"

His fingers tightened on the cup, the nails showing the strain. He let a full minute pass before he came to a decision. He said, "Can you imagine how many persons are looking for this—killer?"

"I've been in the business too, friend."

"All right. I'll tell you this. I know nothing of Richie's last mission and I doubt if I'll find out. But this much I do know —he wasn't supposed to be back here at all. He disobeyed orders and would have been on the carpet had he not been killed."

I said, "Cole wasn't a novice."

And for the first time Rickerby lost his composure. His eyes looked puzzled, bewildered at this sudden failure of something he had built himself. "That's the strange part about it."

"Oh?"

"Richie was forty-five years old. He had been with one department or another since '41 and his record was perfect. He was a book man through and through and wouldn't bust a reg for any reason. He could adapt if the situation necessitated it, but it would conform to certain regulations." He stopped, looked across his cup at me and shook his head slowly. "I— just can't figure it."

"Something put him here."

This time his eyes went back to their bland expression. He had allowed himself those few moments and that was all. Now he was on the job again, the essence of many years of self-discipline, nearly emotionless to the casual observer. "I know," he said.

And he waited and watched for me to give him the one word that might send him out on a kill chase. I used my own coffee cup to cover what I thought, ran through the possibilities until I knew what I wanted and leaned back in my chair. "I need more time," I told him.

"Time isn't too important to me. Richie's dead. Time would be important only if it meant keeping him alive."

"It's important to me."

"How long do you need before telling me?"

"Telling what?"

"What Richie thought important enough to tell you."

I grinned at him. "A week, maybe."

His eyes were deadly now. Cold behind the glasses, each one a deliberate ultimatum. "One week, then. No more. Try to go past it and I'll show you tricks you never thought of when it comes to making a man miserable."

"I could turn up the killer in that time."

"You won't."

"There were times when I didn't do so bad."

"Long ago, Hammer. Now you're nothing. Just don't mess anything up. The only reason I'm not pushing you hard is because you couldn't take the gaff. If I thought you could, my approach would be different."

I stood up and pushed my chair back. "Thanks for the consideration. I appreciate it."

"No trouble at all."

"I'll call you."

"Sure. I'll be waiting."

The same soft rain had come in again, laying a blanket over the city. It was gentle and cool, not heavy enough yet to send the sidewalk crowd into the bars or running for cabs. It was a good rain to walk in if you weren't in a hurry, a good rain to think in.

So I walked to Forty-fourth and turned west toward Broadway, following a pattern from seven years ago I had forgotten, yet still existed. At the Blue Ribbon I went into the bar, had a stein of Prior's dark beer, said hello to a few familiar faces, then went back toward the glow of lights that marked the Great White Way.

The night man in the Hackard Building was new to me, a sleepy-looking old guy who seemed to just be waiting time out so he could leave life behind and get comfortably dead. He watched me sign the night book, hobbled after me into the elevator and let me out where I wanted without a comment, anxious for nothing more than to get back to his chair on the ground floor.

I found my key, turned the lock and opened the door.

*I was thinking of how funny it was that some things could transcend all others, how from the far reaches of your mind something would come, an immediate reaction to an immediate stimulus. I was thinking it and falling, knowing that I had been hit, but not hard, realizing that the cigarette smoke I smelled meant but one thing, that it wasn't mine, and if somebody were still there he had heard the elevator stop, had time to cut the lights and wait—and act. But time had not changed habit and my reaction was quicker than his act.*

Metal jarred off the back of my head and bit into my neck. Even as I fell I could sense him turn the gun around in his hand and heard the click of a hammer going back. I hit face down, totally limp, feeling the warm spill of blood seeping into my collar. The light went on and a toe touched me gently. Hands felt my pockets, but it was a professional touch and the gun was always there and I couldn't move without being suddenly dead, and I had been dead too long already to invite it again.

The blood saved me. The cut was just big and messy enough to make him decide it was useless to push things any further. The feet stepped back, the door opened, closed, and I heard the feet walk away.

I got to the desk as fast as I could, fumbled out the .45,

loaded it and wrenched the door open. The guy was gone. I knew he would be. He was long gone. Maybe I was lucky, because he was a real pro. He could have been standing there waiting, just in case, and his first shot would have gone right where he wanted it to. I looked at my hand and it was shaking too hard to put a bullet anywhere near a target. Besides, I had forgotten to jack a shell into the chamber. So some things did age with time, after all.

Except luck. I still had some of that left.

I walked around the office slowly, looking at the places that had been ravaged in a fine search for something. The shakedown had been fast, but again, in thoroughness, the marks of the complete professional were apparent. There had been no time or motion lost in the wrong direction and had I hidden anything of value that could have been tucked into an envelope, it would have been found. Two places I once considered original with me were torn open expertly, the second, and apparently last, showing a touch of annoyance.

Even Velda's desk had been torn open and the last thing she had written to me lay discarded on the floor, ground into a twisted sheet by a turning foot and all that was left was the heading.

It read, *Mike Darling*—and that was all I could see.

I grinned pointlessly, and this time I jacked a shell into the chamber and let the hammer ease down, then shoved the .45 into my belt on the left side. There was a sudden familiarity with the weight and the knowledge that here was life and death under my hand, a means of extermination, of quick vengeance, and of remembrance of the others who had gone down under that same gun.

*Mike Darling*—

Where was conscience when you saw those words?

Who *really* were the dead: those killing, or those already killed?

Then suddenly I felt like myself again and knew that the road back was going to be a long one alive or a short one dead and there wasn't even time enough to count the seconds.

Downstairs an old man would be dead in his chair because he alone could identify the person who came up here. The name in the night book would be fictitious and cleverly disguised if it had even been written there, and unless a motive were proffered, the old man's killing would be another one of those unexplainable things that happen to lonely people or alone people who stay too close to a terroristic world and are subject to the things that can happen by night.

I cleaned up the office so that no one could tell what had happened, washed my head and mopped up the blood spots on the floor, then went down the stairwell to the lobby.

The old man was lying dead in his seat, his neck broken neatly by a single blow. The night book was untouched, so his deadly visitor had only faked a signing. I tore the last page out, made sure I was unobserved and walked out the door. Someplace near Eighth Avenue I ripped up the page and fed the pieces into the gutter, the filthy trickle of rainwater swirling them into the sewer at the corner.

I waited until a cab came along showing its top light, whistled it over and told the driver where to take me. He hit the flag, pulled away from the curb and loafed his way down to the docks until he found the right place. He took his buck with another silent nod and left me there in front of Benny Joe Grissi's bar where you could get a program for all the trouble shows if you wanted one or a kill arranged or a broad made or anything at all you wanted just so long as you could get in the place.

But best of all, if there was anything you wanted to know about the stretch from the Battery to Grant's Tomb that constitutes New York's harbor facilities on either side of the river, or the associated unions from the NMU to the Teamsters, or wanted a name passed around the world, you could do it here. There was a place like it in London and Paris and Casablanca and Mexico City and Hong Kong and, if you looked hard enough, a smaller, more modified version would be in every city in the world. You just had to know where to look. And this was my town.

At the table near the door the two guys scrutinizing the customers made their polite sign which meant stay out. Then the little one got up rather tiredly and came over and said, "We're closing, buddy. No more customers."

When I didn't say anything he looked at my face and threw a finger toward his partner. The other guy was real big, his face suddenly ugly for having been disturbed. We got eye to eye and for a second he followed the plan and said, "No trouble, pal. We don't want trouble."

"Me either, kid."

"So blow."

I grinned at him, teeth all the way. "Scram."

My hand hit his chest as he swung and he went on his can swinging like an idiot. The little guy came in low, thinking he was pulling a good one, and I kicked his face all out of shape with one swipe and left him whimpering against the wall.

The whole bar had turned around by then, all talk ended. You could see the excitement in their faces, the way they all thought it was funny because somebody had nearly jumped the moat—but not quite. They were waiting to see the rest, like when the big guy got up off the floor and earned his keep and the big guy was looking forward to it too.

Out of the sudden quiet somebody said, "Ten to one on Sugar Boy," and, just as quietly, another one said, "You're on for five."

Again it was slow motion, the bar looking down at the funny little man at the end, wizened and dirty, but liking the odds, regardless of the company. Somebody laughed and said, "Pepper knows something."

"That I do," the funny little man said.

But by then the guy had eased up to his feet, his face showing how much he liked the whole deal, and just for the hell of it he let me have the first swing.

I didn't hurt him. He let me know it and came in like I knew he would and I was back in that old world since seven years ago, tasting floor dirt and gagging on it, feeling my guts fly apart and the wild wrenching of bones sagging under even greater bones and while they laughed and yelled at the bar, the guy slowly killed me until the little bit of light was there like I knew that would be too and I gave him the foot in the crotch and, as if the world had collapsed on his shoulders, he crumpled into a vomiting heap, eyes bulging, hating, waiting for the moment of incredible belly pain to pass, and when it did, reached for his belt and pulled out a foot-long knife and it was all over, all over for everybody because I reached too and no blade argues with that great big bastard of a .45 that makes the big boom so many times, and when he took one look at my face his eyes bulged again, said he was sorry, Mac, and to deal him out, I was the wrong guy, he knew it and don't let the boom go off. He was close for a second and knew it, then I put the gun back without letting the hammer down, stepped on the blade and broke it and told him to get up.

The funny little guy at the bar said, "That's fifty I got coming."

The one who made the bet said, "I told you Pepper knew something."

The big guy got up and said, "No offense, Mac, it's my job."

The owner came over and said, "Like in the old days, hey Mike?"

I said, "You ought to clue your help, Benny Joe."

"They need training."

"Not from me."

"You did lousy tonight. I thought Sugar Boy had you."

"Not when I got a rod."

"So who knew? All this time you go clean? I hear even Gary Moss cleaned you one night. You, even. Old, Mike."

Around the bar the eyes were staring at me curiously, wondering. "They don't know me, Benny Joe."

The little fat man shrugged. "Who would? You got skinny. Now how about taking off."

"Not you, Benny Joe," I said, "Don't tell me you're pushing too."

"Sure. Tough guys I got all the time. Old tough guys I don't want. They always got to prove something. So with you I call the cops and you go down. So blow, okay?"

I hadn't even been looking at him while he talked, but now I took the time to turn around and see the little fat man, a guy I had known for fifteen years, a guy who should have known better, a guy who was on the make since he began breathing but a guy who had to learn the hard way.

So I looked at him, slow, easy, and in his face I could see my own face and I said, "How would you like to get deballed, Benny Joe? You got nobody to stop me. You want to sing tenor for that crib you have keeping house for you?"

Benny Joe almost did what he started out to do. The game was supposed to have ended in the Old West, the making of a reputation by one man taking down a big man. He almost took the .25 out, then he went back to being Benny Joe again and he was caught up in something too big for him. I picked the .25 out of his fingers, emptied it, handed it back and told him, "Don't die without cause, Benny Joe."

The funny little guy at the bar with the new fifty said, "You don't remember me, do you, Mike?"

I shook my head.

"Ten, fifteen years ago—the fire at Carrigan's?"

Again, I shook my head.

"I was a newspaperman then. Bayliss Henry of the *Telegram*. Pepper, they call me now. You had that gunfight with Cortez Johnson and his crazy bunch from Red Hook."

"That was long ago, feller."

"Papers said it was your first case. You had an assignment from Aliet Insurance."

"Yeah," I told him, "I remember the fire. Now I remember you too. I never did get to say thanks. I go through the whole damn war without a scratch and get hit in a lousy heist and almost burn to death. So thanks!"

"My pleasure, Mike. You got me a scoop bonus."

"Now what's new?"

"Hell, after what guys like us saw, what else *could* be new?"

I drank my beer and didn't say anything.

Bayliss Henry grinned and asked, "What's with you?"

"What?" I tried to sound pretty bored.

It didn't take with him at all. "Come on, Big Mike. You've always been my favorite news story. Even when I don't write, I follow the columns. Now you just don't come busting in this place anymore without a reason. How long were you a bum, Mike?"

"Seven years."

"Seven years ago you never would have put a gun on Sugar Boy."

"I didn't need it then."

"Now you need it?"

"Now I need it," I repeated.

Bayliss took a quick glance around. "You got no ticket for that rod, Mike."

I laughed, and my face froze him. "Neither had Capone. Was he worried?"

The others had left us. The two guys were back at their table by the door watching the rain through the windows, the music from the overlighted juke strangely soft for a change, the conversation a subdued hum above it.

A rainy night can do things like that. It can change the entire course of events. It seems to rearrange time.

I said, "What?"

"Jeez, Mike, why don't you listen once? I've been talking for ten minutes."

"Sorry, kid."

"Okay, I know how it is. Just one thing."

"What?"

"When you gonna ask it?"

I looked at him and took a pull of the beer.

"The big question. The one you came here to ask somebody."

"You think too much, Bayliss, boy."

He made a wry face. "I can think more. You got a big one on your mind. This is a funny place, like a thieves' market.

Just anybody doesn't come here. It's a special place for special purposes. You want something, don't you?"

I thought a moment, then nodded. "What can you supply?"

His wrinkled face turned up to mine with a big smile. "Hell, man, for you just about anything."

"Know a man named Richie Cole?" I asked.

"Sure," he said, casually, "he had a room under mine. He was a good friend. A damn smuggler who was supposed to be small-time, but he was better than that because he had loot small smugglers never get to keep. Nice guy, though."

And that is how a leech line can start in New York if you know where to begin. The interweaving of events and personalities can lead you to a crossroad eventually where someone stands who, with one wave of a hand, can put you on the right trail—if he chooses to. But the interweaving is not a simple thing. It comes from years of mingling and mixing and kneading, and although the answer seems to be an almost casual thing, it really isn't at all.

I said, "He still live there?"

"Naw. He got another place. But he's no seaman."

"How do you know?"

Bayliss grunted and finished his beer. "Now what seaman will keep a furnished room while he's away?"

"How do you know this?"

The little guy shrugged and waved the bartender over. "Mike—I've been there. We spilled plenty of beer together." He handed me a fresh brew and picked up his own. "Richie Cole was a guy who made plenty of bucks, friend, and don't you forget it. You'd like him."

"Where's his place?"

Bayliss smiled broadly, "Come on, Mike. I said he was a friend. If he's in trouble I'm not going to make it worse."

"You can't," I told him. "Cole's dead."

Slowly, he put the beer down on the bar, turned and looked at me with his forehead wrinkling in a frown. "How?"

"Shot."

"You know something, Mike? I thought something like that would happen to him. It was in the cards."

"Like how?"

"I saw his guns. He had three of them in a trunk. Besides, he used me for a few things."

When I didn't answer, he grinned and shrugged.

"I'm an old-timer, Mike. Remember? Stuff I know hasn't been taught some of the fancy boys on the papers yet. I still got connections that get me a few bucks here and there. No trouble, either. I did so many favors that now it pays off and, believe me, this retirement pay business isn't what it looks like. So I pick up a few bucks with some well chosen directions or clever ideas. Now, Cole, I never did figure just what he was after, but he sure wanted some peculiar information."

"How peculiar?"

"Well, to a thinking man like me, it was peculiar because no smuggler the size he was supposed to be would want to know what he wanted."

"Smart," I told him. "Did you mention it to Cole?"

"Sure," Bayliss grinned, "but we're both old at what we were doing and could read eyes. I wouldn't pop on him."

"Suppose we go see his place."

"Suppose you tell me what he really was first."

Right then he was real roostery, a Bayliss Henry from years ago before retirement and top dog on the news beat, a wizened little guy, but one who wasn't going to budge an inch. I wasn't giving a damn for national security as the book describes it, at all, so I said, "Richie Cole was a Federal agent and he stayed alive long enough to ask me in on this."

He waited, watched me, then made a decisive shrug with his shoulders and pulled a cap down over his eyes. "You know what you could be getting into?" he asked me.

"I've been shot before," I told him.

"Yeah, but you haven't been dead before," he said.

The place was a brownstone building in Brooklyn that stood soldier-fashion shoulder to shoulder in place with fifty others, a row of facelike oblongs whose windows made dull, expressionless eyes of the throttled dead, the bloated tongue of a stone stoop hanging out of its gaping mouth.

The rest wasn't too hard, not when you're city-born and have nothing to lose anyway. Bayliss said the room was ground-floor rear so we simply got into the back through a cellarway three houses down, crossed the slatted fences that divided one pile of garbage from another until we reached the right window, then went in. Nobody saw us. If they did, they stayed quiet about it. That's the kind of place it was.

In a finger-thick beam of the pencil flash I picked out the sofa bed, an inexpensive contour chair, a dresser and a desk. For a furnished room it had a personal touch that fitted in with what Bayliss suggested. There were times when Richie Cole had desired a few more of the creature comforts than he could normally expect in a neighborhood like this.

There were a few clothes in the closet; a military raincoat, heavy dungaree jacket and rough-textured shirts. An old pair of hip boots and worn high shoes were in one corner. The dresser held changes of underwear and a few sports shirts, but nothing that would suggest that Cole was anything he didn't claim to be.

It was in the desk that I found the answer. To anyone else it would have meant nothing, but to me it was an answer. A terribly cold kind of answer that seemed to come at me like a cloud that could squeeze and tear until I thought I was going to burst wide open.

Cole had kept a simple, inexpensive photo album. There were the usual pictures of everything from the Focking Distillery to the San Francisco Bridge with Cole and girls and other guys and girls and just girls alone the way a thousand other seamen try to maintain a visual semblance of life.

But it was in the first few pages of the album that the fist hit me in the gut because there was Cole a long time ago sitting at a table in a bar with some RAF types in the background and a couple of American GI's from the 8th Air Force on one side and with Richie Cole was Velda.

Beautiful, raven hair in a long pageboy, her breasts swelling tautly against the sleeveless gown, threatening to free themselves. Her lips were wet with an almost deliberate gesture and her smile was purposely designing. One of the GIs was looking at her with obvious admiration.

Bayliss whispered, "What'd you say, Mike?"

I shook my head and flipped a page over. "Nothing."

She was there again, and a few pages further on. Once they were standing outside a pub, posing with a soldier and a WREN, and in another they stood beside the bombed-out ruins of a building with the same soldier, but a different girl.

There was nothing contrived about the album. Those pictures had been there a long time. So had the letters. Six of them dated in 1944, addressed to Cole at a P.O. box in New York, and although they were innocuous enough in content, showed a long-standing familiarity between the two of them. And there was Velda's name, the funny "V" she made, the green ink she always used and, although I hadn't even known her then, I was hating Cole so hard it hurt. I was glad he was dead but wished I could have killed him, then I took a fat breath, held it once and let it out slowly and it wasn't so bad any more.

I felt Bayliss touch my arm and he said, "You okay, Mike?"

"Sure."

"You find anything?"

"Nothing important."

He grunted under his breath. "You're full of crap."

"A speciality of mine," I agreed. "Let's get out of here."

"What about those guns? He had a trunk some place."

"We don't need them. Let's go."

"So you found something. You could satisfy my curiosity."

"Okay," I told him, "Cole and I had a mutual friend."

"It means something?"

"It might. Now move."

He went out first, then me, and I let the window down. We took the same route back, going over the fences where we had crossed earlier, me boosting Bayliss up then following him. I was on top of the last one when I felt the sudden jar of wood beside my hand, then a tug at my coat between my arm and rib cage and the instinct and reaction grabbed me again and I fell on top of Bayliss while I hauled the .45 out and, without even knowing where the silenced shots were coming from, I let loose with a tremendous blast of that fat musket that tore the night wide open with a rolling thunder that let the world know the pigeon was alive and had teeth.

From a distance came a clattering of cans, of feet, then windows slammed open and voices started yelling and the two of us got out fast. We were following the same path of the one who had followed us, but his start was too great. Taillights were already diminishing down the street and in another few minutes a prowl car would be turning the corner.

We didn't wait for it.

Six blocks over we picked up a cab, drove to Ed Dailey's bar and got out. I didn't have to explain a thing to Bayliss. He had been through it all too often before. He was shaking all over and couldn't seem to stop swallowing. He had two double ryes before he looked at me with a peculiar expression and said softly, "Jeez, I'll never learn to keep my mouth shut."

Peerage Brokers could have been anything. The desks and chairs and filing cabinets and typewriters represented nothing, yet represented everything. Only the gray man in the glasses sitting alone in the corner drinking coffee represented something.

Art Rickerby said, "Now?" and I knew what he meant.

I shook my head. He looked at me silently a moment, then sipped at the coffee container again. He knew how to wait, this one. He wasn't in a hurry now, not rushing to prevent something. He was simply waiting for a moment of vengeance because the thing was done and sooner or later time would be on his side.

I said, "Did you know Richie pretty well?"

"I think so."

"Did he have a social life?"

For a moment his face clouded over, then inquisitiveness replaced anger and he put the coffee container down for a reason, to turn his head away. "You'd better explain."

"Like girls," I said.

When he turned back he was expressionless again. "Richie

had been married," he told me. "In 1949 his wife died of cancer."

"Oh? How long did he know her?"

"They grew up together."

"Children?"

"No. Both Richie and Ann knew about the cancer. They married after the war anyway but didn't want to leave any children a difficult burden."

"How about before that?"

"I understood they were both pretty true to each other."

"Even during the war?"

Again there was silent questioning in his eyes. "What are you getting at, Mike?"

"What was Richie during the war?"

The thought went through many channels before it was properly classified. Art said, "A minor O.S.I. agent. He was a Captain then based in England. With mutual understanding, I never asked, nor did he offer, the kind of work he did."

"Let's get back to the girls."

"He was no virgin, if that's what you mean."

He knew he reached me with that one but didn't know why. I could feel myself tighten up and had to relax deliberately before I could speak to him again.

"Who did he go with when he was here? When he wasn't on a job."

Rickerby frowned and touched his glasses with an impatient gesture. "There were—several girls. I really never inquired. After Ann's death—well, it was none of my business, really."

"But you knew them?"

He nodded, watching me closely. Once more he thought quickly, then decided. "There was Greta King, a stewardess with American Airlines that he would see occasionally. And there was Pat Bender over at the Craig House. She's a manicurist there and they had been friends for years. Her brother, Lester, served with Richie but was killed just before the war ended."

"It doesn't sound like he had much fun."

"He didn't look for fun. Ann's dying took that out of him. All he wanted was an assignment that would keep him busy. In fact, he rarely ever got to see Alex Bird, and if—"

"Who's he?" I interrupted.

"Alex, Lester and Richie were part of a team throughout the war. They were great friends in addition to being experts in their work. Lester got killed, Alex bought a chicken farm in Marlboro, New York, and Richie stayed in the service. When Alex went civilian he and Richie sort of lost communication. You know the code in this work—no friends, no relatives—it's a lonely life."

When he paused I said, "That's all?"

Once again, he fiddled with his glasses, a small flicker of annoyance showing in his eyes. "No. There was someone else he used to see on occasions. Not often, but he used to look forward to the visit."

My voice didn't sound right when I asked, "Serious?"

"I—don't think so. It didn't happen often enough and generally it was just a supper engagement. It was an old friend, I think."

"You couldn't recall the name?"

"It was never mentioned. I never pried into his business."

"Maybe it's about time."

Rickerby nodded sagely. "It's about time for you to tell me a few things too."

"I can't tell you what I don't know."

"True." He looked at me sharply and waited.

"If the information isn't classified, find out what he really did during the war, who he worked with and who he knew."

For several seconds he ran the thought through his mental file, then: "You think it goes back that far?"

"Maybe." I wrote my number down on a memo pad, ripped off the page and handed it to him. "My office. I'll be using it from now on."

He looked at it, memorized it and threw it down. I grinned, told him so-long and left.

Over in the west Forties I got a room in a small hotel, got a box, paper and heavy cord from the desk clerk, wrapped my .45 up, addressed it to myself at the office with a buck's worth of stamps and dropped it in the outgoing mail, then sacked out until it was almost noon in a big new tomorrow.

Maybe I still had that look because they thought I was another cop. Nobody wanted to talk, and if they had, there would have been little they could have said. One garrulous old broad said she saw a couple of men in the back court and later a third. No, she didn't know what they were up to and didn't care as long as they weren't in *her* yard. She heard the shot and would show me the place, only she didn't know why I couldn't work with the rest of the cops instead of bothering everybody all over again.

I agreed with her, thanked her and let her take me to where I almost had it going over the fence. When she left, wheezing and muttering, I found where the bullet had torn through the slats and jumped the fence, and dug it out of the two-by-four frame in the section on the other side of the yard. There was still enough of it to show the rifling marks, so I dropped it in my pocket and went back to the street.

Two blocks away I waved down a cab and got in. Then I felt the seven years, and the first time back I had to play it hard and almost stupid enough to get killed. There was a time when I never would have missed with the .45, but now I was happy to make a noise with it big enough to start somebody running. For a minute I felt skinny and shrunken inside the suit and cursed silently to myself.

*If she was alive, I was going to have to do better than I was doing now. Time, damn it. There wasn't any. It was like when the guy in the porkpie hat had her strung from the rafters and the whip in his hand had stripped her naked flesh with bright red welts, the force of each lash stroke making her spin so that the lush beauty of her body and the deep-space blackness of her hair and the wide sweep of her breasts made an obscene kaleidoscope and then I shot his arm off with the tommy gun and it dropped with a wet thud in the puddle of clothes around her feet like a pagan sacrifice and while he was dying I killed the rest of them, all of them, twenty of them, wasn't it? And they called me those terrible names, the judge and the jury did.*

Damn. Enough.

# CHAPTER 7

The body was gone, but the police weren't. The two detectives interrogating Nat beside the elevators were patiently listening to everything he said, scanning the night book one held open. I walked over, nodded and said, "Morning, Nat."

Nat's eyes gave me a half-scared, half-surprised look followed by a shrug that meant it was all out of his hands.

"Hello, Mike." He turned to the cop with the night book. "This is Mr. Hammer. In 808."

"Oh?" The cop made me in two seconds. "Mike Hammer. Didn't think you were still around."

"I just got back."

His eyes went up and down, then steadied on my face. He could read all the signs, every one of them. "Yeah," he said sarcastically. "Were you here last night?"

"Not me, buddy. I was out on the town with a friend."

The pencil came into his hand automatically. "Would you like to—"

"No trouble. Bayliss Henry, an old reporter. I think he lives—"

He put the pencil away with a bored air. "I know where Bayliss lives."

"Good," I said. "What's the kick here?"

Before the pair could tell him to shut up, Nat blurted, "Mike—it was old Morris Fleming. He got killed."

I played it square as I could. "Morris Fleming?"

"Night man, Mike. He started working here after—you left."

The cop waved him down. "Somebody broke his neck."

"What for?"

He held up the book. Ordinarily he never would have answered, but I had been around too long in the same business. "He could have been identified. He wanted in the easy way so he signed the book, killed the old man later and ripped the page out when he left." He let me think it over and added, "Got it figured yet?"

"You don't kill for fun. Who's dead upstairs?"

Both of them threw a look back and forth and stared at me again. "Clever boy."

"Well?"

"No bodies. No reported robberies. No signs of forcible entry. You're one of the last ones in. Maybe you'd better check your office."

"I'll do that," I told him.

But I didn't have to bother. My office had already been checked. Again. The door was open, the furniture pushed around, and in my chair behind the desk was Pat, his face cold and demanding, his hands playing with the box of .45 shells he had found in the niche in the desk.

Facing him with her back to me, the light from the window

making a silvery halo around the yellow of her hair was Laura Knapp.

I said, "Having fun?"

Laura turned quickly, saw me and a smile made her mouth beautiful. "Mike!"

"Now how did you get here?"

She took my hand, held it tightly a moment with a grin of pleasure and let me perch on the end of the desk. "Captain Chambers asked me to." She turned and smiled at Pat, but the smile was lost on him. "He came to see me not long after you did."

"I told you that would happen."

"It seems that since you showed some interest in me he did too, so we just reviewed all—the details of what happened— to Leo." Her smile faded then, her eyes seeming to reflect the hurt she felt.

"What's the matter, Pat, don't you keep files any more?"

"Shut up."

"The manual says to be nice to the public." I reached over and picked up the box of .45's. "Good thing you didn't find the gun."

"You're damn right. You'd be up on a Sullivan charge right now."

"How'd you get in, Pat?"

"It wasn't too hard. I know the same tricks you do. And don't get snotty." He flipped a paper out of his pocket and tossed it on the desk. "A warrant, mister. When I heard there was a kill in this particular building I took this out first thing."

I laughed at the rage in his face and rubbed it in a little. "Find what you were looking for?"

Slowly, he got up and walked around the desk, and though

he stood there watching me it was to Laura that he spoke. "If you don't mind, Mrs. Knapp, wait out in the other room. And close the door."

She looked at him, puzzled, so I nodded to her and she stood up with a worried frown creasing her eyes and walked out. The door made a tiny *snick* as it closed and we had the place all to ourselves. Pat's face was still streaked with anger, but there were other things in his eyes this time. "I'm fed up, Mike. You'd just better talk."

"And if I don't?"

The coldness took all the anger away from his face now. "All right, I'll tell you the alternative. You're trying to do something. Time is running against you. Don't give me any crap because I know you better than you know yourself. This isn't the first time something like this cropped up. You pull your connections on me, you try to play it smart—okay—I'll make time run out on you. I'll use every damn regulation I know to harass you to death. I'll keep a tail on you all day, and every time you spit I'll have your ass hauled into the office. I'll hold you on every pretext possible and if it comes to doing a little high-class framing I can do that too."

Pat wasn't lying. Like he knew me, I knew him. He was real ready to do everything he said and time was one thing I didn't have enough of. I got up and walked around the desk to my chair and sat down again. I pulled out the desk drawer, stowed the .45's back in the niche without trying to be smug about what I did with the gun. Then I sat there groping back into seven years, knowing that instinct went only so far, realizing that there was no time to relearn and that every line had to be straight across the corners.

I said, "Okay, Pat. Anything you want. But first a favor."

"No favors."

"It's not exactly a favor. It's an or else." I felt my face go as cold as his was. "Whether you like it or not I'm ready to take my chances."

He didn't answer. He couldn't. He was ready to throw his fist at my face again and would have, only he was too far away. Little by little he relaxed until he could speak, then all those years of being a cop took over and he shrugged, but he wasn't fooling me any. "What is it?"

"Nothing I couldn't do if I had the time. It's all a matter of public record."

He glanced at me shrewdly and waited.

"Look up Velda's P.I. license."

His jaw dropped open stupidly for a brief second, then snapped shut and his eyes followed suit. He stood there, knuckles white as they gripped the edge of the desk and he gradually leaned forward so that when he swung he wouldn't be out of reach this time.

"What kind of crazy stunt are you pulling?" His voice was almost hoarse.

I shook my head. "The New York State law says that you must have served three or more years in an accredited police agency, city, state, or federal in a rating of sergeant or higher to get a Private Investigator's license. It isn't easy to get and takes a lot of background work."

Quietly, Pat said, "She worked for you. Why didn't you ask?"

"One of the funny things in life. Her ticket was good enough for me at first. Later it never occurred to me to ask. I was always a guy concerned with the present anyway and you damn well know it."

"You bastard. What are you trying to pull?"

"Yes or no, Pat."

His grin had no humor in it. Little cords in his neck stood out against his collar and the pale blue of his eyes was deadly. "No," he said. "You're a wise guy, punk. Don't pull your tangents on me. You got this big feeling inside you that you're coming back at me for slapping you around. You're using *her* now as a pretty little oblique switch—but, mister, you're pulling your crap on the wrong soldier. You've just about had it, boy."

Before he could swing I leaned back in my chair with as much insolence as I could and reached in my pocket for the slug I had dug out of the fence. It was a first-class gamble, but not quite a bluff. I had the odds going for me and if I came up short, I'd still have a few hours ahead of him.

I reached out and laid the splashed-out bit of metal on the desk. "Don't *punk* me, man. Tell ballistics to go after that and tell me what I want and I'll tell you where that came from."

Pat picked it up, his mind putting ideas together, trying to make one thing fit another. It was hard to tell what he was thinking, but one thing took precedence over all others. He was a cop. First-rate. He wanted a killer. He had to play his own odds too.

"All right," he told me, "I can't take any chances. I don't get your point, but if it's a phony, you've had it."

I shrugged. "When will you know about the license?"

"It won't take long."

"I'll call you," I said.

He straightened up and stared out the window over my head, still half in thought. Absently, he rubbed the back of his neck. "You do that," he told me. He turned away, putting his hat on, then reached for the door.

I stopped him. "Pat—"

"What?"

"Tell me something."

His eyes squinted at my tone. I think he knew what I was going to ask.

"Did you love Velda too?"

Only his eyes gave the answer, then he opened the door and left.

"May I come in?"

"Oh, Laura—please."

"Was there—trouble?"

"Nothing special." She came back to the desk and sat down in the client's chair, her face curious. "Why?"

With a graceful motion, she crossed her legs and brushed her skirt down over her kness. "Well, when Captain Chambers was with me—well, he spoke constantly of you. It was as if you were right in the middle of everything." She paused, turning her head toward me. "He hates you, doesn't he?"

I nodded. "But we were friends once."

Very slowly, her eyebrows arched. "Aren't most friendships only temporary at best?"

"That's being pretty cynical."

"No—only realistic. There are childhood friendships. Later those friends from school, even to the point of nearly blood brotherhood fraternities, but how long do they last? Are your Army or Navy friends still your friends or have you forgotten their names?"

I made a motion with my shoulders.

"Then your friends are only those you have at the moment. Either you outgrow them or something turns friendship into hatred."

"It's a lousy system," I said.

"But there it is, nevertheless. In 1945 Germany and Japan

were our enemies and Russia and the rest our allies. Now our former enemies are our best friends and the former allies the direct enemies."

She was so suddenly serious I had to laugh at her. "Beautiful blondes aren't generally philosophers."

But her eyes didn't laugh back. "Mike—it really isn't that funny. When Leo was—alive, I attended to all his affairs in Washington. I still carry on, more or less. It's something he would have wanted me to do. I *know* how people who run the world think. I served cocktails to people making decisions that rocked the earth. I saw wars start over a drink and the friendship of generations between nations wiped out because one stupid, pompous political appointee wanted to do things his way. Oh, don't worry, I *know* about friendships."

"So this one went sour."

"It hurts you, doesn't it?"

"I guess so. It never should have happened that way."

"Oh?" For a few moments she studied me, then she knew. "The woman—we talked about—you both loved her?"

"I thought only I did." She sat there quietly then, letting me finish. "We both thought she was dead. He still thinks so and blames me for what happened."

"Is she, Mike?"

"I don't know. It's all very strange, but if there is even the most remote possibility that some peculiar thing happened seven years ago and that she is still alive somewhere, I want to know about it."

"And Captain Chambers?"

"He could never have loved her as I did. She was mine."

"If—you are wrong—and she is dead, maybe it would be better not to know."

My face was grinning again. Not me, just the face part. I

stared at the wall and grinned idiotically. "If she is alive, I'll
find her. If she is dead, I'll find who killed her. Then slowly,
real slowly, I'll take him apart, inch by inch, joint by joint,
until dying will be the best thing left for him."

I didn't realize that I was almost out of the chair, every
muscle twisted into a monstrous spasm of murder. Then I felt
her hands pulling me back and I let go and sat still until the
hate seeped out of me.

"Thanks."

"I know what you feel like, Mike."

"You do?"

"Yes." Her hand ran down the side of my face, the fingers
tracing a warm path along my jaw. "It's the way I felt about
Leo. He was a great man, then suddenly for no reason at all he
was dead."

"I'm sorry, Laura."

"But it's not over for me anymore, either."

I swung around in the chair and looked up at her. She was
magnificent then, a study in symmetry, each curve of her wonderful body coursing into another, her face showing the full
beauty of maturity, her eyes and mouth rich with color.

She reached out her hand and I stood up, tilted her chin up
with my fingers and held her that way. "You're thinking,
kitten."

"With you I have to."

"Why?"

"Because somehow you know Leo's death is part of her, and
I feel the same way you do. Whoever killed Leo is going to die
too."

I let go of her face, put my hands on her shoulders and
pulled her close to me. "If he's the one I want I'll kill him for
you, kid."

"No, Mike. I'll do it myself." And her voice was as cold and as full of purpose as my own when she said it. Then she added, "You just find that one for me."

"You're asking a lot, girl."

"Am I? After you left I found out all about you. It didn't take long. It was very fascinating information, but nothing I didn't know the first minute I saw you."

"That was me of a long time ago. I've been seven years drunk and I'm just over the bum stage now. Maybe I could drop back real easy. I don't know."

"I know."

"Nobody knows. Besides, I'm not authorized to pursue investigations."

"That doesn't seem to stop you."

A grin started to etch my face again. "You're getting to a point, kid."

She laughed gently, a full, quiet laugh. Once again her hand came up to my face. "Then I'll help you find your woman, Mike, if you'll find who killed Leo."

"Laura—"

"When Leo died the investigation was simply routine. They were more concerned about the political repercussions than in locating his killer. *They* forgot about that one, but I haven't. I thought I had, but I really hadn't. Nobody would look for me—they all promised and turned in reports, but they never really cared about finding that one. But you do, Mike, and somehow I know you will. Oh, you have no license and no authority, but I have money and it will put many things at your disposal. You take it. You find your woman, and while you're doing it, or before, or after, whatever you like, you find the one I want. Tomorrow I'll send you five thousand dollars in cash. No questions. No paperwork. No reports. Even if nothing comes of it there is no obligation on you."

Under my hands she was trembling. It didn't show on her face, but her shoulders quivered with tension. "You loved him very much," I stated.

She nodded. "As you loved her."

We were too close then, both of us feeling the jarring impact of new and sudden emotions. My hands were things of their own, leaving her shoulders to slide down to her waist, then reaching behind her to bring her body close to mine until it was touching, then pressing until a fusion was almost reached.

She had to gasp to breathe, and fingers that were light on my face were suddenly as fierce and demanding as my own as she brought me down to meet her mouth and the scalding touch of her tongue that worked serpentlike in a passionate orgy that screamed of release after so long a time.

She pulled away, her breasts moving spasmodically against my chest. Her eyes were wet and shimmering with a glow of disbelief that it could ever happen again and she said softly: "You, Mike—I want a man. It could never be anybody but—a man." She turned her eyes on mine, pleading. "Please, Mike."

"You never have to say please," I told her, then I kissed her again and we found our place in time and in distance, lost people who didn't have to hurry or be cautious and who could enjoy the sensual discomfort of a cold leather couch on naked skin and take pleasure in the whispering of clothing and relish the tiny sounds of a bursting seam; two whose appetites had been stifled for much too long, yet who loved the food of flesh enough not to rush through the first offering, but to taste and become filled course by course until in an explosion of delight, the grand finale of the whole table, was served and partaken.

We were gourmets, the body satisfied, but the mind knowing that it was only a momentary filling and that there would be other meals, each different, each more succulent than the last in a never-ending progression of enjoyment. The banquet was over so we kissed and smiled at each other, neither having been the guest, but rather, one the host, the other the hostess, both having the same startling thought of *where was the past now? Could the present possibly be more important?*

When she was ready I said, "Let's get you home now, Laura."

"Must I?"

"You must."

"I could stay in town."

"If you did it would be a distraction I can't afford."

"But I live a hundred and ten miles from your city."

"That's only two hours up the Thruway and over the hills."

She grinned at me. "Will you come?"

I grinned back. "Naturally."

I picked up my hat and guided her to the outer office. For a single, terrible moment I felt a wash of shame drench me with guilt. There on the floor where it had been squashed underfoot by the one who killed old Morris Fleming and who had taken a shot at me was the letter from Velda that began, *"Mike Darling—"*

We sat at the corner of the bar in P. J. Moriarty's steak and chop house on Sixth and Fifty-second and across the angle his eyes were terrible little beads, magnified by the lenses of his glasses. John, the Irish bartender, brought us each a cold Blue

Ribbon, leaving without a word because he could feel the thing that existed there.

Art Rickerby said, "How far do you think you can go?"

"All the way," I said.

"Not with me."

"Then alone."

He poured the beer and drank it as if it were water and he was thirsty, yet in a perfunctory manner that made you realize he wasn't a drinker at all, but simply doing a job, something he had to do.

When he finished he put the glass down and stared at me blandly. "You don't realize just how alone you really are."

"I know. Now do we talk?"

"Do you?"

"You gave me a week, buddy."

"Uh-huh." He poured the rest of the bottle into the glass and made a pattern with the wet bottom on the bar. When he looked up he said, "I may take it back."

I shrugged. "So you found something out."

"I did. About you too."

"Go ahead."

From overhead, the light bounced from his glasses so I couldn't see what was happening to his eyes. He said, "Richie was a little bigger than I thought during the war. He was quite important. Quite."

"At his age?"

"He was your age, Mike. And during a war age can be as much of a disguise as a deciding factor."

"Get to it."

"My pleasure." He paused, looked at me and threw the rest of the beer down. "He commanded the Seventeen Group."

When I didn't give him the reaction he looked for he asked me, "Did you ever hear of Butterfly Two?"

I covered the frown that pulled at my forehead by finishing my own beer and waving to John for another. "I heard of it. I don't know the details. Something to do with the German system of total espionage. They had people working for them ever since the First World War."

There was something like respect in his eyes now. "It's amazing that you even heard of it."

"I have friends in amazing places."

"Yes, you had."

As slowly as I could I put the glass down. "What's that supposed to mean?"

And then his eyes came up, fastened on my face so as not to lose sight of even the slightest expression and he said, "It was your girl, the one called Velda, that he saw on the few occasions he was home. She was something left over from the war."

The glass broke in my hand and I felt a warm surge of blood spill into my hand. I took the towel John offered me and held it until the bleeding stopped. I said, "Go on."

Art smiled. It was the wrong kind of smile, with a gruesome quality that didn't match his face. "He last saw her in Paris just before the war ended and at that time he was working on Butterfly Two."

I gave the towel back to John and pressed on the Band-Aid he gave me.

"Gerald Erlich was the target then. At the time his name wasn't known except to Richie—and the enemy. Does it make sense now?"

"No." My guts were starting to turn upside down. I reached for the beer again, but it was too much. I couldn't do anything except listen.

"Erlich was the head of an espionage ring that had been instituted in 1920. Those agents went into every land in the world to get ready for the next war and even raised their children to be agents. Do you think World War II was simply the result of a political turnover?"

"Politics are not my speciality."

"Well, it wasn't. There was another group. It wasn't part of the German General Staff's machinations either. They utilized this group and so did Hitler—or better still, let's say vice versa."

I shook my head, not getting it at all.

"It was a world conquest scheme. It incorporated some of the greatest military and corrupt minds this world has ever known and is using global wars and brush-fire wars to its own advantage until one day when everything is ready *they* can take over the world for their own."

"You're nuts!"

"I am?" he said softly. "How many powers were involved in 1918?"

"All but a few."

"That's right. And in 1945?"

"All of them were—"

"Not quite. I mean, who were the major powers?"

"We were. England, Germany, Russia, Japan—"

"That narrows it down a bit, doesn't it? And now, right now, how many *major powers* are there really?"

What he was getting at was almost inconceivable. "Two. Ourselves and the Reds."

"Ah—now we're getting to the point. And they hold most of the world's land and inhabitants in their hands. They're the antagonists. They're the ones pushing and we're the ones holding."

"Damn it, Rickerby—"

"Easy, friend. Just think a little bit."

"Ah, think my ass. What the hell are you getting to? Velda's part of that deal? You have visions, man, you got the big bug! Damn, I can get better than that from them at a jag dance in the Village. Even the bearded idiots make more sense."

His mouth didn't smile. It twisted. "Your tense is unusual. You spoke as if she were alive."

I let it go. I deliberately played the beer into the glass until the head was foaming over the rim, then drank it off with a grimace of pleasure and put the glass down.

When I was ready I said, "So now the Reds are going to take over the world. They'll bury us. Well, maybe they will, buddy, but there won't be enough Reds around to start re-populating again, that's for sure."

"I didn't say that," Art told me.

His manner had changed again. I threw him an annoyed look and reached for the beer.

"I think the world conquest parties changed hands. The conqueror has been conquered. The Reds have located and are using this vast fund of information, this great organization we call Butterfly Two, and that's why the free world is on the defensive."

John asked me if I wanted another Blue Ribbon and I said yes. He brought two, poured them, put the bar check in the register and returned it with a nod. When he had gone I half swung around, no longer so filled with a crazy fury that I couldn't speak. I said, "You're lucky, Rickerby. I didn't know whether to belt you in the mouth or listen."

"You're fortunate you listened."

"Then finish it. You think Velda's part of Butterfly Two."

Everything, yet nothing, was in his shrug. "I didn't ask that many questions. I didn't care. All I want is Richie's killer."

"That doesn't answer my question. What do you *think?*"

Once again he shrugged. "It looks like she was," he told me.

So I thought my way through it and let the line cut all the corners off because there wasn't that much time and I asked him, "What was Richie working on when he was killed?"

Somehow, he knew I was going to ask that one and shook his head sadly. "Not that at all. His current job had to do with illegal gold shipments."

"You're sure."

"I'm sure."

"Then what about this Erlich?"

Noncommittally, Art shrugged. "Dead or disappeared. Swallowed up in the aftermath of war. Nobody knows."

"Somebody does," I reminded him. "The Big Agency boys don't give up their targets that easily. Not if the target is so big it makes a lifetime speciality of espionage."

He reflected a moment and nodded. "Quite possible. However, it's more than likely Erlich is dead at this point. He'd be in his sixties now if he escaped the general roundup of agents after the war. When the underground organizations of Europe were free of restraint they didn't wait on public trials. They knew who their targets were and how to find them. You'd be surprised at just how many people simply disappeared, big people and little people, agents and collaborators both. Many a person we wanted badly went into a garbage pit somewhere."

"Is that an official attitude?"

"Don't be silly. We don't reflect on attitudes to civilians. Occasionally it becomes necessary—"

"Now, for instance," I interrupted.

"Yes, like now. And believe me, they're better off knowing nothing."

Through the glasses his eyes tried to read me, then lost whatever expression they had. There was a touch of contempt and disgust in the way he sat there, examining me like a specimen under glass, then the last part of my line cut across the last corner and I asked him casually, "Who's The Dragon?"

Art Rickerby was good. Damn, but he was good. It was as if I had asked what time it was and he had no watch. But he just wasn't that good. I saw all the little things happen to him that nobody else would have noticed and watched them grow and grow until he could contain them no longer and had to sluff them off with an aside remark. So with an insipid look that didn't become him at all he said, "Who?"

"Or is it whom? Art?"

I had him where the hair was short and he knew it. He had given me all the big talk but this one was one too big. It was even bigger than he was and he didn't quite know how to handle it. You could say this about him: he was a book man. He put all the facts through the machine in his head and took the risk alone. He couldn't tell what I knew, yet he couldn't tell what I didn't know. Neither could he take a chance on having me clam up.

Art Rickerby was strictly a statesman. A federal agent, true, a cop, a dedicated servant of the people, but foremost he was a statesman. He was dealing with big security now and all the wraps were off. We were in a bar drinking beer and somehow the world was at our feet. What was it Laura had said— *"I saw wars start over a drink—"* and now it was almost the same thing right here.

"You didn't answer me," I prodded.

He put his glass down, and for the first time his hand wasn't steady. "How did you know about that?"

"Tell me, is it a big secret?"

His voice had an edge to it. *"Top secret."*

"Well, whatta you know."

"Hammer—"

"Nuts, Rickerby. You tell me."

Time was on my side now. I could afford a little bit of it. He couldn't. He was going to have to get to a phone to let someone bigger than he was know that The Dragon wasn't a secret any longer. He flipped the mental coin and that someone lost. He turned slowly and took his glasses off, wiping them on a handkerchief. They were all fogged up. "The Dragon is a team."

"So is Rutgers."

The joke didn't go across. Ignoring it, he said, "It's a code name for an execution team. There are two parts, Tooth and Nail."

I turned the glass around in my hand, staring at it, waiting. I asked, "Commies?"

"Yes." His reluctance was almost tangible. He finally said, "I can name persons throughout the world in critical positions in government who have died lately, some violently, some of natural causes apparently. You would probably recognize their names."

"I doubt it. I've been out of circulation for seven years."

He put the glasses on again and looked at the backbar. "I wonder," he mused to himself.

"The Dragon, Rickerby, if it were so important, how come the name never appeared. With a name like that it was bound to show."

"Hell," he said, "it was *our* code name, not theirs." His

hands made an innocuous gesture, then folded together. "And now that you know something no one outside our agency knows, perhaps you'll tell *me* a little something about The Dragon."

"Sure," I said, and I watched his face closely. "The Dragon killed Richie."

Nothing showed.

"Now The Dragon is trying to kill Velda."

Still nothing showed, but he said calmly, "How do you know?"

"Richie told me. That's what he told me before he died. So she couldn't be tied up with the other side, could she?"

Unexpectedly, he smiled, tight and deadly and you really couldn't tell what he was thinking. "You never know," Art answered. "When their own kind slip from grace, they too become targets. We have such in our records. It isn't even unusual."

"You bastard."

"You know too much, Mr. Hammer. You might become a target yourself."

"I wouldn't be surprised."

He took a bill from his pocket and put it on the bar. John took it, totaled up the check and hit the register. When he gave the change back Art said, "Thanks for being so candid. Thank you for The Dragon."

"You leaving it like that?"

"I think that's it, don't you?"

"Sucker," I said.

He stopped halfway off his stool.

"You don't think I'd be that stupid, do you? Even after seven years I wouldn't be that much of a joker."

For a minute he was the placid little gray man I had first

met, then almost sorrowfully he nodded and said, "I'm losing my insight. I thought I had it all. What else do you know?"

I took a long pull of the Blue Ribbon and finished the glass. When I put it down I said to him, "Richie told me something else that could put his killer in front of a gun."

"And just what is it you want for this piece of information?"

"Not much," I grinned. "Just an official capacity in some department or another so that I can carry a gun."

"Like in the old days," he said.

"Like in the old days," I repeated.

# CHAPTER 8

Hy Gardner was taping a show and I didn't get to see him until it was over. We had a whole empty studio to ourselves, the guest chairs to relax in and for a change a quiet that was foreign to New York.

When he lit his cigar and had a comfortable wreath of smoke over his head he said, "How's things going, Mike?"

"Looking up. Why, what have you heard?"

"A little here and there," he shrugged. "You've been seen around." Then he laughed with the cigar in his teeth and put his feet up on the coffee table prop. "I heard about the business down in Benny Joe Grissi's place. You sure snapped back in a hurry."

"Hell, I don't have time to train. Who put you on the bit?"

"Old Bayliss Henry still has his traditional afternoon drink at Ted's with the rest of us. He knew we were pretty good friends."

"What did he tell you?"

Hy grinned again. "Only about the fight. He knew that

would get around. I'd sooner hear the rest from you anyway."

"Sure."

"Should I tape notes?"

"Not yet. It's not that big yet, but you can do something for me."

"Just say it."

"How are your overseas connections?"

Hy took the cigar out, studied it and knocked off the ash. "I figure the next question is going to be a beauty."

"It is."

"Okay," he nodded. "In this business you have to have friends. Reporters aren't amateurs, they have sources of information and almost as many ways of getting what they want as Interpol has."

"Can you code a request to your friends and get an answer back the same way?"

After a moment he nodded.

"Swell. Then find out what anybody knows about The Dragon."

The cigar went back, he dragged on it slowly and let out a thin stream of smoke.

I said, "That's a code name too. Dragon is an execution team. Our side gave it the tag and it's a top secret bit, but that kind of stew is generally the easiest to stir once you take the lid off the kettle."

"You don't play around, do you?"

"I told you, I haven't got time."

"Damn, Mike, you're really sticking it out, aren't you?"

"You'll get the story."

"I hope you're alive long enough to give it to me. The kind of game you're playing has put a lot of good men down for keeps."

"I'm not exactly a patsy," I said.

"You're not the same Mike Hammer you were either, friend."

"When can you get the information off?" I asked him.

"Like now," he told me.

There was a pay phone in the corridor outside. The request went through Bell's dial system to the right party and the relay was assured. The answer would come into Hy's office at the paper coded within a regular news transmission and the favor was expected to be returned when needed.

Hy hung up and turned around. "Now what?"

"Let's eat, then take a run down to the office of a cop who used to be a friend."

I knocked and he said to come in and when he saw who it was his face steeled into an expression that was so noncommittal it was pure betrayal. Behind it was all the resentment and animosity he had let spew out earlier, but this time it was under control.

Dr. Larry Snyder was sprawled out in a wooden desk chair left over from the gaslight era, a surprised smile touching the corner of his mouth as he nodded to me.

I said, "Hy Gardner, Dr. Larry Snyder. I think you know Pat Chambers."

"Hi, Larry. Yes, I know Captain Chambers."

They nodded all around, the pleasantries all a fat fake, then Hy took the other chair facing the desk and sat down. I just stood there looking down at Pat so he could know that I didn't give a damn for him either if he wanted it that way.

Pat's voice had a cutting edge to it and he took in Hy with a curt nod. "Why the party?"

"Hy's got an interest in the story end."

"We have a procedure for those things."

"Maybe you have, but I don't and this is the way it's going to be, old buddy."

"Knock it off."

Quietly, Larry said, "Maybe it's a good thing I brought my medical bag, but if either one of you had any sense you'd keep it all talk until you find the right answers."

"Shut up, Larry," Pat snarled, "you don't know anything about this."

"You'd be surprised at what I know," he told him. Pat let his eyes drift to Larry's and he frowned. Then all his years took hold and his face went blank again.

I said, "What did ballistics come up with?"

He didn't answer me and didn't have to. I knew by his silence that the slug matched the others. He leaned on the desk, his hands folded together and when he was ready he said, "Okay, where did you get it?"

"We had something to trade, remember?"

His grin was too crooked. "Not necessarily."

But my grin was just as crooked. "The hell it isn't. Time isn't working against me any more, kiddo. I can hold out on you as long as I feel like it."

Pat half started to rise and Larry said cautioningly, "Easy, Pat."

He let out a grunt of disgust and sat down again. In a way he was like Art, always thinking, but covering the machinery of his mind with clever little moves. But I had known Pat too long and too well. I knew his play and could read the signs. When he handed me the photostat I was smiling even dirtier and he let me keep on with it until I felt the grin go tight as a drum, then pull into a harsh grimace. When I looked at Pat his face mirrored my own, only his had hate in it.

"Read it out loud," he said.

"Drop dead."

"No," he insisted, his voice almost paternal, a woodshed voice taking pleasure in the whipping, "go ahead and read it."

Silently, I read it again. Velda had been an active agent for the O.S.I. during the war, certain code numbers in the Washington files given for reference, and her grade and time in that type of service had qualified her for a Private Investigator's ticket in the State of New York.

Pat waited, then finally, "Well?"

I handed back the photostat. It was my turn to shrug, then I gave him the address in Brooklyn where Cole had lived and told him where he could find the hole the slug made. I wondered what he'd do when he turned up Velda's picture.

He let me finish, picked up the phone and dialed an extension. A few minutes later another officer laid a folder on his desk and Pat opened it to scan the sheet inside. The first report was enough. He closed the folder and rocked back in the chair. "There were two shots. They didn't come from the same gun. One person considered competent said the second was a large-bore gun, most likely a .45."

"How about that," I said.

His eyes were tight and hard now. "You're being cute, Mike. You're playing guns again. I'm going to catch you at it and then your ass is going to be hung high. You kill anybody on this prod and I'll be there to watch them strap you in the hot squat. I could push you a little more on this right now and maybe see you take a fall, but if I do it won't be enough to satisfy me. When you go down, I want to see you fall all the way, a six-foot fall like the man said."

"Thanks a bunch."

"No trouble," he smiled casually.

I glanced at Larry, then nodded toward Pat. "He's a sick man, Doctor. He won't admit it, but he *was* in love with her too."

Pat's expression didn't change a bit.

"Weren't you?" I asked him.

He waited until Hy and I were at the door and I had turned around to look at him again and this time I wasn't going to leave until he had answered me. He didn't hesitate. Softly, he said, "Yes, damn you."

On the street Hy steered me toward a bar near the Trib Building. We picked a booth in the back, ordered a pair of frigid Blue Ribbons and toasted each other silently when they came. Hy said, "I'm thinking like Alice in Wonderland now, that things keep getting curiousier and curiousier. You've given me a little bit and now I want more. It's fun writing a Broadway column and throwing out squibs about famous people and all that jazz, but essentially I'm a reporter and it wouldn't feel bad at all to do a little poking and prying again for a change."

"I don't know where to start, Hy."

"Well, give it a try."

"All right. How about this one. *Butterfly Two, Gerald Erlich.*"

The beer stopped halfway to his mouth. "How did you know about Butterfly Two?"

"How did *you* know about it?"

"That's war stuff, friend. Do you know what I was then?"

"A captain in special services, you told me."

"That's right. I was. But it was a cover assignment at times too. I was also useful in several other capacities besides."

"Don't tell me you were a spy."

"Let's say I just kept my ear to the ground regarding certain activities. But what's this business about Butterfly Two and Erlich? That's seventeen years old now and out of style."

"Is it?"

"Hell, Mike, when that Nazi war machine—" then he got the tone of my voice and put the glass down, his eyes watching me closely. "Let's have it, Mike."

"Butterfly Two isn't as out of style as you think."

"Look—"

"And what about Gerald Erlich?"

"Presumed dead."

"Proof?"

"None, but damn it, Mike—"

"Look, there are too many suppositions."

"What are you driving at, anyway? Man, don't tell me about Gerald Erlich. I had contact with him on three different occasions. The first two I knew him only as an allied officer, the third time I saw him in a detention camp after the war but didn't realize who he was until I went over it in my mind for a couple of hours. When I went back there the prisoners had been transferred and the truck they were riding in had hit a land mine taking a detour around a bombed bridge. It was the same truck Giesler was on, the SS Colonel who had all the prisoners killed during the Battle of the Bulge."

"You saw the body?"

"No, but the survivors were brought in and he wasn't among them."

"Presumed dead?"

"What else do you need? Listen, I even have a picture of the guy I took at that camp and some of those survivors when they were brought back. He wasn't in that bunch at all."

I perched forward on my chair, my hands flat on the table. "You have *what?*"

Surprised at the edge in my voice, he pulled out another one of those cigars. "They're in my personal stuff upstairs." He waved a thumb toward the street.

"Tell me something, Hy," I said, "Are you cold on these details?"

He caught on quick. "When I got out of the army, friend, I got out. All the way. I was never that big that they called me back as a consultant."

"Can we see those photos?"

"Sure. Why not?"

I picked up my beer, finished it, waited for him to finish his, then followed him out. We went back through the press section of the paper, took the service elevator up and got out at Hy's floor. Except for a handful of night men, the place was empty, a gigantic echo chamber that magnified the sound of our feet against the tiled floor. Hy unlocked his office, flipped on the light and pointed to a chair.

It took him five minutes of rummaging through his old files, but he finally came up with the photos. They were 120 contact sheets still in a military folder that was getting stiff and yellow around the edges and when he laid them out he pointed to one in the top left-hand corner and gave me an enlarging glass to bring out the image.

His face came in loud and clear, chunky features that bore all the physical traits of a soldier with overtones of one used to command. The eyes were hard, the mouth a tight slash as they looked contemptuously at the camera.

*Almost as if he knew what was going to happen,* I thought.

Unlike the others, there was no harried expression, no trace of fear. Nor did he have the stolid composure of a prisoner. Again, it was as if he were not really a prisoner at all.

Hy pointed to the shots of the survivors of the accident. He wasn't in any of those. The mangled bodies of the dead were unrecognizable.

Hy said, "Know him?"

I handed the photos back. "No."

"Sure?"

"I never forget faces."

"Then that's one angle out."

"Yeah," I said.

"But where did you ever get hold of that bit?"

I reached for my hat. "Have you ever heard of a red herring?"

Hy chuckled and nodded. "I've dropped a few in my life."

"I think I might have picked one up. It stinks."

"So drop it. What are you going to do now?"

"Not drop it, old buddy. It stinks just a little too bad to be true. No, there's another side to this Erlich angle I'd like to find out about."

"Clue me."

"Senator Knapp."

"The Missile Man, Mr. America. Now how does he come in?"

"He comes in because he's dead. The same bullet killed him as Richie Cole and the same gun shot at me. That package on Knapp that you gave me spelled out his war record pretty well. He was a light colonel when he went in and a major general when he came out. I'm wondering if I could tie his name in with Erlich's anyplace."

Hy's mouth came open and he nearly lost the cigar. *"Knapp working for another country?"*

"Hell no," I told him. "Were you?"

"But—"

"He could have had a cover assignment too."

"For Pete's sake, Mike, if Knapp had a job other than what was known he could have made political capital of it and—"

"Who knew about yours?"

"Well—nobody, naturally. At least, not until now," he added.

"No friends?"

"No."

"Only authorized personnel."

"Exactly. And they were mighty damn limited."

"Does Marilyn know about it now?"

"Mike—"

"Does she?"

"Sure, I told her one time, but all that stuff is seventeen years old. She listened politely like a wife will, made some silly remark and that was it."

"The thing is, she knows about it."

"Yes. So what?"

"Maybe Laura Knapp does too."

Hy sat back again, sticking the cigar in his mouth. "Boy," he said, "you sure are a cagy one. You'll rationalize anything just to see that broad again, won't you?"

I laughed back at him. "Could be," I said. "Can I borrow that photo of Erlich?"

From his desk Hy pulled a pair of shears, cut out the shot of the Nazi agent and handed it to me. "Have fun, but you're chasing a ghost now."

"That's how it goes. But at least if you run around long enough something will show up."

"Yeah, like a broad."

"Yeah," I repeated, then reached for my hat and left.

Duck-Duck Jones told me that they had pulled the cop off Old Dewey's place. A relative had showed up, some old dame who claimed to be his half sister and had taken over Dewey's affairs. The only thing she couldn't touch was the newsstand which he had left to Duck-Duck in a surprise letter held by Bucky Harris who owned the Clover Bar. Even Duck-Duck could hardly believe it, but now pride of ownership had taken hold and he was happy to take up where the old man left off.

When I had his ear I said, "Listen, Duck-Duck, before Dewey got bumped a guy left something with him to give to me."

"Yeah? Like what, Mike?"

"I don't know. A package or something. Maybe an envelope. Anyway, did you see anything laying around here with my name on it? Or just an unmarked thing."

Duck folded a paper and thrust it at a customer, made change and turned back to me again. "I don't see nuttin', Mike. Honest. Besides, there ain't no place to hide nuttin' here. You wanna look around?"

I shook my head. "Naw, you would have found it by now."

"Well what you want I should do if somethin' shows up?"

"Hang onto it, Duck. I'll be back." I picked up a paper and threw a dime down.

I started to leave and Duck stopped me. "Hey, Mike, you still gonna do business here? Dewey got you down for some stuff."

"You keep me on the list, Duck. I'll pick up everything in a day or two."

I waved, waited for the light and headed west across town. It was a long walk, but at the end of it was a guy who owed me two hundred bucks and had the chips to pay off on the spot. Then I hopped a cab to the car rental agency on Forty-ninth, took my time about picking out a Ford coupé and turned toward the West Side Drive.

It had turned out to be a beautiful day, it was almost noon, the sun was hot, and once on the New York Thruway I had the wide concrete road nearly to myself. I stayed at the posted sixty and occasionally some fireball would come blasting by, otherwise it was smooth run with only a few trucks to pass. Just before I reached Harriman I saw the other car behind me close to a quarter mile and hold there. Fifteen miles further at the Newburgh entrance it was still there so I stepped it up to seventy. Momentarily, the distance widened, then closed and we stayed like that. Then just before the New Paltz exit the car began to close the gap, reached me, passed and kept on going. It was a dark blue Buick Special with a driver lazing behind the wheel and as he went by all the tension left my shoulders. What he had just pulled was a typical tricky habit of a guy who had driven a long way—staying behind a car until boredom set in, then running for it to find a new pacer for a while. I eased off back to sixty, turned through the toll gate at Kingston, picked up Route 28 and loafed my way up to the chalet called The Willows and when I cut the motor of the car I could hear music coming through the trees from behind the house and knew that she was waiting for me.

She was lying in the grass at the edge of the pool, stretched out on an oversize towel with her face cradled in her inter-twined fingers. Her hair spilled forward over her head, letting the sun tan her neck, her arms pulled forward so that lines of muscles were in gentle bas-relief down her back into her hips. Her legs were stretched wide in open supplication of the inveterate sun worshipper and her skin glistened with a fine, golden sweat.

Beside her the shortwave portable boomed in a symphony, the thunder of it obliterating any sound of my feet. I sat there beside her, quietly, looking at the beauty of those long legs and the pert way her breasts flattened against the towel, and after long minutes passed the music became muted and drifted off into a finale of silence.

I said, "Hello, Laura," and she started as though suddenly awakened from sleep, then realizing the state of affairs, reached for the edge of the towel to flip it around her. I let out a small laugh and did it for her.

She rolled over, eyes wide, then saw me and laughed back. "Hey, you."

"You'll get your tail burned lying around like that."

"It's worse having people sneak up on you."

I shrugged and tucked my feet under me. "It was worth it. People like me don't get to see such lovely sights very often."

Her eyes lit up impishly. "That's a lie. Besides, I'm not that new to you," she reminded me.

"Out in the sunlight you are, kitten. You take on an entirely new perspective."

"Are you making love or being clinical?" she demanded.

"I don't know. One thing could lead into another."

"Then maybe we should just let nature take its course."

"Maybe."

"Feel like a swim."

"I didn't bring a suit."

"Well . . ." and she grinned again.

I gave her a poke in the ribs with my forefinger and she grunted. "There are some things I'm prudish about, baby."

"Well I'll be damned," she whispered in amazement. "You never can tell, can you?"

"Sometimes never."

"There are extra suits in the bathhouse."

"That sounds better."

"Then let me go get into one first. I'm not going to be all skin while you play coward."

I reached for her but she was too fast, springing to her feet with the rebounding motion of a tumbler. She swung the towel sari-fashion around herself and smiled, knowing she was suddenly more desirable then than when she was naked. She let me eat her with my eyes for a second, then ran off boyishly, skirting the pool, and disappeared into the dressing room on the other side.

She came back out a minute later in the briefest black bikini I had ever seen, holding up a pair of shorts for me. She dropped them on a chair, took a run for the pool and dove in. I was a nut for letting myself feel like a colt, but the day was right, the woman was right and those seven years had been a long, hard grind. I walked over, picked up the shorts and without bothering to turn on the overhead light got dressed and went back out to the big, big day.

Underwater she was like an eel, golden brown, the black of the bikini making only the barest slashes against her skin. She was slippery and luscious and more tantalizing than a woman had a right to be. She surged up out of the water and sat on the edge of the pool with her stomach sucked in so that a muscular valley ran from her navel up into the cleft of her breasts whose curves arched up in proud nakedness a long way before feeling the constraint of the miniature halter.

She laughed, stuck her tongue out at me and walked to the grass by the radio and sat down. I said, "Damn," softly, waited a bit, then followed her.

When I was comfortable she put her hand out on mine, making me seem almost prison-pale by comparison. "Now we can talk, Mike. You didn't come all the way up here just to see me, did you?"

"I didn't think so before I left."

She closed her fingers over my wrist. "Can I tell you something very frankly?"

"Be my guest."

"I like you, big man."

I turned my head and nipped at her forearm. "The feeling's mutual, big girl. It shouldn't be though."

"Why not?" Her eyes were steady and direct, deep and warm as they watched and waited for the answer.

"Because we're not at all alike. We're miles apart in the things we do and the way we think. I'm a trouble character, honey. It's always been that way and it isn't going to change. So be smart. Don't encourage me because I'll only be too anxious to get in the game. We had a pretty hello and a wonderful beginning and I came up here on a damn flimsy pretext because I was hungry for you and now that I've had a taste again I feel like a pig and want it all."

"Ummmm," Laura said.

"Don't laugh," I told her. "White eyes is not speaking with forked tongue. This old soldier has been around."

"There and back?"

"All the way, buddy."

Her grin was the kind they paint on pixie dolls. "Okay, old soldier, so kill me."

"It'll take days and days."

"Ummm," she said again. "But tell me your pretext for coming in the first place."

I reached out and turned the radio down. "It's about Leo."

The smile faded and her eyes crinkled at the corners. "Oh?"

"Did he ever tell you about his—well, job let's say, during the war?"

She didn't seem certain of what I asked. "Well, he was a general. He was on General Stoeffler's staff."

"I know that. But what did he *do*? Did he ever speak about what his job was?"

Again, she looked at me, puzzled. "Yes. Procurement was their job. He never went into great detail and I always thought it was because he never saw any direct action. He seemed rather ashamed of the fact."

I felt myself make a disgusted face.

"Is there—anything specific—like—"

"No," I said bluntly, "it's just that I wondered if he could possibly have had an undercover job."

"I don't understand, Mike." She propped herself up on one elbow and stared at me. "Are you asking if Leo was part of the cloak-and-dagger set?"

I nodded.

The puzzled look came back again and she moved her head in easy negative. "I think I would have known. I've seen all his old personal stuff from the war, his decorations, his photos, his letters of commendation and heard what stories he had to tell. But as I said, he always seemed to be ashamed that he wasn't on the front line getting shot at. Fortunately, the country had a better need for him."

"It was a good try," I said and sat up.

"I'm sorry, Mike."

Then I thought of something, told her to wait and went back to the bathhouse. I got dressed and saw the disappointment in her eyes from all the way across the pool when I came out, but the line had to be drawn someplace.

Laura gave me a look of mock disgust and patted the grass next to her. When I squatted down I took out the photo of Gerald Erlich and passed it over. "Take a look, honey. Have you ever seen that face in any of your husband's effects?"

She studied it, her eyes squinting in the sun, and when she had made sure she handed it back. "No, I never have. Who is he?"

"His name used to be Gerald Erlich. He was a trained espionage agent working for the Nazis during the war."

"But what did he have to do with Leo?"

"I don't know," I told her. "His name has been coming up a little too often to be coincidental."

"Mike—" She bit her lip, thinking, then: "I have Leo's effects in the house. Do you think you might find something useful in them? They might make more sense to you than they do to me."

"It sure won't hurt to look." I held out my hand to help her up and that was as far as I got. The radio between us suddenly burst apart almost spontaneously and slammed backward into the pool.

I gave her a shove that threw her ten feet away, rolled the other way and got to my feet running like hell for the west side of the house. It had to have been a shot and from the direction the radio skidded I could figure the origin. It had to be a silenced blast from a pistol because a rifle would have had either Laura or me with no trouble at all. I skirted the trees, stopped and listened, and from almost directly ahead I heard a door slam and headed for it wishing I had kept the .45 on me and to hell with Pat. The bushes were too thick to break through so I had to cut down the driveway, the gravel crunching under my feet. I never had a chance. All I saw was

the tail end of a dark blue Buick special pulling away to make
a turn that hid it completely.

And now the picture was coming out a little clearer. It
hadn't been a tired driver on the Thruway at all. The bastard
had picked me up at Duck's stand, figured he had given me
something when he had handed me the paper, probably hired
a car the same time I did with plenty of time to do it in since
I wasn't hurrying at all. He followed me until he was sure he
knew where I was headed and waited me out.

*Damn. It was too close. But what got me was, how many
silenced shots had he fired before hitting that radio? He had
been too far away for accurate shooting apparently, but he
could have been plunking them all around us hoping for a
hit until he got the radio. Damn!*

*And I was really important. He knew where I was heading.
Ever since I had started to operate I had had a tail on me and
it had almost paid off for him. But if I were important dead,
so was Laura, because now that killer could never be sure I
hadn't let her in on the whole business. Another damn.*

She stood over the wreckage of the portable she had fished
from the pool, white showing at the corners of her mouth.
Her hands trembled so that she clasped them in front of her
and she breathed as though she had done the running, not
me. Breathlessly, she said, "Mike—what was it? Please,
Mike—"

I put my arm around her shoulder and with a queer sob
she buried her face against me. When she looked up she had
herself under control. "It was a shot, wasn't it?"

"That's right. A silenced gun."

"But—"

"It's the second time he's tried for me."

"Do you think—"

"He's gone for now," I said.

"But who was he?"

"I think he was The Dragon, sugar."

For a few seconds she didn't answer, then she turned her face up toward mine. "Who?"

"Nobody you know. He's an assassin. Up until now his record has been pretty good. He must be getting the jumps."

"My gracious, Mike, this is crazy! It's absolutely crazy."

I nodded in agreement. "You'll never know, but now we have a real problem. You're going to need protection."

"*Me!*"

"Anybody I'm close to is in trouble. The best thing we can do is call the local cops."

She gave me a dismayed glance. "But I can't—I have to be in Washington— Oh, Mike!"

"It won't be too bad in the city, kid, but out here you're too alone."

Laura thought about it, then shrugged. "I suppose you're right. After Leo was killed the police made me keep several guns handy. In fact, there's one in each room."

"Can you use them?"

Her smile was wan. "The policeman you met the last time showed me."

"Swell, but what about out here?"

"There's a shotgun in the corner of the bathhouse."

"Loaded?"

"Yes."

"A shotgun isn't exactly a handgun."

"Leo showed me how to use it. We used to shoot skeet together at the other end of the property."

"Police protection would still be your best bet."

"Can it be avoided?"

"Why stick your neck out?"

"Because from now on I'm going to be a very busy girl,
Mike. Congress convenes this week and the race is on for
hostess of the year."

"That stuff is a lot of crap."

"Maybe, but that's what Leo wanted."

"So he's leaving a dead hand around."

There was a hurt expression on her face. "Mike—I did love
him. Please . . . ?"

"Sorry, kid. I don't have much class. We bat in different
leagues."

She touched me lightly, her fingers cool. "Perhaps not. I
think we are really closer than you realize."

I grinned and squeezed her hand, then ran my palm along
the soft swell of her flanks.

Laura smiled and said, "Are you going to—do anything
about that shot?"

"Shall I?"

"It's up to you. This isn't my league now."

I made the decision quickly. "All right, we'll keep it quiet.
If that slob has any sense he'll know we won't be stationary
targets again. From now on I'll be doing some hunting myself."

"You sure, Mike?"

"I'm sure."

"Good. Then let's go through Leo's effects."

Inside she led me upstairs past the bedrooms to the end of
the hall, opened a closet and pulled out a small trunk. I took
it from her, carried it into the first bedroom and dumped the
contents out on the dresser.

When you thought about it, it was funny how little a man
actually accumulated during the most important years of his

life. He could go through a whole war, live in foreign places with strange people, be called upon to do difficult and unnatural work, yet come away from those years with no more than he could put in a very small trunk.

Leo Knapp's 201 file was thick, proper and as military as could be. There was an attempt at a diary that ran into fifty pages, but the last third showed an obvious effort being made to overcome boredom, then the thing dwindled out. I went through every piece of paperwork there was, uncovering nothing, saving the photos until last.

Laura left me alone to work uninterruptedly, but the smell of her perfume was there in the room and from somewhere downstairs I could hear her talking on the phone. She was still tense from the experience outside and although I couldn't hear her conversation I could sense the strain in her voice. She came back in ten minutes later and sat on the edge of the bed, quiet, content just to be there, then she sighed and I knew the tension had gone out of her.

I don't know what I expected, but the results were a total negative. Of the hundreds of photos, half were taken by G.I. staff photogs and the rest an accumulation of camp and tourist shots that every soldier who ever came home had tucked away in his gear. When you were old and fat you could take them out, reminisce over the days when you were young and thin and wonder what had happened to all the rest in the picture before putting them back in storage for another decade.

Behind me Laura watched while I began putting things back in the trunk and I heard her ask, "Anything, Mike?"

"No." I half threw his medals in the pile. "Everything's as mundane as a mud pie."

"I'm sorry, Mike."

"Don't be sorry. Sometimes the mundane can hide some peculiar things. There's still a thread left to pull. If Leo had anything to do with Erlich I have a Fed for a friend who just might come up with the answer." I snapped the lock shut on the trunk. "It just gives me a pain to have everything come up so damn hard."

"Really?" Her voice laughed.

I glanced up into the mirror on the dresser and felt that wild warmth steal into my stomach like an ebullient catalyst that pulled me taut as a bowstring and left my breath hanging in my throat.

"Something should be made easy for you then," she said.

Laura was standing there now, tall and lovely, the sun still with her in the rich loamy color of her skin, the nearly bleached white tone of her hair.

At her feet the bikini made a small puddle of black like a shadow, then she walked away from it to me and I was waiting for her.

# CHAPTER 9

Night and the rain had come back to New York, the air musty with dust driven up by the sudden surge of the downpour. The bars were filled, the sheltered areas under marquees crowded and an empty taxi a rare treasure to be fought over.

But it was a night to think in. There is a peculiar anonymity you can enjoy in the city on a rainy night. You're alone, yet not alone. The other people around you are merely motion and sound and the sign of life whose presence averts the panic of being truly alone, yet who observe the rules of the city and stay withdrawn and far away when they are close.

*How many times had Velda and I walked in the rain? She was big and our shoulders almost touched. We'd deliberately walk out of step so that our inside legs would touch rhythmically and if her arm wasn't tucked underneath mine we'd hold hands. There was a ring I had given her. I'd feel it under my fingers and she'd look at me and smile because she knew what that ring meant.*

145

Where was she now? What had really happened? Little hammers would go at me when I thought of the days and hours since they had dragged me into Richie Cole's room to watch him die, but could it have been any other way?

Maybe not seven years ago. Not then. I wouldn't have had a booze-soaked head then. I would have had a gun and a ticket that could get me in and out of places and hands that could take care of anybody.

But now. Now I was an almost-nothing. Not quite, because I still had years of experience going for me and a reason to push. I was coming back little by little, but unless I stayed cute about it all I could be a pushover for any hardcase.

What I had to do now was think. I still had a small edge, but how long it would last was anybody's guess. So think, Mike, old soldier. Get your head going the way it's supposed to. You know who the key is. You've known it all along. Cole died with her name on his lips and ever since then she's been the key. But why? But why?

How could she still be alive?

Seven years is a long time to hide. Too long. Why? Why?

So think, old soldier. Go over the possibilities.

The rain came down a little harder and began to run off the brim of my hat. In a little while it seeped through the top of the cheap trench coat and I could feel the cold of it on my shoulders. And then I had the streets all alone again and the night and the city belonged only to me. I walked, so I was king. The others who huddled in the doorways and watched me with tired eyes were the lesser ones. Those who ran for the taxis were the scared ones. So I walked and I was able to think about Velda again. She had suddenly become *a case* and it had to be that way. It had to be cold and logical, otherwise it would vaporize into incredibility and there would be nothing left except to go back to where I had come from.

*Think.*

Who saw her die? No one. It was an assumption. Well assumed, but an assumption nevertheless.

Then, after seven years, who saw her alive? Richie Cole.

Sure, he had reason to know her. They were friends. War buddies. They had worked together. Once a year they'd meet for supper and a show and talk over old times. Hell, I'd done it myself with George and Earle, Ray, Mason and the others. It was nothing you could talk about to anybody else, though. Death and destruction you took part in could be shared only with those in range of the same enemy guns. With them you couldn't brag or lie. You simply recounted and wondered that you were still alive and renewed a friendship.

Cole couldn't have made a mistake. *He knew her.*

And Cole had been a pro. Velda was a pro. He had come looking for me because she had told him I was a pro and he had been disappointed at what he had seen. He had taken a look at me and his reason for staying alive died right then. Whatever it was, he didn't think I could do it. He saw a damned drunken bum who had lost every bit of himself years before and he died thinking she was going to die too and he was loathing me with eyes starting to film over with the nonexistence of death.

Richie Cole just didn't know me very well at all.

He had a chance to say the magic word and that made all the difference.

*Velda.*

Would it still be the same? How will *you* look after seven years? Hell, you should see me. You should see the way *I* look. And what's inside *you* after a time span like that?

Things happen in seven years; things build, things dissolve. What happens to people in love? Seven years ago that's the way we were. In Love. Capital *L*. Had we stayed together time would only have lent maturity and quality to that which it served to improve.

But my love, my love, how could you look at me, me after seven years? You knew what I had been and called for me at last, but I wasn't what you expected at all. That big one you knew and loved is gone, kid, long gone, and you can't come back that big any more. Hell, Velda, you know that. You can't come back . . . you should have known what would happen to me. Damn, you knew me well enough. And it happened. So how can you yell for me now? *I know you knew what I'd be like, and you asked for me anyway.*

I let out a little laugh and only the rain could enjoy it with me. She knew, all right. You can't come back just as big. Either lesser or bigger. There was no other answer. She just didn't know the odds against the right choice.

There was a new man on the elevator now. I signed the night book, nodded to him and gave him my floor. I got off at eight and went down the hall, watching my shadow grow longer and longer from the single light behind me.

I had my keys in my hand, but I didn't need them at all. The door to 808 stood wide open invitingly, the lights inside throwing a warm glow over the dust and the furniture and when I closed it behind me I went through the anteroom to my office where Art Rickerby was sitting and picked up the sandwich and Blue Ribbon beer he had waiting for me and sat down on the edge of the couch and didn't say a word until I had finished both.

Art said, "Your friend Nat Drutman gave me the key."

"It's okay."

"I pushed him a little."

"He's been pushed before. If he couldn't read you right you wouldn't have gotten the key. Don't sell him short."

"I figured as much."

I got up, took off the soggy coat and hat and threw them across a chair. "What's with the visit? I hope you're not getting too impatient."

"No. Patience is something inbred. Nothing I can do will bring Richie back. All I can do is play the angles, the curves, float along the stream of time, then, my friend, something will bite, even on an unbaited hook."

"Shit."

"You know it's like that. You're a cop."

"A long time ago."

He watched me, a funny smile on his face. "No. *Now.* I know the signs. I've been in this business too long."

"So what do you want here?"

Rickerby's smile broadened. "I told you once. I'll do anything to get Richie's killer."

"Oh?"

He reached in his pocket and brought out an envelope. I took it from him, tore it open and read the folded card it contained on all four of its sides, then slid it into my wallet and tucked it away.

"Now I can carry a gun," I said.

"Legally. In any state."

"Thanks. What did you give up to get it?"

"Not a thing. Favors were owed me too. Our department is very—wise."

"They think it's smart to let me carry a rod again?"

"There aren't any complaints. You have your—ticket."

"It's a little different from the last one this state gave me."

"Don't look a gift horse in the mouth, my friend."

"Okay. Thanks."

"No trouble. I'm being smug."

"Why?"

He took off his glasses again, wiped them and put them back on. "Because I have found out all about you a person could find. You're going to do something I can't possibly do because you have the key to it all and won't let it go. Whatever your motives are, they aren't mine, but they encompass what I want and that's enough for me. Sooner or later you're going to name Richie's killer and that's all I want. In the meantime, rather than interfere with your operation, I'll do everything I can to supplement it. Do you understand?"

"I think so," I said.

"Good. Then I'll wait you out." He smiled, but there was nothing pleasant in his expression. "Some people are different from others. You're a killer, Mike. You've always been a killer. Somehow your actions have been justified and I think righteously so, but nevertheless, you're a killer. You're on a hunt again and I'm going to help you. There's just one thing I ask."

"What?"

"If you do find Richie's murderer before me, don't kill him."

I looked up from the fists I had made. "Why?"

"I want him, Mike. Let him be mine."

"What will you do with him?"

Rickerby's grin was damn near inhuman. It was a look I had seen before on other people and never would have expected from him. "A quick kill would be too good, Mike," he told me slowly. "But the law—this supposedly just, merciful provision—this is the most cruel of all. It lets you rot in a death cell for months and deteriorate slowly until you're only an accumulation of living cells with the consciousness of knowing you are about to die; then the creature is tied in a chair and jazzed with a hot shot that wipes him from the face of the earth with one big jolt and that's that."

"Pleasant thought," I said.

"Isn't it, though? Too many people think the sudden kill is the perfect answer for revenge. Ah, no, my friend. It's the waiting. It's the knowing beforehand that even the merciful provisions of a public trial will only result in what you already know—more waiting and further contemplation of that little room where you spend your last days with death in an oaken chair only a few yards away. And do you know what? I'll see that killer every day. I'll savor his anguish like a fine drink and be there as a witness when he burns and he'll see me and know why I'm there and when he's finished I'll be satisfied."

"You got a mean streak a yard wide, Rickerby."

"But it doesn't quite match yours, Mike."

"The hell it doesn't."

"No—you'll see what I mean some day. You'll see yourself express the violence of thought and action in a way I'd never do. True violence isn't in the deed itself. It's the contemplation and enjoyment of the deed."

"Come off it."

Rickerby smiled, the intensity of hatred he was filled with a moment ago seeping out slowly. If it had been me I would have been shaking like a leaf, but now he casually reached out for the can of beer, sipped at it coolly and put it down.

"I have some information you requested," he told me.

While I waited I walked behind the desk, sat down and

pulled open the lower drawer. The shoulder holster was still supple although it had lain there seven years. I took off my jacket, slipped it on and put my coat back.

Art said, "I—managed to find out about Gerald Erlich."

I could feel the pulse in my arm throb against the arm of the chair. I still waited.

"Erlich is dead, my friend."

I let my breath out slowly, hoping my face didn't show how I felt.

"He died five years ago and his body was positively identified."

*Five years ago! But he was supposed to have died during the war!*

"He was found shot in the head in the Eastern Zone of Germany. After the war he had been fingerprinted and classified along with other prisoners of note so there was no doubt as to his identity." Art stopped a moment, studied me, then went on. "Apparently this man was trying to make the Western Zone. On his person were papers and articles that showed he had come out of Russia, there were signs that he had been under severe punishment and if you want to speculate, you might say that he had escaped from a prison and was tracked down just yards from freedom."

"That's pretty good information to come out of the Eastern Zone," I said.

Rickerby nodded sagely. "We have people there. They purposely investigate things of this sort. There's nothing coincidental about it."

"There's more."

His eyes were funny. They had an oblique quality as if they watched something totally foreign, something they had never realized could exist before. They watched and waited. Then

he said, "Erlich had an importance we really didn't understand until lately. He was the nucleus of an organization of
espionage agents the like of which had never been developed
before and whose importance remained intact even after the
downfall of the Third Reich. It was an organization so ruthless that its members, in order to pursue their own ends,
would go with any government they thought capable of winning a present global conflict and apparently they selected
the Reds. To oppose them and us meant fighting two battles,
so it would be better to support one until the other lost, then
undermine that one until it could take over."

"Crazy," I said.

"Is it?"

"They can't win."

"But they can certainly bring on some incredible devas-
tation."

"Then why kill Erlich?"

Art sat back and folded his hands together in a familiar
way. "Simple. He defected. He wanted out. Let's say he got
smart in his late years and realized the personal futility of
pushing this thing any further. He wanted to spend a few
years in peace."

It was reasonable in a way. I nodded.

"But he had to die," Art continued. "There was one thing
he knew that was known only to the next in line in the chain
of command, the ones taking over the organization."

"Like what?"

"He knew every agent in the group. He could bust the
whole shebang up if he spilled his guts to the West and the
idea of world conquest by the Reds or the others would go
smack down the drain."

"This you know?" I asked.

He shook his head. "No. Let's say I'm sure of it, but I don't *know* it. At this point I really don't care. It's the rest of the story I pulled out of the hat I'm interested in." And now his eyes cocked themselves up at me again. "He was tracked down and killed by one known to the Reds as their chief assassin agent Gorlin, but to us as The Dragon."

If he could have had his hand on my chest, or even have touched me anywhere he would have known what was happening. My guts would knot and churn and my head was filled with a wild flushing sensation of blood almost bursting through their walls. But he didn't touch me and he couldn't tell from my face so his eyes looked at me even a little more obliquely expecting even the slightest reaction and getting none. None at all.

"You're a cold-blooded bastard," he nearly whispered.

"You said that before."

He blinked owlishly behind his glasses and stood up, his coat over his arm. "You know where to reach me."

"I know."

"Do you need anything?"

"Not now. Thanks for the ticket."

"No trouble. Will you promise me something?"

"Sure."

"Just don't use that gun on The Dragon."

"I won't kill him, Art."

"No. Leave that for me. Don't spoil my pleasure or yours either."

He went out, closing the doors softly behind him. I pulled the center desk drawer out, got the extra clip and the box of shells from the niche and closed the drawer.

The package I had mailed to myself was on the table by the

door where Nat always put my packages when he had to take them from the mailman. I ripped it open, took out the .45, checked the action and dropped it in the holster.

*Now it was just like old times.*

I turned off the light in my office and went outside. I was reaching for the door when the phone on Velda's desk went off with a sudden jangling that shook me for a second before I could pick it up.

Her voice was rich and vibrant when she said hello and I wanted her right there with me right then. She knew it too, and her laugh rippled across the miles. She said, "Are you going to be busy tonight, Mike?"

Time was something I had too little of, but I had too little of her too. "Well—why?"

"Because I'm coming into your big city."

"Isn't it kind of late?"

"No. I have to be there at 10 P.M. to see a friend of yours and since I see no sense of wasting the evening I thought that whatever you have to do you can do it with me. Or can you?"

"It takes two to dance, baby."

She laughed again. "I didn't mean it *that* way."

"Sure, come on in. If I said not to I'd be lying. Who's my friend you have a date with?"

"An old friend and new enemy. Captain Chambers."

"What is this?"

"I don't know. He called and asked if I could come in. It would simplify things since his going out of his jurisdiction requires a lot of work."

"For Pete's sake—"

"Mike—I don't mind, really. If it has to do with Leo's death, well, I'll do anything. You know that."

"Yeah, but—"

"Besides, it gives me an excuse to see you even sooner than I hoped. Okay?"

"Okay."

"See you in a little while, Mike. Any special place?"

"Moriarty's at Sixth and Fifty-second. I'll be at the bar."

"Real quick," she said and hung up.

I held the disconnect bar down with my finger. Time. Seven years' worth just wasted and now there was none left. I let the bar up and dialed Hy Gardner's private number at the paper, hoping I'd be lucky enough to catch him in. I was.

He said, "Mike, if you're not doing anything, come on up here. I have to get my column out and I'll be done before you're here. I have something to show you."

"Important?"

"Brother, one word from you and everybody flips. Shake it up."

"Fifteen minutes."

"Good."

I hung up and pushed the phone back. When I did I uncovered a heart scratched in the surface with something sharp. Inside it was a *V* and an *M. Velda and Mike.* I pulled the phone back to cover it, climbed into my coat and went outside. Just to be sure I still had the night to myself I walked down, out the back way through the drugstore then headed south on Broadway toward Hy's office.

Marilyn opened the door and hugged me hello, a pretty grin lighting her face up. She said, "Hy's inside waiting for you. He won't tell me what it's all about."

"You're his wife now, not his secretary anymore. You don't work for him."

"The heck I don't. But he still won't tell me."

"It's man talk, sugar."

"All right, I'll let you be. I'll get some coffee—and Mike—" I turned around.

"It's good to have you back."

When I winked she blew me a kiss and scurried out the door.

Hy was at his desk inside with his glasses up on his forehead, frowning at some sheets in his hand. They were covered with penciled notations apparently culled from another batch beside his elbow.

I pulled up a chair, sat down and let Hy finish what he was doing. Finally he glanced up, pulling his glasses down. "I got your message across."

"So?"

"So it was like I dropped a bomb in HQ. Over there they seem to know things we don't read in the paper here." He leaned forward and tapped the sheets in his hand. "This bit of The Dragon is the hottest item in the cold war, buddy. Are you sure you know what you're up to?"

"Uh-huh."

"Okay, I'll go along with you. The Reds are engaged in an operation under code name REN. It's a chase thing. Behind the Iron Curtain there has been a little hell to pay the last few years. Somebody was loose back there who could rock the whole Soviet system and that one had to be eliminated. That's where The Dragon came in. This one has been on that chase and was close to making his hit. Nobody knows what the score really is." He stopped then, pushed his glasses back up and said seriously, "or do they, Mike?"

"They?"

I should have been shaking. I should have been feeling some emotion, some wildness like I used to. What had happened? But maybe it was better this way. I could feel the weight of the .45 against my side and tightened my arm down on it lovingly. "They're after Velda," I said. "It's her. They're hunting her."

Hy squeezed his mouth shut and didn't say anything for a full minute. He laid the papers down and leaned back in his chair. "Why, Mike?"

"I don't know, Hy. I don't know why at all."

"If what I heard is true she doesn't have a chance."

"She has a chance," I told him softly.

"Maybe it really isn't her at all, Mike."

I didn't answer him. Behind us the door opened and Marilyn came in. She flipped an envelope on Hy's desk and set down the coffee container. "Here's a picture that just came off the wires. Del said you requested it."

Hy looked at me a little too quickly, opened the envelope and took out the photo. He studied it, then passed it across.

It really wasn't a good picture at all. The original had been fuzzy to start with and transmission electrically hadn't improved it any. She stood outside a building, a tall girl with seemingly black hair longer than I remembered it, features not quite clear and whose shape and posture were hidden under bulky Eastern European style clothing. Still, there was that indefinable something, some subtlety in the way she stood, some trait that came through the clothing and poor photography that I couldn't help but see.

I handed the photo back. "It's Velda."

"My German friend said the picture was several years old."

"Who had it?"

"A Red agent who was killed in a skirmish with some West German cops. It came off his body. I'd say he had been assigned to REN too and the picture was for identification purposes."

"Is this common information?"

Hy shook his head. "I'd say no. Rather than classify this thing government sources simply refuse to admit it exists. We came on it separately."

I said, "The government knows it exists."

"You know too damn much, Mike."

"No, not enough. I don't know where she is now."

"I can tell you one thing," Hy said.

"Oh?"

"She isn't in Europe any longer. The locale of REN has changed. The Dragon has left Europe. His victim got away somehow and all indications point to them both being in this country."

Very slowly, I got up, put my coat and hat on and stretched the dampness out of my shoulders. I said, "Thanks, Hy."

"Don't you want your coffee?"

"Not now."

He opened a drawer, took out a thick Manila envelope and handed it to me. "Here. You might want to read up a little more on Senator Knapp. It's confidential stuff. Gives you an idea of how big he was. Save it for me."

"Sure." I stuck it carelessly in my coat pocket. "Thanks."

Marilyn said, "You all right, Mike?"

I grinned at her a little crookedly. "I'm okay."

"You don't look right," she insisted.

Hy said, "Mike—"

And I cut him short. "I'll see you later, Hy." I grinned at

him too. "And thanks. Don't worry about me." I patted the
gun under my coat. "I have a friend along now. Legally."

While I waited, I read about just how great a guy Leo
Knapp had been. His career had been cut short at a tragic spot
because it was evident that in a few more years he would have
been the big man on the political scene. It was very evident
that here had been one of the true powers behind the throne,
a man initially responsible for military progress and missile
production in spite of opposition from the knotheaded lib-
erals and "better-Red-than-dead" slobs. He had thwarted
every attack and forced through the necessary programs and
in his hands had been secrets of vital importance that made
him a number one man in the Washington setup. His death
came at a good time for the enemy. The bullet that killed him
came from the gun of The Dragon. A bullet from the same
gun killed Richie Cole and almost killed me twice. A bullet
from that same gun was waiting to kill Velda.

She came in then, the night air still on her, shaking the
rain from her hair, laughing when she saw me. Her hand was
cool when she took mine and climbed on the stool next to me.
John brought her a Martini and me another Blue Ribbon.
We raised the glasses in a toast and drank the top off them.

"Good to see you," I said.

"You'll never know," she smiled.

"Where are you meeting Pat?"

She frowned, then, "Oh, Captain Chambers. Why, right
here." She glanced at her watch. "In five minutes. Shall we sit
at a table?"

"Let's." I picked up her glass and angled us across the room
to the far wall. "Does Pat know I'll be here?"

"I didn't mention it."

"Great. Just great."

Pat was punctual, as usual. He saw me but didn't change expression. When he said hello to Laura he sat beside her and only then looked at me. "I'm glad you're here too."

"That's nice."

He was a mean, cold cop if ever there was one, his face a mask you couldn't penetrate until you looked into his eyes and saw the hate and determination there. "Where do you find your connections, Mike?"

"Why?"

"It's peculiar how a busted private dick, a damn drunken pig in trouble up to his ears can get a gun-carrying privilege we can't break. How do you do it, punk?"

I shrugged, not feeling like arguing with him. Laura looked at the two of us, wondering what was going on.

"Well, you might need it at that if you keep getting shot at. By the way, I got a description of your back alley friend. He was seen by a rather observant kid in the full light of the street lamp. Big guy, about six-two with dark curly hair and a face with deep lines in the cheeks. His cheekbones were kind of high so he had kind of an Indian look. Ever see any-body like that?"

*He was pushing me now, doing anything to set me off so he'd have a reason to get at me but sure, I saw a guy like that. He drove past me on the Thruway and I thought he was a tired driver, then he shot at me later and now I know damn well who he is. You call him The Dragon. He had a face I'd see again someday, a face I couldn't miss.*

I said, "No, I don't know him." It wasn't quite a lie.

Pat smiled sardonically, "I have a feeling you will."

"So okay, I'll try to catch up with him for you."

"You do that, punk. Meanwhile I'll catch up with you. I'm putting you into this thing tighter than ever."

"Me?"

"That's right. That's why I'm glad you're here. It saves seeing you later." He had me curious now and knew it, and he was going to pull it out all the way. "There is a strange common denominator running throughout our little murder puzzle here. I'm trying to find out just what it all means."

"Please go on," Laura said.

"Gems. For some reason I can't get them out of my mind. Three times they cross in front of me." He looked at me, his eyes narrowed, "The first time when my old friend here let a girl die because of them, then when Senator Knapp was killed a batch of paste jewels were taken from the safe, and later a man known for his gem smuggling was killed with the same gun. It's a recurrent theme, isn't it, Mike? You're supposed to know about these things. In fact, it must have occurred to you too. You were quick enough about getting upstate to see Mrs. Knapp here."

"Listen, Pat."

"Shut up. There's more." He reached in his pocket and tugged at a cloth sack. "We're back to the gems again." He pulled the top open, spilled the sack upside down and watched the flood of rings, brooches and bracelets make a sparkling mound of brilliance on the table between us.

"Paste, pure paste, Mrs. Knapp, but I think they are yours."

Her hand was shaking when she reached out to touch them. She picked up the pieces one by one, examining them, then shaking her head. "Yes—they're mine! But where—"

"A pathetic old junkman was trying to peddle them in a pawnshop. The broker called the cops and we grabbed the guy. He said he found them in a garbage can a long time ago and kept them until now to sell. He figured they were stolen, all right, but didn't figure he'd get picked up like he did."

"Make your connection, Pat. So far all you showed was that a smart crook recognized paste jewelry and dumped it."

His eyes had a vicious cast to them this time. "I'm just wondering about the original gem robbery, the one your agency was hired to prevent. The name was Mr. and Mrs. Rudolph Civac. I'm wondering what kind of a deal was really pulled off there. You sent in Velda but wouldn't go yourself. I'm thinking that maybe you turned sour away back there and tried for a big score and fouled yourself up in it somehow."

His hands weren't showing so I knew one was sitting on a gun butt. I could feel myself going around the edges but hung on anyway. "You're nuts," I said, "I never even saw Civac. He made the protection deal by phone. I never laid eyes on him."

Pat felt inside his jacket and came out with a four-by-five glossy photo. "Well take a look at what your deceased customer looked like. I've been backtracking all over that case, even as cold as it is. Something's going to come up on it, buddy boy, and I hope you're square in the middle of it." He forgot me for a moment and turned to Laura. "Do you positively identify these, Mrs. Knapp?"

"Oh, yes. There's an accurate description of each piece on file and on the metal there's—"

"I saw the hallmarks."

"This ring was broken—see here where this prong is off— yes, these are mine."

"Fine. You can pick them up at my office tomorrow if you want to. I'll have to hold them until then though."

"That's all right."

He snatched the picture out of my fingers and put it back in his pocket. "You I'll be seeing soon," he told me.

I didn't answer him. I nodded, but that was all. He looked at me a moment, scowled, went to say something and changed his mind. He told Laura goodbye and walked to the door.

Fresh drinks came and I finished mine absently. Laura chuckled once and I glanced up. "You've been quiet a long time. Aren't we going to do the town?"

"Do you mind if we don't?"

She raised her eyebrows, surprised, but not at all unhappy. "No, do you want to do something else?"

"Yes. Think."

"Your place?" she asked mischievously.

"I don't have a place except my office."

"We've been there before," she teased.

But I had kissed Velda there too many times before too. "No," I said.

Laura leaned forward, serious now. "It's important, isn't it?"

"Yes."

"Then let's get out of the city entirely. Let's go back upstate to where it's cool and quiet and you can think right. Would you like to do that?"

"All right."

I paid the bill and we went outside to the night and the rain to flag down a cab to get us to the parking lot. She had to do it for me because the only thing I could think of was the face in that picture Pat had showed me.

*Rudolph Civac was the same as Gerald Erlich.*

# CHAPTER 10

I couldn't remember the trip at all. I was asleep before we reached the West Side Drive and awakened only when she shook me. Her voice kept calling to me out of a fog and for a few seconds I thought it was Velda, then I opened my eyes and Laura was smiling at me. "We're home, Mike."

The rain had stopped, but in the stillness of the night I could hear the soft dripping from the shadows of the blue spruces around the house. Beyond them a porch and inside light threw out a pale yellow glow. "Won't your servants have something to say about me coming in?"

"No, I'm alone at night. The couple working for me come only during the day."

"I haven't seen them yet."

"Each time you were here they had the day off."

I made an annoyed grimace. "You're nuts, kid. You should keep somebody around all the time after what happened."

Her hand reached out and she traced a line around my mouth. "I'm trying to," she said. Then she leaned over and brushed me with lips that were gently damp and sweetly warm, the tip of her tongue a swift dart of flame, doing it too quickly for me to grab her to make it last.

"Quit brainwashing me," I said.

She laughed at me deep in her throat. "Never, Mister Man. I've been too long without you."

Rather than hear me answer she opened the door and slid out of the car. I came around from the other side and we went up the steps into the house together. It was a funny feeling, this coming home sensation. There was the house and the woman and the mutual desire, an instinctive demanding passion we shared, one for the other, yet realizing that there were other things that came first and not caring because there was always later.

There was a huge couch in the living room of soft, aged leather, a hidden hi-fi that played Dvorak, Beethoven and Tchaikovsky and somewhere in between Laura had gotten into yards of flowing nylon that did nothing to hide the warmth of her body or restrain the luscious bloom of her thighs and breasts. She lay there in my arms quietly, giving me all of the moment to enjoy as I pleased, only her sometimes-quickened breathing indicating her pleasure as I touched her lightly, caressing her with my fingertips. Her eyes were closed, a small satisfied smile touched the corners of her mouth and she snuggled into me with a sigh of contentment.

How long I sat there and thought about it I couldn't tell. I let it drift through my mind from beginning to end, the part I knew and the part I didn't know. Like always, a pattern was there. You can't have murder without a pattern. It weaves in and out, fabricating an artful tapestry, and while the background colors were apparent from the beginning it is only at the last that the picture itself emerges. But who was the weaver? Who sat invisibly behind the loom with shuttles of death in one hand and skeins of lives in the other? I fell asleep trying to peer behind the gigantic framework of that murder factory, a sleep so deep, after so long, that there was nothing I thought about or remembered afterward.

I was alone when the bright shaft of sunlight pouring in the room awakened me. I was stretched out comfortably, my shoes off, my tie loose and a light Indian blanket over me. I threw it off, put my shoes back on and stood up. It took me a while to figure out what was wrong, then I saw the .45 in the shoulder holster draped over the back of a chair with my coat over it and while I was reaching for it she came in with all the exuberance of a summer morning, a tray of coffee in her hands and blew me a kiss.

"Well hello," I said.

She put the tray down and poured the coffee. "You were hard to undress."

"Why bother?"

Laura looked up laughing. "It's not easy to sleep with a man wearing a gun." She held out a cup. "Here, have some coffee. Sugar and milk?"

"Both. And I'm glad it's milk and not cream."

She fixed my cup, stirring it too. "You're a snob, Mike. In your own way you're a snob." She made a face at me and grinned. "But I love snobs."

"You should be used to them. You travel in classy company."

"They aren't snobs like you. They're just scared people putting on a front. You're the real snob. Now kiss me good morning—or afternoon. It's one o'clock." She reached up offering her mouth and I took it briefly, but even that quick touch bringing back the desire again.

Laura slid her hand under my arm and walked me through the house to the porch and out to the lawn by the pool. The sun overhead was brilliant and hot, the air filled with the smell of the mountains. She said, "Can I get you something to eat?"

I tightened my arm on her hand. "You're enough for right now."

She nuzzled my shoulder, wrinkled her nose and grinned. We both pulled out aluminum and plastic chairs, and while she went inside for the coffeepot I settled down in mine.

Now maybe I could think.

She poured another cup, knowing what was going through my mind. When she sat down opposite me she said, "Mike, would it be any good to tell me about it? I'm a good listener. I'll be somebody you can aim hypothetical questions at. Leo did this with me constantly. He called me his sounding board. He could think out loud, but doing it alone he sounded foolish to himself so he'd do it with me." She paused, her eyes earnest, wanting to help. "I'm yours for anything if you want me, Mike."

"Thanks, kitten."

I finished the coffee and put the cup down.

"You're afraid of something," she said.

"Not of. *For*. Like for you, girl. I told you once I was a trouble character. Wherever I am there's trouble and when you play guns there are stray shots and I don't want you in the way of any."

"I've already been there, remember?"

"Only because I wasn't on my toes. I've slowed up. I've been away too damn long and I'm not careful."

"Are you careful now?"

My eyes reached hers across the few feet that separated us.

"No. I'm being a damn fool again. I doubt if we were tailed here, but it's only a doubt. I have a gun in the house, but we could be dead before I reached it."

She shrugged unconcernedly. "There's the shotgun in the bathhouse."

"That's still no good. It's a pro game. There won't be any more second chances. You couldn't reach the shotgun either. It's around the pool and in the dark."

"So tell me about it, Mike. Think to me and maybe it will end even faster and we can have ourselves to ourselves. If you want to think, or be mad or need a reaction, think to me."

I said, "Don't you like living?"

A shadow passed across her face and the knuckles of her hand on the arms of the chair went white. "I stopped living when Leo died. I thought I'd never live again."

"Kid—"

"No, it's true, Mike. I know all the objections you can put up about our backgrounds and present situations but it still doesn't make any difference. It doesn't alter a simple fact that I knew days ago. I fell in love with you, Mike. I took one look at you and fell in love, knowing then that objections would come, troubles would be a heritage and you might not love me at all."

"Laura—"

"Mike—I started to live again. I thought I was dead and I started to live again. Have I pushed you into anything?"

"No."

"And I won't. You can't push a man. All you can do is try, but you just can't push a man and a woman should know that. If she can, then she doesn't have a man."

She waved me to be quiet and went on. "I don't care how you feel toward me. I hope, but that is all. I'm quite content

knowing I can live again and no matter where you are you'll
know that I love you. It's a peculiar kind of courtship, but
these are peculiar times and I don't care if it has to be like
this. Just be sure of one thing. You can have anything you
want from me, Mike. Anything. There's nothing you can ask
me to do that I won't do. Not one thing. That's how completely yours I am. There's a way to be sure. Just ask me. But
I won't push you. If you ask me never to speak of it again,
then I'll do that too. You see, Mike, it's a sort of hopeless
love, but I'm living again, I'm loving, and you can't stop me
from loving you. It's the only exception to what you can ask
—I won't stop loving you.

"But to answer your question, yes, I like living. You
brought me alive. I was dead before."

There was a beauty about her then that was indescribable.
I said, "Anything you know can be too much. You're a target
now. I don't want you to be an even bigger one."

"I'll only die if you die," she said simply.

"Laura—"

She wouldn't let me finish. "Mike—do you love me—at all?"

The sun was a honeyed cloud in her hair, bouncing off the
deep brown of her skin to bring out the classic loveliness of
her features. She was so beautifully deep-breasted, her
stomach molding itself hollow beneath the outline of her
ribs, the taut fabric of the sleeveless playsuit accentuating the
timeless quality that was Laura.

I said, "I think so, Laura. I don't know for sure. It's just
that I—can't tell anymore."

"It's enough for now," she said. "That little bit will grow
because it has to. You were in love before, weren't you?"

I thought of Charlotte and Velda and each was like being
suddenly shot low down when knowledge precedes breath-

lessness and you know it will be a few seconds before the real pain hits.

"Yes," I told her.

"Was it the same?"

"It's never the same. You are—different."

She nodded. "I know, Mike. I know." She waited, then added, "It will be—the other one—or me, won't it?"

There was no sense lying to her. "That's right."

"Very well. I'm satisfied. So now do you want to talk to me? Shall I listen for you?"

I leaned back in the chair, let my face look at the sun with my eyes closed and tried to start at the beginning. Not the beginning the way it happened, but the beginning the way I thought it could have happened. It was quite a story. Now I had to see if it made sense.

I said:

"There are only principals in this case. They are odd persons, and out of it entirely are the police and the Washington agencies. The departments only know results, not causes, and although they suspect certain things they are not in a position to be sure of what they do. We eliminate them and get to basic things. They may be speculative, but they are basic and lead to conclusions.

"The story starts at the end of World War I with an espionage team headed by Gerald Erlich who, with others, had visions of a world empire. Oh, it wasn't a new dream. Before him there had been Alexander and Caesar and Napoleon so he was only picking up an established trend. So Erlich's prime mover was nullified and he took on another— Hitler. Under that regime he became great and his organization became more nearly perfected, and when Hitler died and the Third Reich became extinct this was nothing too, for now the world was more truly divided. Only two parts remained, the East and the West and he chose, for the moment, to side with the East. Gerald Erlich picked the Red Government as his next prime mover. He thought they would be the ultimate victors in the conquest of the world, then, when the time was right, he would take over from them.

"Ah, but how time and circumstances can change. He didn't know that the Commies were equal to him in *their* dreams of world empire. He didn't realize that they would find *him* out and use *him* while he thought they were in *his* hands. They took over his organization. Like they did the rest of the world they control, they took his corrupt group and corrupted it even further. But an organization they could control. The leader of the organization, a fanatical one, they knew they couldn't. He had to go. Like dead.

"However, Erlich wasn't quite that stupid. He saw the signs and read them right. He wasn't young any longer and his organization had been taken over. His personal visions of world conquest didn't seem quite so important anymore and the most important thing was to stay alive as best he could and the place to do it was in the States. So he came here. He married well under the assumed name of Rudy Civac to a rich widow and all was well in his private world for a time.

"Then, one day, they found him. His identity was revealed. He scrambled for cover. It was impossible to ask for police protection so he did the next best thing, he called a private detective agency and as a subterfuge, used his wife's jewels as the reason for needing security. Actually, he wanted guns around. He wanted shooting protection.

"Now here the long arm of fate struck a second time. Not coincidence—but fate, pure unblemished fate. I sent Velda. During the war she had been young, beautiful, intelligent, a perfect agent to use against men. She was in the O.S.S., the O.S.I. and another highly secretive group and assigned to Operation Butterfly Two which was nailing Gerald Erlich and breaking down his organization. The war ended before it could happen, she was discharged, came with me into the agency because it was a work she knew and we stayed together until Rudy Civac called for protection. He expected me. He got her.

"Fate struck for sure when she saw him. She knew who he was. She knew that a man like that had to be stopped because he might still have his purposes going for him. There was the one thing she knew that made Gerald Erlich the most important man in the world right then. He knew the names and identities of every major agent he ever had working for him and these were such dedicated people they never stopped working—and now they were working for the Reds.

"Coincidence here. Or Fate. Either will do. This was the night the Red agents chose to act. They hit under the guise of burglars. They abducted Rudy Civac, his wife and Velda. They killed the wife, but they needed Rudy to find out exactly what he knew.

"And Velda played it smart. She made like she was part of Civac's group just to stay alive and it was conceivable that she had things they must know too. This we can't forget— Velda was a trained operative—she had prior experience even I didn't know about. Whatever she did she made it stick. They got Civac and her back into Europe and into Red territory and left the dead wife and the stolen jewels as a red herring that worked like a charm, and while Velda was in that goddamn Russian country I was drinking myself into a lousy pothole—"

She spoke for the first time. She said, "Mike—" and I squeezed open my eyes and looked at her.

"Thanks."

"It's all right. I understand."

I closed my eyes again and let the picture form.

"The Commies aren't the greatest brains in the world, though. Those stupid peasants forgot one thing. Both Civac —or Erlich—and Velda were pros. Someplace along the line they slipped and both of them cut out. They got loose inside the deep Iron Curtain and from then on the chase was on.

"Brother, I bet heads rolled after that. Anyway, when they knew two real hotshots were on the run they called in the top man to make the chase. *The Dragon.* Comrade Gorlin. But I like The Dragon better. I'll feel more like St. George when I kill him. *And won't Art hate me for that, I thought.*

"The chase took seven years. I think I know what happened during that time. Civac and Velda had to stay together to pool their escape resources. One way or another Velda was able to get things from Civac—or Erlich—and the big thing was those names. I'll bet she made him recount every one and she committed them to memory and carried them in her head all the way through so that she was fully as important now as Civac was.

"Don't underplay the Reds. They're filthy bastards, every one, but they're on the ball when it comes to thinking out the dirty work. They're so used to playing it themselves that it's second nature to them. Hell, they knew what happened. They knew Velda was as big as Erlich now—perhaps even bigger. Erlich's dreams were on the decline . . . what Velda knew would put us on the upswing again, so above all, she had to go.

"So The Dragon in his chase concentrated on those two.

Eventually he caught up with Erlich and shot him. That left Velda. Now he ran into a problem. During her war years she made a lot of contacts. One of them was Richie Cole. They'd meet occasionally when he was off assignment and talk over the old days and stayed good friends. She knew he was in Europe and somehow or other made contact with him. There wasn't time enough to pass on what she had memorized and it wasn't safe to write it down, so the answer was to get Velda back to the States with her information. There wasn't even time to assign the job to a proper agency.

"Richie Cole broke orders and took it upon himself to protect Velda and came back to the States. He knew he was followed. He knew The Dragon would make him a target—he knew damn well there wouldn't be enough time to do the right thing, but Velda had given him a name. She gave him me and a contact to make with an old newsie we both knew well.

"Sure, Cole tried to make the contact, but The Dragon shot him first. Trouble was, Cole didn't die. He told off until they got hold of me because Velda told him I was so damn big I could break the moon apart in my bare hands and he figured if she said it I really could. Then he saw me."

I put my face in my hands to rub out the picture. *"Then he saw me!"*

"Mike—"

"Let's face it, kid. I was a drunk."

"Mike—"

"Shut up. Let me talk."

Laura didn't answer, but her eyes hoped I wasn't going off the deep end, so I stopped a minute, poured some coffee, drank it, then started again.

"Once again those goddamn Reds were smart. They backtracked Velda and found out about me. They knew what Richie Cole was trying to do. Richie knew where Velda was and wanted to tell me. He died before he did. They thought he left the information with Old Dewey and killed the old man. They really thought I knew and they put a tail on me to see if I made a contact. They tore Dewey's place and my place apart looking for information they thought Cole might have passed to me. Hell, The Dragon even tried to kill me because he thought I wasn't really important at all and was better out of the way."

I leaned back in the chair, my insides feeling hollow all of a sudden. Laura asked, "Mike, what's the matter?"

"Something's missing. Something big."

"Please don't talk any more."

"It's not that. I'm just tired, I guess. It's hard to come back to normal this fast."

"If we took a swim it might help."

I opened my eyes and looked at her and grinned. "Sick of hearing hard luck stories?"

"No."

"Any questions?"

She nodded. "Leo. Who shot him?"

I said, "In this business guns can be found anywhere. I'm never surprised to see guns with the same ballistics used in different kills. Did you know the same gun that shot your husband and Richie Cole was used in some small kill out West?"

"No, I didn't know that."

"There seemed to be a connection through the jewels. Richie's cover was that of a sailor and smuggler. Your jewels were missing. Pat made that a common factor. I don't believe it."

"Could Leo's position in government—well, as you intimated—"

"There is a friend of mine who says no. He has reason to know the facts. I'll stick with him."

"Then Leo's death is no part of what you are looking for?"

"I don't think so. In a way I'm sorry. I wish I could help avenge him too. He was a great man."

"Yes, he was."

"I'll take you up on that swim."

"The suits are in the bathhouse."

"That should be fun," I said.

In the dim light that came through the ivy-screened windows we turned our backs and took off our clothes. When you do that deliberately with a woman, it's hard to talk and you are conscious only of the strange warmth and the brief, fiery contact when skin meets skin and a crazy desire to turn around and watch or to grab and hold or do anything except what you said you'd do when the modest moment was in reality a joke—but you didn't quite want it to be a joke at all.

Then before we could turn it into something else and while we could still treat it as a joke, we had the bathing suits on and she grinned as she passed by me. I reached for her, stopped her, then turned because I saw something else that left me cold for little *ticks* of time.

Laura said, "What is it, Mike?"

I picked the shotgun out of the corner of the room. The building had been laid up on an extension of the tennis court outside and the temporary floor was clay. Where the gun rested by the door water from the outside shower had seeped in and wet it down until it was a semi-firm substance, a blue putty you could mold in your hand.

*She had put the shotgun down muzzle first and both barrels*

*were plugged with clay and when I picked it up it was like
somebody had taken a bite out of the blue glop with a cookie
cutter two inches deep!*

Before I opened it I asked her, "Loaded?"

"Yes."

I thumbed the lever and broke the gun. It fell open and I
picked out the two twelve-gauge Double O shells, then
slapped the barrels against my palm until the cores of clay
emerged far enough for me to pull them out like the deadly
plugs they were.

She saw the look on my face and frowned, not knowing
what to say. So I said it instead. "Who put the gun here?"

"I did."

"I thought you knew how to handle it?" There was a rasp
in my voice you could cut with a knife.

"Leo—showed me how to shoot it."

"He didn't show you how to handle it, apparently."

"Mike—"

"Listen, Laura, and you listen good. You play with guns
and you damn well better *know* how to handle them. You
went and stuck this baby's nose down in the muck and do you
know what would happen if you ever tried to shoot it?"

Her eyes were frightened at what she saw in my face and
she shook her head. "Well, damn it, you listen then. Without
even thinking you stuck this gun in heavy clay and plugged
both barrels. It's loaded with high-grade sporting ammuni-
tion of the best quality and if you ever pulled the trigger
you would have had one infinitesimal span of life between the
big then and the big now because when you did the back blast
in that gun would have wiped you right off the face of the
earth."

"Mike—"

"No—keep quiet and listen. It'll do you good. You won't make the mistake again. That barrel would unpeel like a tangerine and you'd get that whole charge right down your lovely throat and if ever you want to give a police medical examiner a job to gag a maggot, that's the way to do it. They'd have to go in and scrape your brains up with a silent butler and pick pieces of your skull out of the woodwork with needle-nosed pliers. I saw eyeballs stuck to a wall one time and if you want to *really* see a disgusting sight, try that. They're bigger than you would expect them to be and they leak fluid all the time they look at you trying to lift them off the boards and then you have no place to put them except in your hand and drop them in the bucket with the rest of the pieces. They float on top and keep watching you until you put on the lid."

*"Mike!"*

"Damn it, shut up! Don't play guns stupidly around me! You did it, now listen!"

Both hands covered her mouth and she was almost ready to vomit.

"The worst of all is the neck because the head is gone and the neck spurts blood for a little bit while the heart doesn't know its vital nerve center is gone—and do you know how high the blood can squirt? No? Then let me tell you. It doesn't just ooze. It goes up under pressure for a couple of feet and covers everything in the area and you wouldn't believe just how much blood the body has in it until you see a person suddenly become headless and watch what happens. I've been there. I've had it happen. *Don't let it happen to you!"*

She let her coffee go on the other side of the door and I didn't give a damn because anybody that careless with a shotgun or any other kind of a gun needs it like that to make them remember. I wiped the barrels clean, reloaded the gun and put it down in place, butt first.

When I came out Laura said, "Man, are you mean."

"It's not a new saying." I still wasn't over my mad.

Her smile was a little cockeyed, but a smile nevertheless. "Mike—I understand. Please?"

"Really?"

"Yes."

"Then you watch it. I play guns too much. It's my business. I hate to see them abused."

"Please, Mike?"

"Okay. I made my point."

"Nobly, to say the least. I usually have a strong stomach."

"Go have some coffee."

"Oh, Mike."

"So take a swim," I told her and grinned. It was the way I felt and the grin was the best I could do. She took a run and a dive and hit the water, came up stroking for the other side, then draped her arms on the edge of the drain and waited for me.

I went in slowly, walking up to the edge, then I dove in and stayed on the bottom until I got to the other side. The water made her legs fuzzy, distorting them to Amazonian proportions, enlarging the cleft and swells and declivities of her belly, then I came up to where all was real and shoved myself to concrete surface and reached down for Laura.

She said, "Better?" when I pulled her to the top.

I was looking past her absently. "Yes. I just remembered something."

"Not about the gun, Mike."

"No, not about the gun."

"Should I know?"

"It doesn't matter. I don't really know myself yet. It's just a point."

"Your eyes look terribly funny."

"I know."

"Mike—"

"What?"

"Can I help?"

"No."

"You're going to leave me now, aren't you?"

"Yes, I am."

"Will you come back?"

I couldn't answer her.

"It's between the two of us, isn't it?"

"The girl hunters are out," I said.

"But will you come back?"

My mind was far away, exploring the missing point. "Yes," I said, "I have to come back."

"You loved her."

"I did."

"Do you love me at all?"

I turned around and looked at this woman. She was mine now, beautiful, wise, the way a woman should be formed for a man like I was, lovely, always naked in my sight, always incredibly blonde and incredibly tanned, the difference in color—or was it comparison—a shocking, sensual thing. I said, "I love you, Laura. Can I be mistaken?"

She said, "No, you can't be mistaken."

"I have to find her first. She's being hunted. Everybody is hunting her. I loved her a long time ago so I owe her that much. She asked for me."

"Find her, Mike."

I nodded. I had the other key now. "I'll find her. She's the most important thing in this old world today. What she knows will decide the fate of nations. Yes, I'll find her."

"Then will you come back?"

"Then I'll come back," I said.

Her arms reached out and encircled me, her hands holding my head, her fingers tight in my hair. I could feel every inch of her body pressed hard against mine, forcing itself to meet me, refusing to give at all. At all.

"I'm going to fight her for you," she said.

"Why?"

"Because you're mine now."

"Girl," I said, "I'm no damn good to anybody. Look good and you'll see a corn ear husked, you know?"

"I know. So I eat husks."

"Damn it, don't fool around!"

"Mike!"

"Laura—"

"You say it nice, Mike—but there's something in your voice that's terrible and I can sense it. If you find her, what will you do?"

"I can't tell."

"Will you still come back?"

"Damn it, I don't know."

"Why don't you know, Mike?"

I looked down at her. "Because I don't know what I'm really like any more. Look—do you know what I *was*? Do you know that a judge and jury took me down and the whole world once ripped me to little bits? It was only Velda who stayed with me then."

"That was then. How long ago was it?"

"Nine years maybe."

"Were you married?"

"No."

"Then I can claim part of you. I've had part of you." She let go of me and stood back, her eyes calm as they looked into mine. "Find her, Mike. Make your decision. Find her and take her. Have you ever had her at all?"

"No."

"You've had *me*. Maybe you're more mine than hers."

"Maybe."

"Then find her." She stepped back, her hands at her side. "If what you said was true then she deserves this much. You find her, Mike. I'm willing to fight you for anybody—but not somebody you think is dead. Not somebody you think you owe a debt to. Let me love you my own way. It's enough for me at least. Do you understand that?"

For a while we stood there. I looked at her. I looked away. I said, "Yes, I understand."

"Come back when you've decided."

"You have all of Washington to entertain."

Laura shook her head. Her hair was a golden swirl and she said, "The hell with Washington. I'll be waiting for you."

*Velda, Laura. The names were so similar. Which one? After seven years of nothingness, which one? Knowing what I did, which one? Yesterday was then. Today was now. Which one?*

I said, "All right, Laura, I'll find out, then I'll come back."

"Take my car."

"Thanks."

And now I had to take her. My fingers grabbed her arms and pulled her close to where I could kiss her and taste the inside of her mouth and feel the sensuous writhing of her tongue against mine because this was the woman I knew I was coming back to.

The *Girl Hunters*. We all wanted the same one and for reasons of a long time ago. We would complete the hunt, but what would we do with the kill?

She said, "After that you shouldn't leave."

"I have to," I said.

"Why?"

"She had to get in this country someway. I think I know how."

"You'll find her then come back?"

"Yes," I said, and let my hands roam over her body so that she knew there could never be anybody else, and when I was done I held her off and made her stay there while I went inside to put on the gun and the coat and go back to the new Babylon that was the city.

# CHAPTER 11

And once again it was night, the city coming into its nether life like a minion of Count Dracula. The bright light of day that could strip away the facade of sham and lay bare the coating of dirt was gone now, and to the onlooker the unreal became real, the dirt had changed into subtle colors under artificial lights and it was as if all of that vast pile of concrete and steel and glass had been built only to live at night.

I left the car at the Sportsmen's Parking Lot on the corner of Eighth and Fifty-second, called Hy Gardner and told him to meet me at the Blue Ribbon on Forty-fourth, then started my walk to the restaurant thinking of the little things I should have thought of earlier.

The whole thing didn't seem possible, all those years trapped in Europe. You could walk around the world half a dozen times in seven years. But you wouldn't be trapped then. The thing was, they *were* trapped. Had Velda or Erlich been amateurs they would have been captured without much trouble, but being pros they edged out. Almost. That made Velda even better than he had been.

Somehow, it didn't seem possible.

But it was.

Hy had reached the Blue Ribbon before me and waited at a table sipping a stein of rich, dark beer. I nodded at the waiter and he went back for mine. We ordered, ate, and only then did Hy bother to give me his funny look over the cigar he lit up. "It's over?"

"It won't be long now."

"Do we talk about it here?"

"Here's as good as any. It's more than you can put in your column."

"You let me worry about space."

So he sat back and let me tell him what I had told Laura, making occasional notes, because now was the time to make notes. I told him what I knew and what I thought and where everybody stood, and every minute or so he'd glance up from his sheets with an expression of pure incredulity, shake his head and write some more. When the implications of the total picture began really to penetrate, his teeth clamped down on the cigar until it was half hanging out of his mouth unlit, then he threw it down on his plate and put a fresh one in its place.

When I finished he said, "Mike—do you realize what you have hold of?"

"I know."

"How can you stay so damn calm?"

"Because the rough part has just started."

"Ye gods, man—"

"You know what's missing, don't you?"

"Sure. You're missing something in the head. You're trying to stand off a whole political scheme that comes at you with every force imaginable no matter where you are. Mike, you don't fight these guys alone!"

"Nuts. It looks like I have to. I'm not exactly an accredited type character. Who would listen to me?"

"Couldn't this Art Rickerby—"

"He has one purpose in mind. He wants whoever killed Richie Cole."

"That doesn't seem likely. He's a trained Federal agent."

"So what? When something hits you personally, patriotism can go by the boards awhile. There are plenty of other agents. He wants a killer and knows I'll eventually come up with him. Like Velda's a key to one thing, I'm a key to another. They think that I'm going to stumble over whatever it was Richie Cole left for me. I know what it was now. So do you, don't you?"

"Yes," Hy said. "It was Velda's location, wherever she is."

"That's right. They don't know if I know or if I'll find out. You can damn well bet that they know he stayed alive waiting for me to show. They can't even be sure if he just clued me. They can't be sure of anything, but they know that I have to stay alive if they want to find Velda too."

Hy's eyes went deep in thought. "Alive? They tried to shoot you twice, didn't they?"

"Fine, but neither shot connected and I can't see a top assassin missing a shot. Both times I was a perfect target."

"Why the attempt then?"

"I'll tell you why," I said. I leaned on the table feeling my hands go open and shut wanting to squeeze the life out of somebody. "Both tries were deliberately sour. They were pushing me. They wanted me to move fast, and if anything

can stir a guy up it's getting shot at. If I had anything to hide
or to work at, it would come out in a hurry."

"But you didn't bring anything out?"

I grinned at him and I could see my reflection in the glass
facing of the autographed pictures behind his head. It wasn't
a pretty face at all, teeth and hate and some wildness hard to
describe. "No, I didn't. So now I'm a real target because I
know too much. They know I *don't* have Velda's location and
from now on I can only be trouble to them. I'll bet you that
right now a hunt is on for me."

"Mike—if you called Pat—"

"Come off it. He's no friend anymore. He'll do anything to
nail my ass down and don't you forget it."

"Does he know the facts?"

"No. The hell with him."

Hy pushed his glasses up on his head, frowning. "Well,
what are you going to do?"

"Do, old buddy? I'll tell you what I'm going to do. I'm
going after the missing piece. If I weren't so damn slow after
all those years I would have caught it before. I'm going after
the facts that can wrap up the ball game and you're going
with me."

"But you said—"

"Uh-uh. I didn't say anything. I *don't* know where she is,
but I do know a few other things. Richie Cole came blasting
back into this country when he shouldn't have and ducked
out to look for me. That had a big fat meaning and I muffed
it. Damn it, I muffed it!"

"But how?"

"Come on, Hy—Richie was a sailor—he smuggled her on
the ship he came in on. *He never left her in Europe! He got
her back in this country!*"

He put the cigar down slowly, getting the implication.

I said, "He had to smuggle her out, otherwise they would have killed her. If they took a plane they would have blown it over the ocean, or if she sailed under an assumed name and cover identity they would have had enough time to locate her and a passenger would simply fall overboard. No, he smuggled her out. He got her on that ship and got her into this country."

"You make it sound easy."

"Sure it's easy! You think there wasn't some cooperation with others in the crew! Those boys love to outfox the captain and the customs. What would they care as long as it was on Cole's head? He was on a tramp steamer and they can do practically anything on those babies if they know how and want to. Look, you want me to cite you examples?"

"I know it could be done."

"All right, then here's the catch. Richie realized how close The Dragon was to Velda when they left. He had no time. He had to act on his own. This was a project bigger than any going in the world at the time, big enough to break regulations for. He got her out—but he didn't underestimate the enemy either. He knew they'd figure it and be waiting.

"They were, too," I continued. "The Dragon was there all right, and he followed Cole thinking he was going to an appointed place where he had already hidden Velda, but when he realized that Cole wasn't doing anything of the kind he figured the angles quickly. He shot Cole, had to leave because of the crowd that collected and didn't have a chance until later to reach Old Dewey, then found out about me. Don't ask me the details about *how* they can do it—they have resources at their fingertips everywhere. Later he went back, killed Dewey, didn't find the note Cole left and had to stick with me to see where I led him."

Hy was frowning again.

I said, "I couldn't lead him to Velda. I didn't know. But before long he'll figure out the same thing I did. Somebody else helped Cole get her off that boat and knows where she is!"

"What are you going to do?" His voice was quietly calm next to mine.

"Get on that ship and see who else was in on the deal."

"How?"

"Be my guest and I'll show you the seamier side of life."

"You know me," Hy said, standing up.

I paid the cabbie outside Benny Joe Grissi's bar and when Hy saw where we were he let out a low whistle and said he hoped I knew what I was doing. We went inside and Sugar Boy and his smaller friend were still at their accustomed places and when Sugar Boy saw me he got a little pasty around the mouth and looked toward the bar with a quick motion of his head.

Benny Joe gave the nod and we walked past without saying a word, and when I got to the bar I held out the card Art Rickerby had given me and let Benny Joe take a long look at it. "In case you get ideas like before, mister. I'll shoot this place apart and you with it."

"Say, Mike, I never—"

"Tone it down," I said. "Bayliss Henry here?"

"Pepper? Yeah. He went in the can."

"Wait here, Hy."

I went down the end to the door stenciled MEN and pushed on in. Old Bayliss was at the washstand drying his hands and saw me in the mirror, his eyes suddenly wary at the recognition. He turned around and put his hands on my chest. "Mike, my boy, no more. Whatever it is, I want none of it. The last time out taught me a lesson I won't forget. I'm old, I scare easy, and what life is left to me I want to enjoy. Okay?"

"Sure."

"Then forget whatever you came in here to ask me. Don't let me talk over my head about the old days or try and make like a reporter again."

"You won't get shot at."

Bayliss nodded and shrugged. "How can I argue with you? What do you want to know?"

"What ship was Richie Cole on?"

"The *Vanessa*."

"What pier?"

"She was at number twelve, but that won't do you any good now."

"Why not?"

"Hell, she sailed the day before yesterday."

What I had to say I did under my breath. Everything was right out the window because I thought too slow and a couple of days had made all the difference.

"What was on it, Mike?"

"I wanted to see a guy."

"Oh? I thought it was the ship. Well maybe you can still see some of the guys. You know the *Vanessa* was the ship they had the union trouble with. Everybody complained about the chow and half the guys wouldn't sign back on. The union really laid into 'em."

Then suddenly there was a chance again and I had to grab at it. "Listen, Bayliss—who did Cole hang around with on the ship?"

"Jeepers, Mike, out at sea—"

"Did he have any friends on board?"

"Well, no, I'd say."

"Come on, damn it, a guy doesn't sail for months and not make some kind of an acquaintance!"

"Yeah, I know—well, Cole was a chess player and there was this one guy—let's see, Red Markham—yeah, that's it, Red Markham. They'd have drinks together and play chess together because Red sure could play chess. One time—"

"Where can I find this guy?"

"You know where Annie Stein's pad is?"

"The flophouse?"

"Yeah. Well, you look for him there. He gets drunk daytimes and flops early."

"Suppose you go along."

"Mike, I told you—"

"Hy Gardner's outside."

Bayliss looked up and grinned. "Well, shoot. If he's along I'll damn well go. He was still running copy when I did the police beat."

Annie Stein's place was known as the Harbor Hotel. It was a dollar a night flop, pretty expensive as flops go, so the trade was limited to occasional workers and itinerant seamen. It was old and dirty and smelled of disinfectant and urine partially smothered by an old-man odor of defeat and decay.

The desk clerk froze when we walked in, spun the book around without asking, not wanting any trouble at all. Red Markham was in the third room on the second floor, his door half open, the sound and smell of him oozing into the corridor.

I pushed the door open and flipped on the light. Overhead

a sixty-watt bulb turned everything yellow. He was curled on the cot, an empty pint bottle beside him, breathing heavily through his mouth. On the chair with his jacket and hat was a pocket-sized chessboard with pegged chessmen arranged in some intricate move.

It took ten minutes of cold wet towels and a lot of shaking to wake him up. His eyes still had a whiskey glassiness and he didn't know what we wanted at all. He was unintelligible for another thirty minutes, then little by little he began to come around, his face going through a succession of emotions. Until he saw Bayliss he seemed scared, but one look at the old man and he tried on a drunken grin, gagged and went into a spasm of dry heaves. Luckily, there was nothing in his stomach, so we didn't have to go through that kind of mess.

Hy brought in a glass of water and I made him sip at it. I said, "What's your name, feller?"

He hiccoughed. "You—cops?"

"No, a friend."

"Oh." His head wobbled, then he looked back to me again. "You play chess?"

"Sorry, Red, but I had a friend who could. Richie Cole."

Markham squinted and nodded solemnly, remembering. "He—pretty damn good. Yessir. Good guy."

I asked him, "Did you know about the girl on the ship?"

Very slowly, he scowled, his lips pursing out, then a bit of clarity returned to him and he leered with a drunken grimace. "Sure. Hell of—joke." He hiccoughed and grinned again. "Joke. Hid—her in—down in—hold."

We were getting close now. His eyes drooped sleepily and I wanted him to hang on. I said, "Where is she now, Red?"

He just looked at me foggily.

"Damn it, think about it!"

For a second he didn't like the way I yelled or my hand on his arm and he was about to balk, then Bayliss said, "Come on, Red, if you know where she is, tell us."

You'd think he was seeing Bayliss for the first time. "Pepper," he said happily, his eyes coming open.

"Come on, Red. The girl on the *Vanessa*. Richie's girl."

"Sure. Big—joke. You know?"

"We know, but tell us where she is."

His shrug was the elaborate gesture of the sodden drunk. "Dunno. I—got her—on deck."

Bayliss looked at me, not knowing where to go. It was all over his head and he was taking the lead from me. Then he got the pitch and shook Red's shoulder. "Is she on shore?"

Red chuckled and his head weaved. "On—shore. Sure—on shore." He laughed again, the picture coming back to his mind. "Dennis—Wallace packed her—in crate. Very funny."

I pushed Bayliss away and sat on the edge of the cot. "It sure was a good joke all right. Now where did the crate go?"

"Crate?"

"She was packed in the crate. This Dennis Wallace packed her in the crate, right?"

"Right!" he said assuredly, slobbering on himself.

"Then who got the crate?"

"Big joke."

"I know, now let us in on it. Who got the crate?"

He made another one of those shrugs. "I—dunno."

"Somebody picked it up," I reminded him.

Red's smile was real foolish, that of the drunk trying to be secretive. "Richie's—joke. He called—a friend. Dennis gave him—the crate." He laughed again. "Very funny."

Hy said, "Cute."

I nodded. "Yeah. Now we have to find this Dennis guy."

"He's got a place not far from here," Bayliss said.

"You know everybody?"

"I've been around a long time, Mike."

We went to leave Red Markham sitting there, but before we could reach the door he called out, "Hey, you."

Bayliss said, "What, Red?"

"How come—everybody wants—old Dennis?"

"I don't—"

My hand stopped the old guy and I walked back to the cot. "Who else wanted Dennis, Red?"

"Guy—gimme this pint." He reached for the bottle, but was unable to make immediate contact. When he did he sucked at the mouth of it, swallowed as though it was filled and put the bottle down.

"What did he look like, Red?"

"Oh—" he lolled back against the wall. "Big guy. Like you."

"Go on."

"Mean. Son of a—he was mean. You ever see—mean ones? Like a damn Indian. Something like Injun Pete on the *Darby Standard*—he—"

I didn't bother to hear him finish. I looked straight at Hy and felt cold all over. "The Dragon," I said. "He's one step up."

Hy had a quiet look on his face. "That's what I almost forgot to tell you about, Mike."

"What?"

"The Dragon. I got inside the code name from our people overseas. There may be two guys because The Dragon code breaks down to *tooth* and *nail*. When they operate as a team they're simply referred to as The Dragon."

"Great," I said. "Swell. That's all we need for odds." My

mouth had a bad taste in it. "Show us Dennis's place, Bayliss.
We can't stay here any longer."

"Not me," he said. "You guys go it alone. Whatever it is
that's going on, I don't like it. I'll tell you where, but I'm not
going in any more dark places with you. Right now I'm going
back to Benny Joe Grissi's bar and get stinking drunk where
you can't get at me and if anything happens I'll read about it
in the papers tomorrow."

"Good enough, old-timer. Now where does Dennis live?"

The rooming house was a brownstone off Ninth Avenue, a
firetrap like all the others on the block, a crummy joint filled
with cubicles referred to as furnished rooms. The landlady
came out of the front floor flat, looked at me and said, "I don't
want no cops around here," and when Hy handed her the ten-
spot her fat face made a brief smile and she added, "So I made
a mistake. Cops don't give away the green. What're you
after?"

"Dennis Wallace. He's a seaman and—"

"Top floor front. Go on up. He's got company."

I flashed Hy a nod, took the stairs with him behind me
while I yanked the .45 out and reached the top floor in seconds. The old carpet under our feet puffed dust with every
step but muffled them effectively and when I reached the
door there was no sound from within and a pencil-thin line
of light seeped out at the sill. I tried the knob, pushed the
door open and was ready to cut loose at anything that moved
wrong.

But there was no need for any shooting, if the little guy on
the floor with his hands tied behind him and his throat slit
wide open was Dennis Wallace, for his killer was long gone.

The fat landlady screeched when she saw the body and told

us it was Dennis all right. She waddled downstairs again and pointed to the wall phone and after trying four different numbers I got Pat and told him I was with another dead man. It wasn't anything startling, he was very proper about getting down the details and told me to stay right there. His voice had a fine tone of satisfaction to it that said he had me where he could make me sweat and maybe even break me like he had promised.

Hy came down as I hung up and tapped my shoulder. "You didn't notice something on the guy up there."

"What's that?"

"All that blood didn't come from his throat. His gut is all carved up and his mouth is taped shut. The blood obscures the tape."

"Tortured?"

"It sure looks that way."

The landlady was in her room taking a quick shot for her nerves and seemed to hate us for causing all the trouble. I asked her when Dennis' guest had arrived and she said a couple of hours ago. She hadn't heard him leave so she assumed he was still there. Her description was brief, but enough. He was a big mean-looking guy who reminded her of an Indian.

There was maybe another minute before a squad car would come along and I didn't want to be here when that happened. I pulled Hy out on the stoop and said, "I'm going to take off."

"Pat won't like it."

"There isn't time to talk about it. You can give him the poop."

"All of it?"

"Every bit. Lay it out for him."

"What about you?"

"Look, you saw what happened. The Dragon put it together the same way I did. He was here when the boat docked and Richie Cole knew it. So Richie called for a friend who knew the ropes, told him to pick up the crate with Velda in it and where to bring it. He left and figured right when he guessed anybody waiting would follow him. He pulled them away from the boat and tried to make contact with Old Dewey at the newsstand and what he had for Dewey was the location of where that friend was to bring the crate."

"Then there's one more step."

"That's right. The friend."

"You can't trace that call after all this time."

"I don't think I have to."

Hy shook his head. "If Cole was a top agent then he didn't have any friends."

"He had one," I said.

"Who?"

"Velda."

"But—"

"So he could just as well have another. Someone who was in the same game with him during the war, someone he knew would realize the gravity of the situation and act immediately and someone he knew would be capable of fulfilling the mission."

"Who, Mike?"

I didn't tell him. "I'll call you when it's over. You tell Pat."

Down the street a squad car turned the corner. I went down the steps and went in the other direction, walking casually, then when I reached Ninth, I flagged a cab and gave him the parking lot where I had left Laura's car.

# CHAPTER 12

If I was wrong, the girl hunters would have Velda. She'd be dead. They wanted nothing of her except that she be dead. Damn their stinking hides anyway. Damn them and their philosophies! Death and destruction were the only things the Kremlin crowd was capable of. They knew the value of violence and death and used it over and over in a wild scheme to smash everything flat but their own kind.

But there was one thing they didn't know. They didn't know how to handle it when it came back to them and exploded in their own faces. Let her be dead, *I thought,* and I'll start a hunt of my own. They think *they* can hunt? Shit. They didn't know how to be *really* violent. Death? I'd get them, every one, no matter how big or little, or wherever they were. I'd cut them down like so many grapes in ways that would scare the living crap out of them and those next in line for my kill would never know a second's peace until their heads went flying every which way.

So I'd better not be wrong.

Dennis Wallace had known who was to pick up the crate. There wouldn't have been time for elaborate exchanges of coded recognition signals and if Dennis had known it was more than just a joke he might conceivably have backed out. No, it had to be quick and simple and not at all frightening. He had turned the crate over to a guy whose name had been given him and since it was big enough a truck would have been used in the delivery. He would have seen lettering on the truck, he would have been able to identify both it and the driver, and with some judicious knife work on his belly he would have had his memory jarred into remembering every single detail of the transaction.

I had to be right.

Art Rickerby had offered the clue.

The guy's name had to be Alex Bird, Richie's old war buddy in the O.S.S. who had a chicken farm up in Marlboro, New York, and who most likely had a pickup truck that could transport a crate. He would do the favor, keep his mouth shut and forget it the way he had been trained to, and it was just as likely he missed any newspaper squibs about Richie's death and so didn't show up to talk to the police when Richie was killed.

By the time I reached the George Washington Bridge the stars were wiped out of the night sky and you could smell the rain again. I took the Palisades Drive and where I turned off to pick up the Thruway the rain came down in fine slanting lines that laid a slick on the road and whipped in the window.

I liked a night like this. It could put a quiet on everything. Your feet walked softer and dogs never barked in the rain. It obscured visibility and overrode sounds that could give you away otherwise and sometimes was so soothing that you could be lulled into a death sleep. Yeah, I remembered other nights like this too. Death nights.

At Newburgh I turned off the Thruway, drove down 17K into town and turned north on 9W. I stopped at a gas station when I reached Marlboro and asked the attendant if he knew where Alex Bird lived.

Yes, he knew. He pointed the way out and just to be sure I sketched out the route then picked up the blacktop road that led back into the country.

I passed by it the first time, turned around at the crossroad cursing to myself, then eased back up the road looking for the mailbox. There was no name on it, just a big wooden cutout of a bird. It was in the shadow of a tree before, but now my lights picked it out and when they did I spotted the drive, turned in, angled off into a cut in the bushes and killed the engine.

The farmhouse stood an eighth of a mile back off the road, an old building restored to more modern taste. In back of it, dimly lit by the soft glow of night lights, were two long chicken houses, the manure odor of them hanging in the wet air. On the right, a hundred feet away, a two-story boxlike barn stood in deep shadow, totally dark.

Only one light was on in the house when I reached it, downstairs on the chimney side and obviously in a living room. I held there a minute, letting my eyes get adjusted to the place. There were no cars around, but that didn't count since there were too many places to hide one. I took out the .45, jacked a shell in the chamber and thumbed the hammer back.

But before I could move another light went on in the opposite downstairs room. Behind the curtains a shadow moved slowly, purposefully, passed the window several times then disappeared altogether. I waited, but the light didn't go out. Instead, one top-floor light came on, but too dimly to do more than vaguely outline the form of a person on the curtains.

Then it suddenly made sense to me and I ran across the distance to the door. Somebody was searching the house.

The door was locked and too heavy to kick in. I hoped the rain covered the racket I made, then laid my trench coat against the window and pushed. The glass shattered inward to the carpeted floor without much noise, I undid the catch, lifted the window and climbed over the sill.

Alex Bird would be the thin, balding guy tied to the straightback chair. His head slumped forward, his chin on his chest and when I tilted his head back his eyes stared at me life-lessly. There was a small lumpy bruise on the side of his head where he had been hit, but outside of a chafing of his wrists and ankles, there were no other marks on him. His body had the warmth of death only a few minutes old and I had seen too many heart-attack cases not to be able to diagnose this one.

The Dragon had reached Alex Bird, all right. He had him right where he could make him talk and the little guy's heart exploded on him. That meant just one thing. He hadn't talked. The Dragon was still searching. *He didn't know where she was yet!*

And right then, right that very second he was upstairs tear-ing the house apart!

The stairs were at a shallow angle reaching to the upper landing and I hugged the wall in the shadows until I could definitely place him from the sounds. I tried to keep from laughing out loud because I felt so good, and although I could hold back the laugh I couldn't suppress the grin. I could feel it stretch my face and felt the pull across my shoulders and back, then I got ready to go.

I knew when he felt it. When death is your business you have a feeling for it; an animal instinct can tell when it's close even when you can't see it or hear it. You just know it's there. And like he knew suddenly that I was there, I realized he knew it too.

Upstairs the sounds stopped abruptly. There was the smallest of metallic *clicks* that could have been made by a gun, but that was all. Both of us were waiting. Both of us knew we wouldn't wait long.

You can't play games when time is so important. You take a chance on being hit and maybe living through it just so you get one clean shot in where it counts. You have to end the play knowing one must die and sometimes two and there's no other way. For the first time you both know it's pro against pro, two cold, calm killers facing each other down and there's no such thing as sportsmanship and if an advantage is offered it will be taken and whoever offered it will be dead.

We came around the corners simultaneously with the rolling thunder of the .45 blanking out the rod in his hand and I felt a sudden torch along my side and another on my arm. It was immediate and unaimed diversionary fire until you could get the target lined up and in the space of four rapid-fire shots I saw him, huge at the top of the stairs, his high-cheekboned face truly Indianlike, the black hair low on his forehead and his mouth twisted open in the sheer enjoyment of what he was doing.

Then my shot slammed the gun out of his hand and the advantage was his because he was up there, a crazy killer with a scream on his lips and like the animal he was he re-

acted instantly and dove headlong at me through the acrid
fumes of the gunsmoke.

The impact knocked me flat on my back, smashing into a
corner table so that the lamp shattered into a million pieces
beside my head. I had my hands on him, his coat tore, a long
tattered slice of it in my fingers, then he kicked free with a
snarl and a guttural curse, rolling to his feet like an acrobat.
The .45 had skittered out of my hand and lay up against the
step. All it needed was a quick movement and it was mine. He
saw the action, figured the odds and knew he couldn't reach
me before I had the gun, and while I grabbed it up he was
into the living room and out the front door. The slide was
forward and the hammer back so there was still one shot left
at least and he couldn't afford the chance of losing. I saw
his blurred shadow racing toward the drive and when my
shadow broke the shaft of light coming from the door he
swerved into the darkness of the barn and I let a shot go at
him and heard it smash into the woodwork.

It was my last. This time the slide stayed back. I dropped
the gun in the grass, ran to the barn before he could pull the
door closed and dived into the darkness.

He was on me like a cat, but he made a mistake in reaching
for my right hand thinking I had the gun there. I got the
other hand in his face and damn near tore it off. He didn't
yell. He made a sound deep in his throat and went for my
neck. He was big and strong and wild mean, but it was
my kind of game too. I heaved up and threw him off, got to my
feet and kicked out to where he was. I missed my aim, but my
toe took him in the side and he grunted and came back with
a vicious swipe of his hand I could only partially block. I felt
his next move coming and let an old-time reflex take over.
The judo bit is great if everything is going for you, but a

terrible right cross to the face can destroy judo or karate or anything else if it gets there first.

My hand smashed into bone and flesh and with the meaty impact I could smell the blood and hear the gagging intake of his breath. He grabbed, his arms like great claws. He just held on and I knew if I couldn't break him loose he could kill me. He figured I'd start the knee coming up and turned to block it with a half-turn. But I did something worse, I grabbed him with my hands, squeezed and twisted and his scream was like a woman's, so high-pitched as almost to be noiseless, and in his frenzy of pain he shoved me so violently I lost that fanatical hold of what manhood I had left him, and with some blind hate driving him he came at me as I stumbled over something and fell on me like a wild beast, his teeth tearing at me, his hands searching and ripping and I felt the shock of incredible pain and ribs break under his pounding and I couldn't get him off no matter what I did, and he was holding me down and butting me with his head while he kept up that whistlelike screaming and in another minute it would be me dead and him alive, then Velda dead.

And when I thought of her name something happened, that little thing you have left over was there and I got my elbow up, smashed his head back unexpectedly, got a short one to his jaw again, then another, and another, and another, then I was on top of him and hitting, hitting, smashing—and he wasn't moving at all under me. He was breathing, but not moving.

I got up and found the doorway somehow, standing there to suck in great breaths of air. I could feel the blood running from my mouth and nose, wetting my shirt, and with each breath my side would wrench and tear. The two bullet burns were nothing compared to the rest. I had been squeezed dry, pulled apart, almost destroyed, but I had won. Now the son of a bitch would die.

Inside the door I found a light switch. It only threw on a small bulb overhead, but it was enough. I walked back to where he lay face up and then spat down on The Dragon. Mechanically, I searched his pockets, found nothing except money until I saw that one of my fists had torn his hair loose at the side and when I ripped the wig off there were several small strips of microfilm hidden there.

Hell, I didn't know what they were. I didn't care. I even grinned at the slob because he sure did look like an Indian now, only one that had been half scalped by an amateur. He was big, big. Cheekbones high, a Slavic cast to his eyes, his mouth a cruel slash, his eyebrows thick and black. Half bald, though, he wouldn't have looked too much like an Indian. Not our kind, anyway.

There was an ax on the wall, a long-handled, double-bitted ax with a finely honed edge and I picked it from the pegs and went back to The Dragon.

Just how *did* you kill a dragon? I could bury the ax in his belly. That would be fun, all right. Stick it right in the middle of his skull and it would look a lot better. They wouldn't come fooling around after seeing pictures of that. How about the neck? One whack and his head would roll like the Japs used to do. But nuts, why be that kind?

This guy was *really* going to die.

I looked at the big pig, put the ax down and nudged him with my toe. What was it Art had said? Like about suffering? I thought he was nuts, but he could be right. Yeah, he sure could be right. Still, there had to be some indication that people were left who treat those Commie slobs like they liked to treat people.

Some indication.

He was Gorlin now, Comrade Gorlin. Dragons just aren't dragons anymore when they're bubbling blood over their chins.

I walked around the building looking for an *indication.*

I found it on a workbench in the back.

A twenty-penny nail and a ball peen hammer. The nail seemed about four inches long and the head big as a dime.

I went back and turned Comrade Gorlin over on his face.

I stretched his arm out palm down on the floor.

I tapped the planks until I found a floor beam and put his hand on it.

It was too bad he wasn't conscious.

Then I held the nail in the middle of the back of his hand and slammed it in with the hammer and slammed and slammed and slammed until the head of that nail dimpled his skin and he was so tightly pinned to the floor like a piece of equipment he'd never get loose until he was pried out and he wasn't going to do it with a ball peen. I threw the hammer down beside him and said, "Better'n handcuffs, buddy," but he didn't get the joke. He was still out.

Outside, the rain came down harder. It always does after a thing like that, trying to flush away the memory of it. I picked up my gun, took it in the house and dismantled it, wiped it dry and reassembled the piece.

Only then did I walk to the telephone and ask the operator to get me New York and the number I gave her was that of the Peerage Brokers.

Art Rickerby answered the phone himself. He said, "Mike?"

"Yes."

For several seconds there was silence. "Mike—"

"I have him for you. He's still alive."

It was as though I had merely told him the time. "Thank you," he said.

"You'll cover for me on this."

"It will be taken care of. Where is he?"

I told him. I gave him the story then too. I told him to call Pat and Hy and let it all loose at once. Everything tied in. It was almost all wrapped up.

Art said, "One thing, Mike."

"What?"

"*Your* problem."

"No trouble. It's over. I was standing here cleaning my gun and it all was like snapping my fingers. It was simple. If I had thought of it right away Dewey and Dennis Wallace and Alex Bird would still be alive. It was tragically simple. I could have found out where Velda was days ago."

"Mike—"

"I'll see you, Art. The rest of The Dragon has yet to fall."

"What?" He didn't understand me.

"*Tooth and Nail.* I just got Tooth— Nail is more subtle."

"We're going to need a statement."

"You'll get it."

"How will—"

I interrupted him with, "I'll call you."

# CHAPTER 13

At daylight the rain stopped and the music of sunlight played off the trees and grass at dawn. The mountains glittered and shone and steamed a little, and as the sun rose the sheen stopped and the colors came through. I ate at an all-night drive-in, parking between the semis out front. I sat through half a dozen cups of coffee before paying the bill and going out to the day, ignoring the funny looks of the carhop.

I stopped again awhile by the Ashokan Reservoir and did nothing but look at the water and try to bring seven years into focus. It was a long time, that. You change in seven years.

*You change in seven days too, I thought.*

I was a bum Pat had dragged into a hospital to look at a dying man. Pat didn't know it, but I was almost as dead as the one on the bed. It depends on where you die. My dying had been almost done. The drying up, the withering, had taken place. Everything was gone except hopelessness and that is the almost death of living.

*Remember, Velda, when we were big together? You must*

*have remembered or you would never have asked for me. And
all these years I had spent trying to forget you while you were
trying to remember me.*

I got up slowly and brushed off my pants, then walked
back across the field to the car. During the night I had gotten
it all muddy driving aimlessly on the back roads, but I didn't
think Laura would mind.

The sun had climbed high until it was almost directly
overhead. When you sit and think time can go by awfully
fast. I turned the key, pulled out on the road and headed
toward the mountains.

When I drove up, Laura heard me coming and ran out to
meet me. She came into my arms with a rush of pure delight
and did nothing for a few seconds except hold her arms
around me, then she looked again, stepped back and said,
"Mike—your face!"

"Trouble, baby. I told you I was trouble."

For the first time I noticed my clothes. My coat swung open
and there was blood down my jacket and shirt and a jagged
tear that was clotted with more blood at my side.

Her eyes went wide, not believing what she saw. "Mike!
You're—you're all—"

"Shot down, kid. Rough night."

She shook her head. "It's not funny. I'm going to call a
doctor!"

I took her hand. "No, you're not. It isn't that bad."

"Mike—"

"Favor, kitten. Let me lie in the sun like an old dog, okay?
I don't want a damn medic. I'll heal. It's happened before. I
just want to be left alone in the sun."

"Oh, Mike, you stubborn fool."

"Anybody home?" I asked her.

"No, you always pick an off day for the servants." She smiled again now. "You're clever and I'm glad."

I nodded. For some reason my side had started to ache and it was getting hard to breathe. There were other places that had pain areas all their own and they weren't going to get better. It had only just started. I said, "I'm tired."

So we went out back to the pool. She helped me off with my clothes and once more I put the trunks on, then eased down into a plastic contour chair and let the sun warm me. There were blue marks from my shoulders down and where the rib was broken a welt had raised, an angry red that arched from front to back. Laura found antiseptic and cleaned out the furrow where the two shots had grazed me and I thought back to the moment of getting them, realizing how lucky I was because the big jerk was too impatient, just like I had been, taking too much pleasure out of something that should have been strictly business.

I slept for a while. I felt the sun travel across my body from one side to the other, then I awoke abruptly because events had compacted themselves into my thoughts and I knew that there was still that one thing more to do.

Laura said, "You were talking in your sleep, Mike."

She had changed back into that black bikini and it was wet like her skin so she must have just come from the water. The tight band of black at her loins had rolled down some from the swim and fitted tightly into the crevasses of her body. The top half was like an artist's brush stroke, a quick motion of impatience at a critical sex-conscious world that concealed by reason of design only. She was more nearly naked dressed than nude.

How lovely.

Large, flowing thighs. Full, round calves. They blended

into a softly concave stomach and emerged, higher, into proud, outthrust breasts. Her face and hair were a composite halo reaching for the perfection of beauty and she was smiling.

Lovely.

"What did I say, Laura?"

She stopped smiling then. "You were talking about dragons."

I nodded. "Today, I'm St. George."

"Mike—"

"Sit down, baby."

"Can we talk again?"

"Yes, we'll talk."

"Would you mind if I got dressed first? It's getting chilly out here now. You ought to get dressed yourself."

She was right. The sun was a thick red now, hanging just over the crest of a mountain. While one side was a blaze of green, the other was in the deep purple of the shadow.

I held out my hand and she helped me up, and together we walked around the pool to the bathhouse, touching each other, feeling the warmth of skin against skin, the motion of muscle against muscle. At the door she turned and I took her in my arms. "Back to back?" she said.

"Like prudes," I told her.

Her eyes grew soft and her lips wet her tongue. Slowly, with an insistent hunger, her mouth turned up to mine and I took it, tasting her again, knowing her, feeling the surge of desire go through me and through her too.

I let her go reluctantly and she went inside with me behind her. The setting sun threw long orange rays through the window, so there was no need of the overhead light. She went into the shower and turned on a soft drizzle while I got dressed slowly, aching and hurting as I pulled on my clothes.

She called out, "When will it all be over, Mike?"

"Today," I said quietly.

"Today?"

I heard her stop soaping herself in the shower. "Are you sure?"

"Yes."

"You were dreaming about dragons," she called out.

"About how they die, honey. They die hard. This one will die especially hard. You know, you wouldn't believe how things come about. Things that were planted long ago suddenly bear fruit now. Like what I told you. Remember all I told you about Velda?"

"Yes, Mike, I do."

"I had to revise and add to the story, Laura."

"Really?" She turned the shower off and stood there behind me soaping herself down, the sound of it so nice and natural I wanted to turn around and watch. I knew what she'd look like: darkly beautiful, blondely beautiful, the sun having turned all of her hair white.

I said, "Pat was right and I was right. Your jewels did come into it. They were like Mrs. Civac's jewels and the fact that Richie Cole was a jewel smuggler."

"Oh?" That was all she said.

"They were all devices. Decoys. Red herrings. How would you like to hear the rest of what I think?"

"All right, Mike."

She didn't see me, but I nodded. "In the government are certain key men. Their importance is apparent to critical eyes long before it is to the public. Your husband was like that. It was evident that he was going to be a top dog one day

and the kind of top dog our Red enemy could hardly afford
to have up there.

"That was Leo Knapp, your husband. Mr. Missile Man.
Mr. America. He sure was a big one. But our wary enemy
knew his stuff. Kill him off and you had a public martyr or a
great investigation that might lead to even greater international stuff and those Reds just aren't the kind who can
stand the big push. Like it or not, they're still a lousy bunch
of peasants who killed to control but who can be knocked into
line by the likes of us. They're shouting slobs who'll run like
hell when class shows and they know this inside their feeble
little heads. So they didn't want Leo Knapp put on a pedestal.

"Control comes other ways, however. For instance, he could
marry a woman who would listen to him as a sounding board
and relay his thoughts and secrets to the right persons so that
whatever he did could be quickly annulled by some other
action. He could marry a woman who, as his official Washington hostess, had the ear of respected persons and could pick
up things here and there that were as important to enemy
ears as any sealed documents. He could find his work being
stymied at every turn.

"Then one day he figured it all out. He pinpointed the
enemy and found it within his own house. He baited a trap
by planting supposedly important papers in his safe and one
night while the enemy, his wife, was rifling his safe with her
compatriot who was to photograph the papers and transport
the photos to higher headquarters, he came downstairs. He
saw her, accused her, but blundered into a game bigger than
he was.

"Let's say she shot him. It doesn't really matter. She was
just as guilty even if it was the other one. At least the other
one carried the gun off—a pickup rod traceable to no one if it

was thrown away printless. His wife delayed long enough so she and her compatriot could fake a robbery, let the guy get away, then call in the cops.

"Nor does it end there. The same wife still acts as the big Washington hostess with her same ear to the same ground and is an important and inexhaustible supply of information to the enemy. Let's say that she is so big as to even be part of The Dragon team. He was Tooth, she was Nail, both spies, both assassins, both deadly enemies of this country."

Behind me the water went on again, a downpour that would rinse the bubbles of soap from her body.

"All went well until Richie Cole was killed. Tooth went and used the same gun again. It tied things in. Like I told you when I let you be *my* sounding board—coincidence is a strange thing. I like the word 'fate' even better. Or is 'consequence' an even better one? Richie and Leo and Velda were all tied into the same big situation and for a long time I was too damn dumb to realize it.

"A guy like me doesn't stay dumb forever, though. Things change. You either die or smarten up. I had The Dragon on my back and when I think about it all the little things make sense too. At least I think so. Remember how when Gorlin shot the radio you shook with what I thought was fear? Hell, baby, that was rage. You were pissed off that he could pull such a stupid stunt and maybe put your hide in danger. Later you gave him hell on the phone, didn't you? That house is like an echo chamber, baby. Talk downstairs and you hear the tones all over. You were mad. I was too interested in going through your husband's effects to pay any attention, that was all.

"Now it's over. Tooth is nailed, but that's a joke you don't understand yet, baby. Let's just say that The Dragon is tethered. He'll sit in the chair and all the world will know why and nations will backtrack and lie and propaganda will tear up the knotheads in the Kremlin and maybe their satellite countries will wise up and blast loose and maybe we'll wise up and blast them, but however it goes, The Dragon is dead. It didn't find Velda. She'll talk, she'll open up the secrets of the greatest espionage organization the world has ever known and Communist philosophy will get the hell knocked out of it.

"You see, baby, I know where Velda is."

The shower stopped running and I could hear her hum as though she couldn't even hear me.

"The catch was this. Richie Cole did make his contact. He gave Old Dewey, the newsstand operator, a letter he had that told where Alex Bird would take Velda. It was a prepared place and she had orders to stay there until either he came for her or I came for her. He'll never come for her.

"Only me," I said. "Dewey put the letter in a magazine. Every month he holds certain magazines aside for me and to make sure I got it he put it inside my copy of *Cavalier*. It will be there when I go back to the city. I'll pick it up and it will tell me where Velda is."

I finished dressing, put on the empty gun and slid painfully into the jacket. The blood was crusty on my clothes, but it really didn't matter anymore.

I said, "It's all speculation. I might be wrong. I just can't take any chances. I've loved other women. I loved Velda. I've loved you and like you said, it's either you or her. I have to go for her, you know that. If she's alive I have to find her. The key is right there inside my copy of that magazine. It will have my name on it and Duck-Duck will hand it over and I'll know where she is."

She stopped humming and I knew she was listening. I heard her make a curious woman-sound like a sob.

"I may be wrong, Laura. I may see her and not want her. I may be wrong about you, and if I am I'll be back, but I have to find out." The slanting beam of the sun struck the other side of the bathhouse leaving me in the shadow then. I knew what I had to do. It had to be a test. They either passed it or failed it. No in-betweens. I didn't want it on my head again.

I reached for the shotgun in the corner, turned it upside down and shoved the barrels deep into the blue clay and twisted them until I was sure both barrels were plugged just like a cookie cutter and I left it lying there and opened the door.

The mountains were in deep shadow, the sun out of sight and only its light flickering off the trees. It was a hundred miles into the city, but I'd take the car again and it wouldn't really be very long at all. I'd see Pat and we'd be friends again and Hy would get his story and Velda—Velda? What would it be like now?

I started up the still wet concrete walk away from the bath-house and she called out, "Mike—*Mike!*"

I turned at the sound of her voice and there she stood in the naked, glossy, shimmering beauty of womanhood, the lovely tan of her skin blossoming and swelling in all the vast hillocks and curves that make a woman, the glinting blond hair throwing tiny lights back into the sunset and over it all those incredible gray eyes.

Incredible.

They watched me over the elongated barrels of the shotgun and seemed to twinkle and swirl in the fanatical delight of murder they come up with at the moment of the kill, the moment of truth.

But for whom? Truth will out, but for whom?

The muzzle of the gun was a pair of yawning chasms but there was no depth to their mouths. Down the length of the blued steel the blood crimson of her nails made a startling and symbolic contrast.

Death red, I thought. The fingers behind them should have been tan but weren't. They were a tense, drawing white and with another fraction of an inch the machinery of the gun would go into motion.

She said, *"Mike—"* and in that one word there was hate and desire, revenge and regret, but above all the timbre of duty long ago instilled into a truly mechanical mind.

I said, "So long, baby."

Then I turned and walked toward the outside and Velda and behind me I heard the unearthly roar as she pulled both triggers at once.